Silk Ribbon Treasures

Smocking and Embroidery

By Martha Campbell Pullen Ph.D.

May God Bless You

Martha Pullen

Dedication

To Margaret Malinda Lee Taylor and William Campbell Crocker

This book wouldn't be in your hands right now if these two individuals hadn't insisted that it was needed and actually started the work without my knowledge. Camp, my son, and Margaret travel to our shows around the country and meet literally thousands of people during the year. Knowing of the popularity of the revival of silk ribbon embroidery they said to me, "Martha, we absolutely have to do a book combining silk ribbon embroidery and smocking." Since we were in the middle of doing 26 *Martha's Sewing Room* television shows per year and writing two show guides to go along with those shows I said, "I think we don't have time to take on another project of this magnitude." I really believed that everyone here was working at full capacity and that we simply didn't have the time or resources to tackle another project. They listened to me politely and paid absolutely no attention to what I had said. They began planning this book and Margaret began to call our designers around the country to ask them to start stitching. Margaret and Camp laid out the plans for this book and the work began.

Margaret Lee Taylor was the first child of Minnie Russell and the late Rocklin Lee. Born in Gurley, Alabama her love of embroidery was started with lessons from her mother. Making pillowcases and tea towels were favorite pastimes for her when she was a young girl. Beginning in the ninth grade her home economics teacher, Helen Glasscock of Gurley High School, had a major impact on Margaret. She taught sewing and Margaret recalls that she "just couldn't get enough of sewing." Margaret made most of her own clothes from high school through young adulthood. At Gurley High School Margaret was the class valedictorian, belonged to the Beta Club and served on the annual staff.

During her young adult years she also began other types of needlework and loved her "quilting stint" best of all. In addition to loving quilting, she also learned bargello, needlepoint, crewel and cross stitch.

She is married to Norman S. Taylor and they have two daughters, Kathy Bentley and Shelia Cantrell. Margaret and Norman have two granddaughters, Taylor Nicole Bentley and Alana Leigh Bentley. Needless to say, these little beauties receive gorgeous clothes for special occasion wearing. Margaret also has a "baby sister" that she adores and feels like that she is "her child." This beloved sister is Deborah Jean Atchley who is thirteen years younger than Margaret. It was on the occasion of the birth of Debbie and Frankie's daughter, Misty Dawn Atchley, that she began taking heirloom sewing classes and once again, "just couldn't get enough of it." In her sewing heirlooms for Misty, she took her embroidery skills and transferred them to smocking, heirloom embroidery and silk ribbon embroidery.

In my traveling with Margaret she is such an inspiration to me and so much help. She can do "Martha Pullen Workshops" as well as Martha Pullen; the students love her excellent instruction as well as her humor. At night we share from the Bible and talk about verses which we don't understand. On the last trip we discussed many passages from the book of James.

My son, Camp Crocker, has such vision concerning this business and the direction in which we should travel. In addition to business planning, he has a wonderful ability to make me stop worrying and start thinking creatively instead. He insisted that silk ribbon embroidery, which was revived in this country by Esther Randall, was the next largest movement in needlework. Our women who love to smock had already begun to combine silk ribbon embroidery with smocking in lovely ways. This needlework marriage seemed inevitable, Camp insisted. Of course, he was correct as I believe you will see in this beautiful book. He and Margaret began to collaborate and the vision started to become a reality.

I dedicate this book to Margaret and Camp with the greatest of thanks for taking on extra responsibility when both of them were already up to their eyeballs in other work. They both are great about saying, "I can do more." Those words are music to a small business owner's ears. 🎔

Acknowledgments

James 1:2-5

2 "My brothers and sisters, whenever you face trials of any kind, consider it nothing but joy,

3 because you know that the testing of your faith produces endurance;

4 and let endurance have its full effect, so that you may be mature and complete, lacking in nothing."

To see in the Bible that God says to welcome stress is relieving to me in many ways. Although I don't like the word stress, I guess I have to admit that my life feels full of it many times. I think this scripture says to "consider it nothing but joy" when we face trials of any kind. I know that my trials have made me stronger and I hope that I face trials and pressures with depth of character and grace. It is easy to be kind to others under good circumstances. How do I treat others when things are going badly? I want to become a more mature Christian and I think grace under pressure offers me much opportunity for personal growth and for demonstrating to others my character. I thank God for being with me during rough times as well as good times. I thank God for giving me the strength for enduring problems, both business and personal. God never leaves me alone during troubled times and for this I am most grateful.

My mother and father, Anna Ruth Dicus Campbell and the late Paul Jones Campbell were my first and greatest teachers. Their example of living a Godly, decent, and hard-working life certainly formed my attitude toward life and what should and could be accomplished. I love them and I thank them.

My children, Camp and Charisse, John and Suzanne, Mark and Sherry Ann, Jeff and Angela and Joanna have always loved me and believed in me. I love them all, and I am so proud of them. Joanna's birth, after having four boys, caused me to go right back to my sewing machine to make her little fancy dresses. Because of my love of making little dresses for her I decided to open this business in August, 1981.

My grandchildren have to be the most beautiful, the smartest, the cutest, and the most creative in the world! Isn't that spoken like a true grandmother? To Campbell, Morgan Ross, Sarah Joy, Rebekah, Marshall and Bradley—I love you dearly, and I thank you for coming into my life bringing such pure joy!

My sisters and brothers-Mary, Dottie, Cliff, and Robin-and their families are beautiful individuals whom I love very much. Brothers and sisters are gifts from God who grow more precious with every year.

My business could not be a reality without the talents of many people.

After this book was conceived by Camp Crocker and Margaret Taylor, Margaret began to enlist the talents of many people around the country for their designs and stitching. I am deeply grateful for each one of their contributions because without them this book would not have happened.

Jack Cooper is so patient in photographing for all of our books. This one is no exception. His details in close–up work as well as his creativity and patience in handling children are wonderful. Jack is an important part of this whole business and his work is beautiful.

Linda Trivers photographed Kathy Harrison's children for this book. Several years ago while I was teaching in Indianapolis, Kathy showed me some of Linda's photographs. Since that day she has done a lot of work for us and it continues to be magical.

Thanks to Sue Pennington for designs and stitching. Sue is a critical part of this whole business and I am amazed at her never–ending stockpile of ideas. She is one of the most creative people that I have ever known and she is much appreciated in every aspect of this business. Sue's designing and teaching are world renowned and she is always there for us in whatever way we need her.

Charlotte Potter did smocking designs and stitching. Charlotte has been working with us for many years and she is much appreciated. Charlotte is very professional and meets deadlines every time. She also contributes to the school each year with her wonderful teaching and assisting.

Donna Marcum has designed and stitched some of the smocking and silk ribbon designs. She has been creating goodies for all aspects of this business for quite some time now and she is fabulous. Donna not only designs for us, she assists at our school here in Huntsville twice a year. We depend on Donna for so many different things.

Jena Blair's never-ending supply of ideas in her creative head add so much to *Sew Beautiful* as well as to this book. She just stitches and stitches more beautifully than the last time. Jena is one of the great smocking designers of this country.

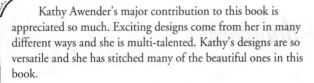

Kathy Awender's major contribution to this book is appreciated so much. Exciting designs come from her in many different ways and she is multi-talented. Kathy's designs are so versatile and she has stitched many of the beautiful ones in this book.

Joyce Catoir stitched until the wee hours when we had some new designs and called her. She is a completely talented needle artist as well as a wonderful seamstress. She is a vital part of many aspects of this business including handling major responsibilities at our school here in Huntsville twice a year.

Kathy Neal contributed the eyeglass case and the exquisite black pillow. Her designs are magical and we so appreciate her generosity. Kathy is a master silk ribbon embroidery teacher as well as stitcher. We love having her teach at our school.

Kathy Pearce, Toni Duggar, Lakanjala Campbell, Angie Daniel, Charisse Crocker, Amy Duggar and Camp Crocker have kept the business running while others worked on this book!

Kris Broom's drawings give great depth to the how to sections of our books. She is a master seamstress and designer and understands exactly how something is constructed with her art. It is wonderful to have an artist on staff who can look at a finished garment and take the written directions and draw the how-to's.

Kathy Brower's instructions on some of the silk ribbon stitches are superb; her illustrations are excellent also and make the stitching so easy. Kathy's teaching of silk ribbon on our television show, *Martha's Sewing Room,* has excited people all over the country to begin this easy type of embroidery.

Kathy Harrison designed the dress for the pattern in the book as well as all of the smocking design plates which are on the dresses. Her work sings and dances with superb construction and creativity. She also made the adorable pillow to match the ecru silk dupioni dress. After meeting Kathy a few years ago, many of my design projects have been executed by her skilled hands. She can listen to my design needs over the phone, and return to me a finished project within a few weeks.

Claudia Newton wrote the instructions for the dress and pattern and helped draft the collars to go on the dress. Her excellence in design and execution is always appreciated. Sometimes a person comes into my life who is destined to do great things to help this business. Claudia is one of those individuals. She can do everything from writing directions, illustrating, drafting patterns, teaching at our schools and on the television show, and sewing.

Kathy McMakin drafted the dress and helped draft the collars. Kathy has helped with all aspects of this book from proofing and advising to drafting to writing instructions. From master seamstress, teacher and writer to advisor and teacher, Kathy is a vital part of all aspects of this business. Kathy wrote the instructions for the dress construction.

Angela Pullen's drawings add life and magic to all of our books. Her illustrations have great depth, detail, and creativity. She designed the alphabet and some of the other designs as well. She always meets deadlines and never complains about the boxes of work that we send her.

Margaret Taylor wrote part of the instructions for this book, designed some of the projects, made all of the phone calls to our other artists, and engineered this book to its completion. Without her it wouldn't be in your hands right now. Since the book is dedicated in part to her, I'll talk more about her contributions in another part of this book.

Ann LeRoy's book design is creative and lends a professional touch to all of the sections. It is not an easy task to take hundreds of drawings and computer disks of information and create a book out of it. To have an element of style and beauty in addition to correctness of directions and pictures is quite a feat. It overwhelms me to think of all the decisions which she had to make concerning the layout of this book.

There is one person to whom I am especially grateful. Next to God, he has been my faithful advisor, my financial partner, my idea person and my mentor. My husband, Joe Ross Pullen, has always believed in me more than I believe in myself. He is a wonderful dentist and has been one of the worldwide pioneers in implant dentistry. He is a wonderful Christian husband and father, and God blessed me beyond my wildest imaginations the day that Joe asked me to marry him. He is my best friend and my partner; I love him, and I thank him.

A number of years ago, I gave this whole business to God. He took it, figured out what to do next, and has given the guidance for moving in the directions in which we are moving. All the credit and glory for any success that we have had in the sewing industry go to Him and Him alone. The path has not been nor is it now an easy one. I don't think He promised us an easy trip through life. He did promise to be with us always and I can testify that He has never failed me. ▧

Table of Contents

Smocking Plate Directory

Projects Directory

Stitch Directory

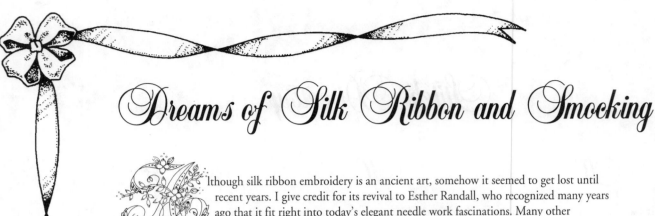

Dreams of Silk Ribbon and Smocking

Although silk ribbon embroidery is an ancient art, somehow it seemed to get lost until recent years. I give credit for its revival to Esther Randall, who recognized many years ago that it fit right into today's elegant needle work fascinations. Many other designers are loving working with these wonderful ribbons and the marketplace is filling with beautiful designs and ideas.

Loving smocking designs which are beautiful, easy and unusual, I began to dream of a book of silk ribbon and smocking designs which fit together in perfect harmony. There is nothing more elegant than smocking with silk ribbons, or smocking with floss with silk ribbon embellishments on top of the pleats. With these two ideas being foremost, we began to commission some of our favorite smocking designers to create the designs for this book.

Of course, Martha Pullen books are known for their incredible value; to make this book even more wonderful, we have designed a beautiful pattern which is wonderful with these smocking designs. It is a pattern that comes to the waist in the back and can be worn with a sash. School age girls tend to like the waisted dresses which hug the waist. This dress has a Peter Pan collar and it can be made as a "very fancy" dress or as a casual dress depending on the fabrics you choose. Of course you can smock any smocking plate of your choice using this very versatile pattern.

Silk ribbon embroidery is so easy to do and that is another reason for wanting an heirloom smocking plus silk ribbon book. On every other show of *Martha's Sewing Room,* our television show for PBS stations around the country, we feature at least one silk ribbon embroidery stitch in living color and live! Silk ribbon is such a popular embroidery technique at this time that we included 30 minutes of silk ribbon stitches on our 1995-1996 subscriber FREE video with *Sew Beautiful* subscriptions!

I love the combination of silk ribbon plus smocking for another reason. Silk ribbon embroidery, which is EASY, makes it possible to put "a picture smocking effect" on your smocking design without actually stacking cables. Another reason I love silk ribbon plus smocking is that it makes smocking very dressy. Smocking is so wonderful because it can be as tailored, sporty, fun and casual as you want it to be. It can also be dressy and used on Sunday School and Portrait clothing. With silk ribbon it becomes especially dressy and ready for that portrait of a lifetime, christening of a lifetime, or museum dress of a lifetime for your little loved one.

With the addition of silk ribbon, smocking becomes very sophisticated for an adult garment such as a blouse, nightgown or robe. What bride of a few hours or 50 years wouldn't love a beautiful smocked nightgown or robe?

There are silk ribbon designs for collars or garments in addition to smocked designs smocked with actual silk ribbons found in this book. There are combinations of smocking with floss and embellishment with silk ribbons in this book. This is a very beautiful book with very creative and elegant ideas.

In this book there are easy to follow smocking instructions, use of the pleater instructions, and silk ribbon instructions. ▧

Left: Kate Irene Dress
  • *Instructions on page 71*

Right: Kelly Michelle Dress
  • *Instructions on page 77*

"Little Lamb, who made thee?
Dost thou know who made thee?
Gave thee life and bid thee feed
By the stream and o'er the mead;
Gave thee clothing of delight,
Softest clothing, woolly bright."

—William Blake, Songs of Innocence

Kelly Michelle Dress
• *Instructions on page 77*

Above: Kelly Michelle Dress
- *Instructions on page 77*
- *Smocking plate on page 78*

Left: Detail of Sleeve from Kelly Michelle Dress
- *Smocking plate on page 79*

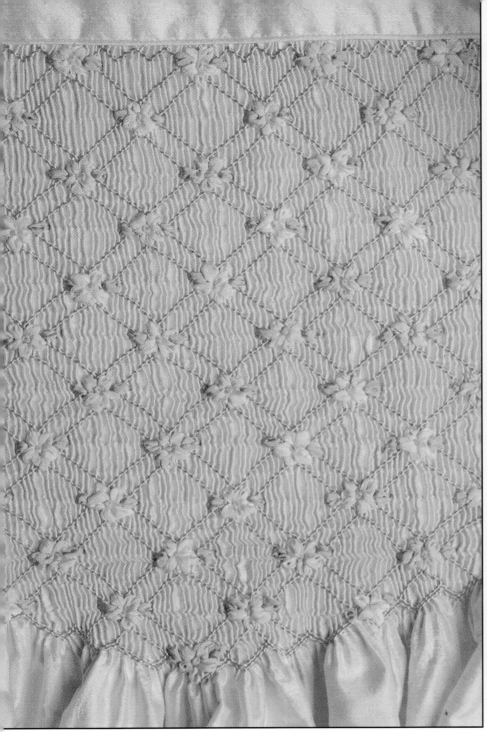

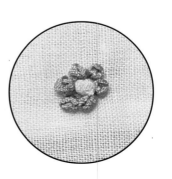

Above Left: Close –up of smocking graph from Kelly Michelle Dress
- *Instructions on page 77*
- *Smocking Graph on page 78*

Above Right: Detail of buttons on back of Kelly Michelle Dress
- *Instructions on page 77*

In Circle: Detail of silk ribbon embroidery on sash tail on Kelly Michelle Dress

Above:
- *Close –up of smocking graph on Kate Irene Dress*
- *Instructions on page 71*
- *Smocking Graph on page 73*

Left: Kate Irene Dress

Above: Close–up of smocking on sleeve of Kate Irene Dress
- *Instructions on page 71*
- *Smocking Graph on page 72*

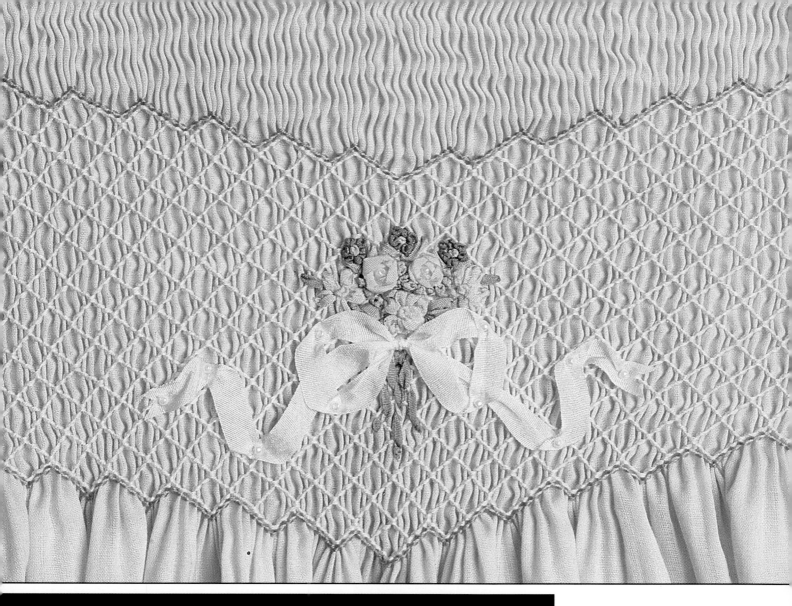

Above: Detail of smocking on Summer Delight Dress

Left: Summer Delight Dress

- *Instructions on page 81*
- *Smocking Graph on page 83*

Above: Misty Dress

Right: Detail of smocking and silk ribbon
on Misty Dress sleeve

  • Instructions on page 75
  • Smocking Graph on page 76

Above: Detail of smocking and silk ribbon on Misty Dress
- *Instructions on page 75*
- *Smocking Graph on page 76*

Emerald Elegance Pillow
• Instructions on page 131

Left: Victorian Boudoir Pillow
• Instructions on page 128

Right: Ring Bearer Pillow
• Instructions on page 125

Above Left: Initial Pillow
  • *Instructions on page 135*

Above Right: Ring Bearer Pillow
  • *Instructions on page 125*

*Below Right: Detail of silk ribbon
embroidery on Initial Pillow*

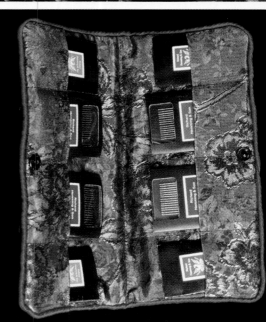

Above: Linen Guest Towel
  • *Instructions on page 137*

Below Left: Victorian Needle Case
  • *Instructions on page 143*

Below Right: Inside of Needle Case

20

Above: Placemat

• *Instructions on page 138*

Left: Grandmother's Favorite Spectacle Case

• *Instructions on page 140*

Round Yoke Christening Gown
• *Instructions on page 65*

Above: Smocking on Round Yoke Christening Gown

Below: Scalloped hem of Round Yoke Christening Gown

• Instructions on page 65

23

Blouse with initial "M"

• See page 151

(Blouse pattern is found in Heirloom Sewing for Women by Martha Pullen)

Above: Sweetheart Collar

- *In Circle: detail of Sweetheart Collar*

- *Instructions on page 123*

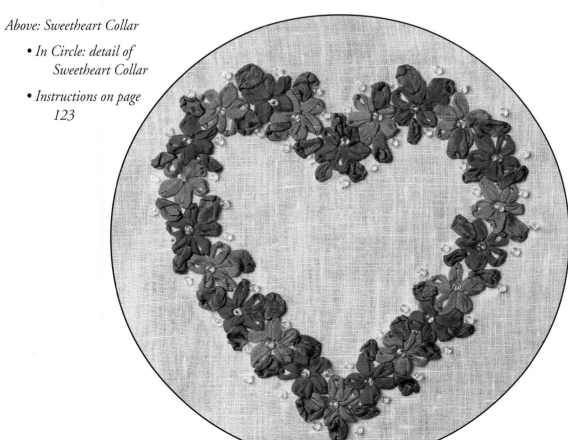

Above: Peek–A–Boo Bunnies Collar

- *In Circle: close up of Peek–A–Boo Collar*

- *Instructions on page 120*

26

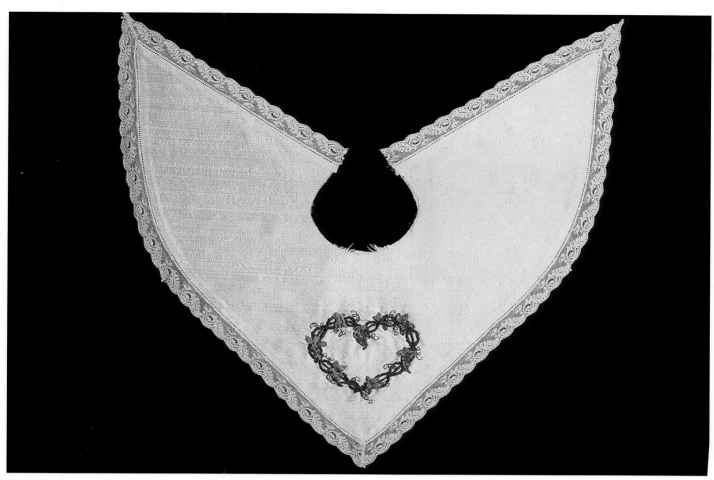

Above: Grapevine Heart Collar

- *In Circle: Close up of Grapevine Heart Collar*

- *Instructions on page 117*

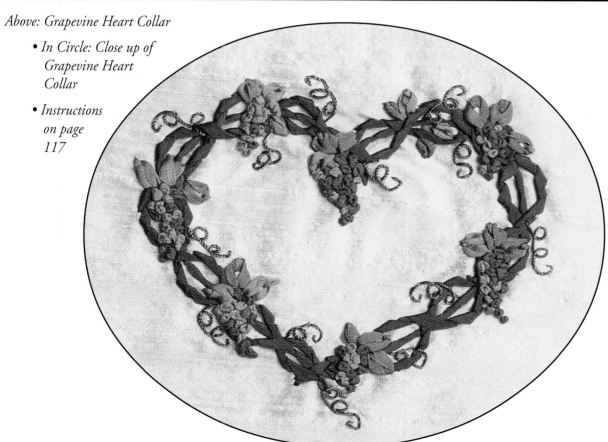

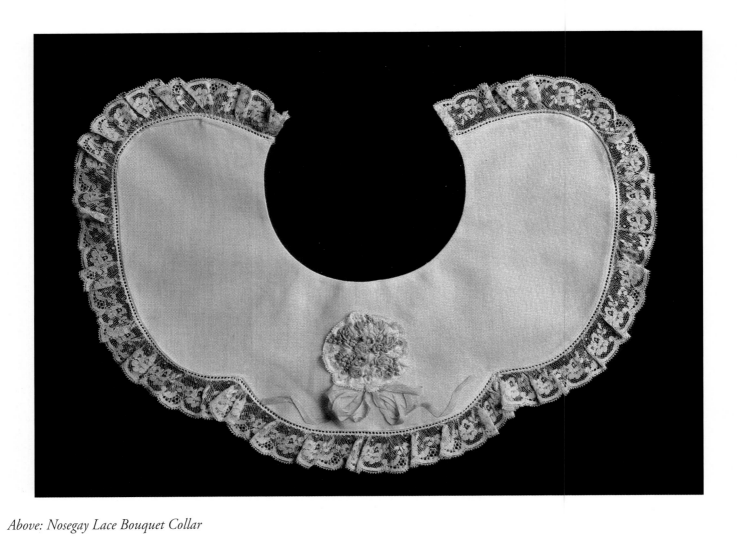

Above: Nosegay Lace Bouquet Collar

Below: Close–up of Nosegay Lace Bouquet Collar

• *Instructions on page 121*

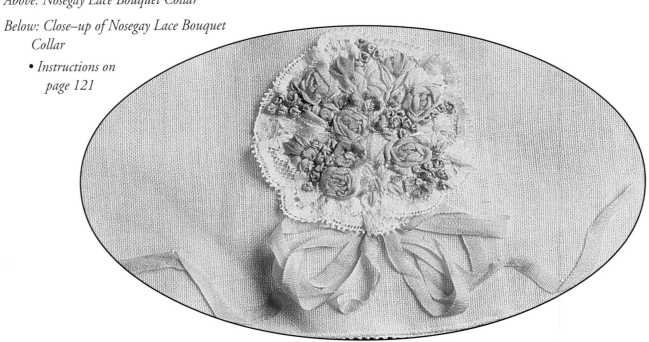

Above: Sophisticated Elegance Collar   *Below: Close–up of Sophisticated Elegance Collar*   • *Instructions on page 122*

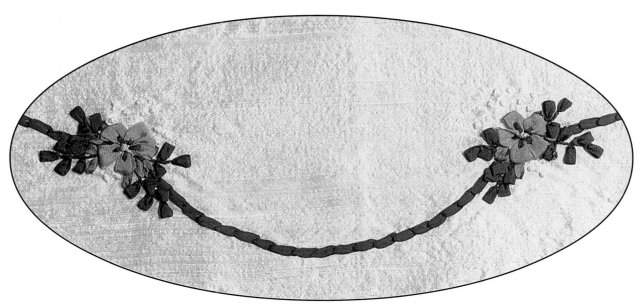

Above: Heartfelt Inspirations Collar

Below: Detail of Heartfelt Inspirations Collar

• *Instructions on page 119*

Above: Daisy Collar

Below: Close—up of Daisy Collar
  • *Instructions on page 116*

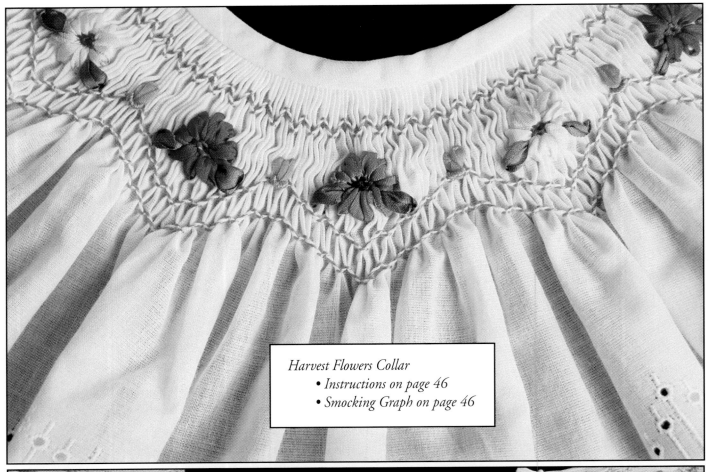

Harvest Flowers Collar
- *Instructions on page 46*
- *Smocking Graph on page 46*

Ribbons and Roses Smocking Plate
- *Instructions on page 47*
- *Smocking Graph on page 47*

Heritage Baskets Smocking Plate
• *Instructions on page 69*
• *Smocking Graph on page 69*

33

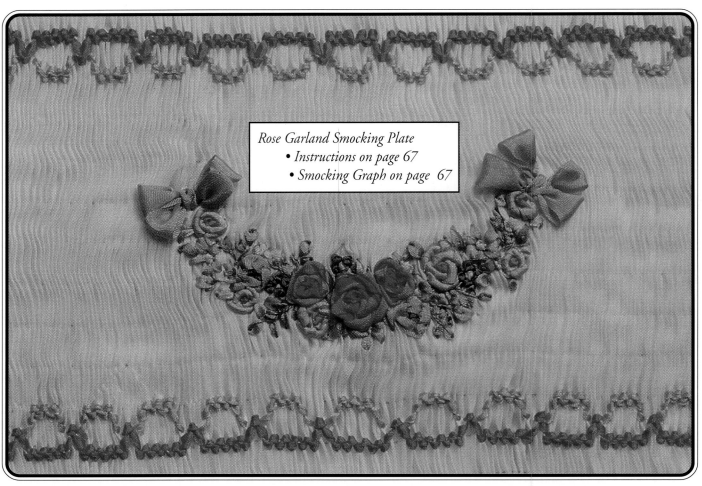

Rose Garland Smocking Plate
* *Instructions on page 67*
* *Smocking Graph on page 67*

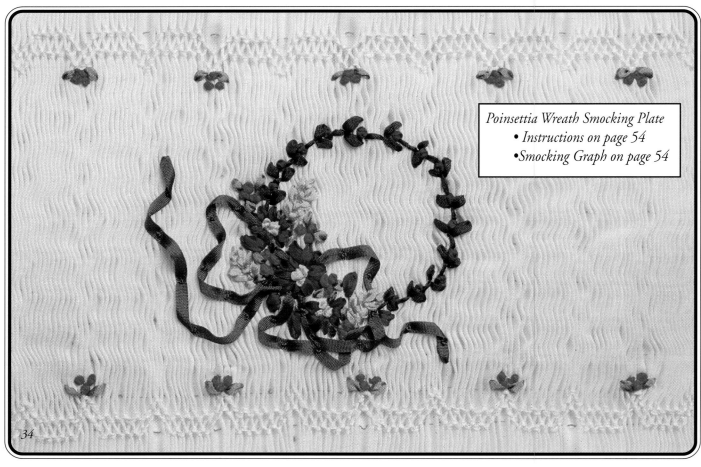

Poinsettia Wreath Smocking Plate
* *Instructions on page 54*
* *Smocking Graph on page 54*

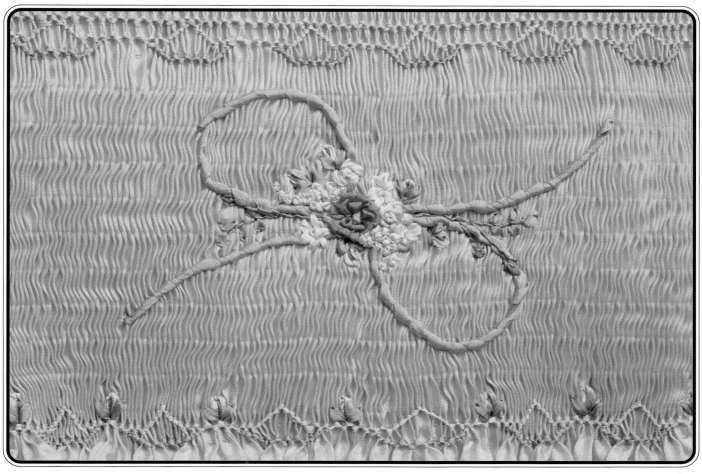

Amy's Bow Smocking Plate
- *Instructions on page 42*
- *Smocking Graph on page 42*

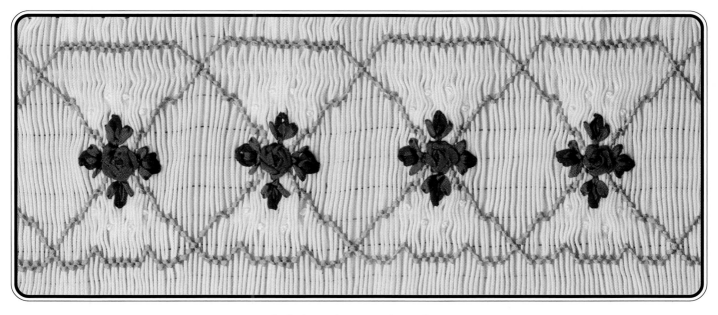

Cathedral Windows Smocking Plate
- *Instructions on page 63*
- *Smocking Graph on page 63*

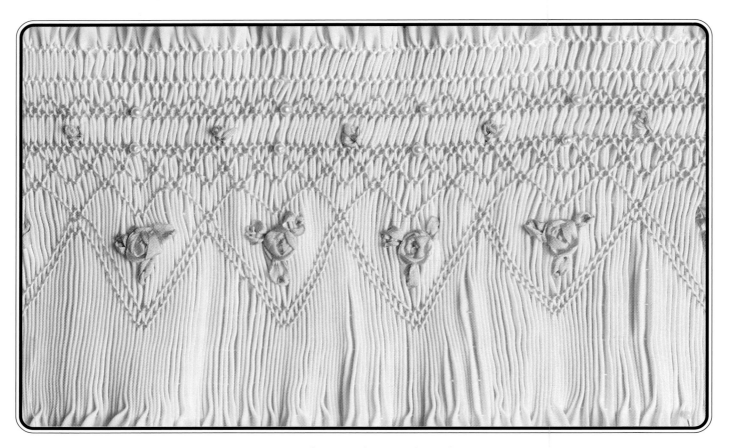

Peach Rose Bishop Smocking Plate
- *Instructions on page 52*
- *Smocking Graph on page 52*

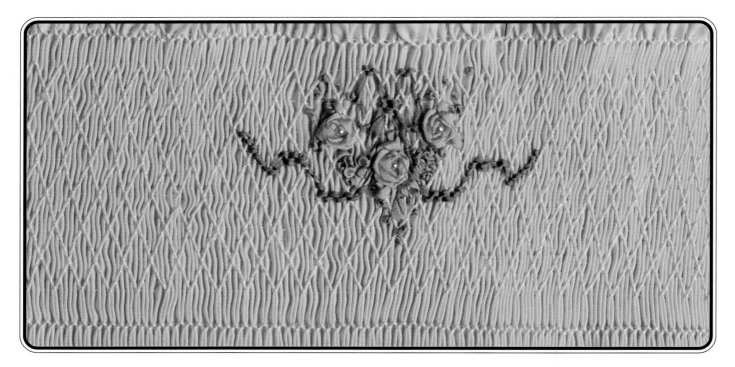

Donna's Crest Smocking Plate
- *Instructions on page 59*
- *Smocking Graph on page 60*

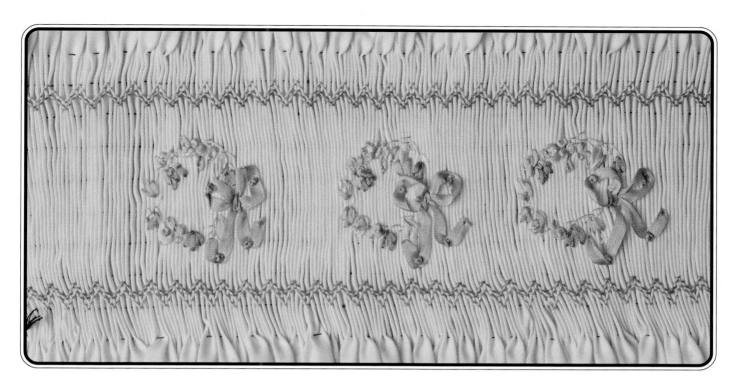

Sarah's Wreath Smocking Plate
- *Instructions on page 61*
- *Smocking Graph on page 61*

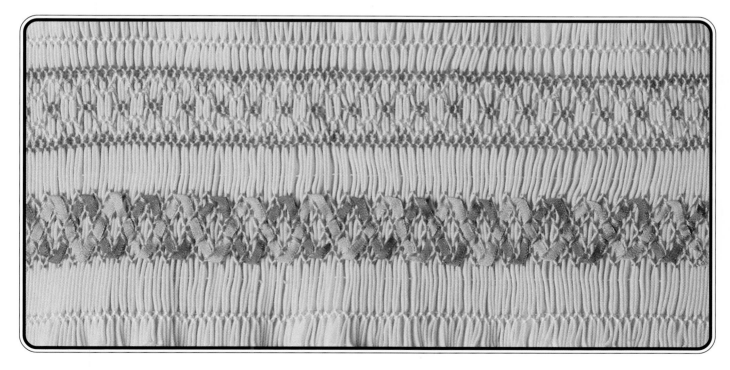

Woven Elegance Smocking Plate
- *Instructions on page 58*
- *Smocking Graph on page 58*

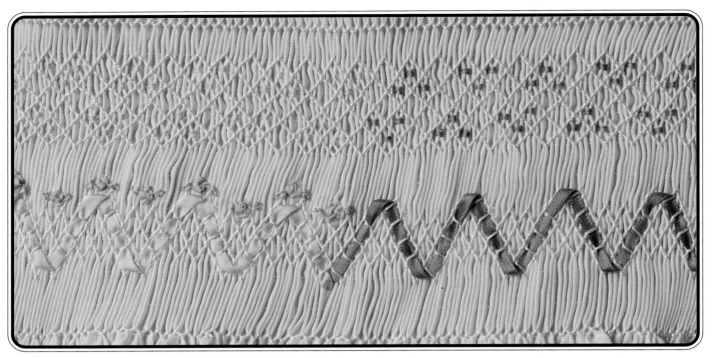

Jack and Jill Smocking Plate
  • *Instructions on page 48*
  • *Smocking Graph on page 48*

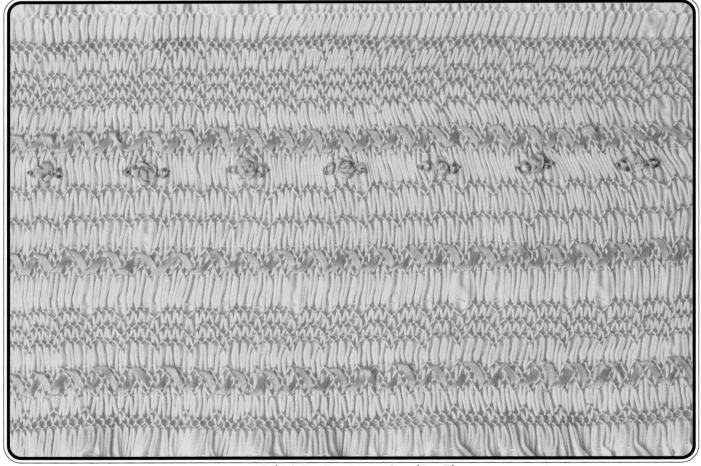

Robin's Egg Renaissance Smocking Plate
  • *Instructions on page 56*
  • *Smocking Graph on page 56*

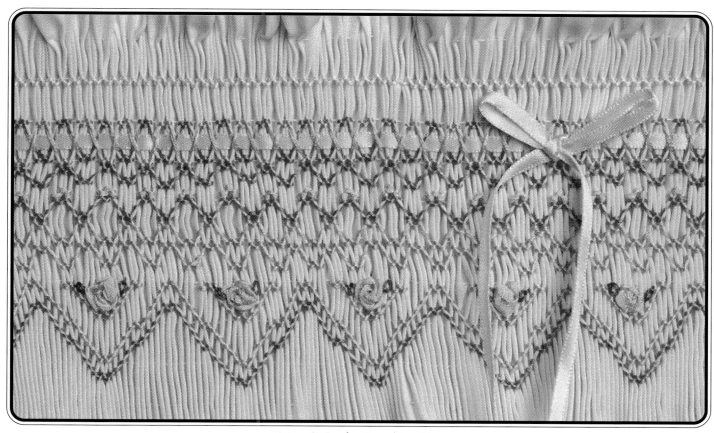

Monet's Garden Smocking Plate
• *Instructions on page 50*   • *Smocking Graph on page 50*

Bouquet Of Roses Smocking Plate
• *Instructions on page 84*
• *Smocking Graph on page 84*

Victorian Garden Smocking Plate
- *Instructions on page 87*
- *Smocking Graph on page 87*

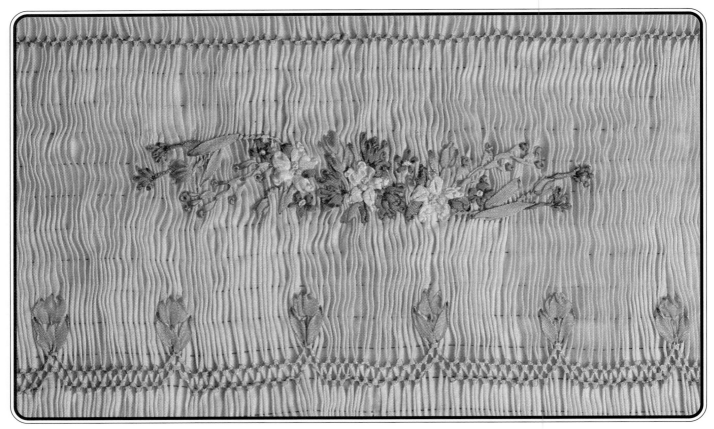

Tulip Garden Smocking Plate
- *Instructions on page 44*
- *Smocking Graph on page 44*

Smocking Graphs

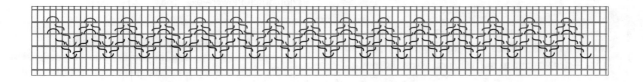

Amy's Bow

Silk ribbon on silk blue fabric seems to be the mode for this beautiful smocking and silk ribbon design. Two shades of pink silk ribbon have been used for the borders; the bottom borders have flowers on the cable rows between the trellis figures. A gorgeous wrapped silk ribbon bow is found in the center with magnificent silk ribbon flowers in deep rose, white, pale pink, yellow, lavender and green lavishly stitched in the center of the bow. The vines are made with green silk thread and the leaves are green silk ribbon. This design is royal in nature and so lush with the ribbon and the silk fabric.

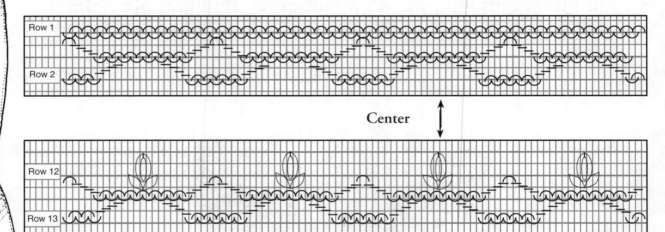

Center

Materials

❈ Silk Ribbon Colors Used:

    2mm: #7 pink, #127 pink

    4mm: #3 white, #5 pink, #13 yellow, #83 orchid, #128 pink, #154 green

❈ Kanagawa Silk Thread: #165 green

❈ DMC floss to match the color of your fabric for backsmocking

❈ Color photo - page 35

Directions

1. Pleat 15 rows. The top and bottom rows are stabilizer rows and are not numbered on the graph. Smock 13 rows.

2. Backsmock rows 2 through 12 with two strands of floss to match your fabric.

3. Beginning beneath row 1 with a down cable, cable across row 1 using 2mm #7 pink silk ribbon.

4. Between rows 1 and $1^{1}/_{2}$, use 2mm #7 pink silk ribbon, work 1 up cable, a 4-step wave down to row $1^{1}/_{2}$, cable 15, a 4-step wave up to row 1. Repeat across the row.

5. Using 2mm #127 pink silk ribbon, work a 4-step wave down to row 2, 9 cables, 4-step combination up to row $1^{1}/_{2}$. Refer to graph for placement. Tie off the ribbon on the wrong side of the fabric. Skip 6 pleats and repeat across the row.

6. Following the instructions given in Step 4, repeat the cable-wave combination between rows 12 and $12^{1}/_{2}$.

7. Following the instructions given in Step 5, repeat the cable wave combination between rows $12^{1}/_{2}$ and l3.

Embroidery Stitches

Colonial Knot - page 161	Running Stitch - page 171
Fly Stitch - page 163	Stem/Outline Stitch - page 173
French Knot - page 164	Straight Stitch - page 173
Japanese Ribbon Stitch - page 167	Wrapped Stitch - page 175
Lazy Daisy Stitch - page 167	
Loop Stitch Flower - page 168	

1. Trace the bow design only on a piece of paper or cardboard. Cut around the outside of the bow design. Place the bow template on top of the pleated fabric and

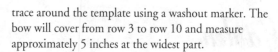

trace around the template using a washout marker. The bow will cover from row 3 to row 10 and measure approximately 5 inches at the widest part.

2. Using 2mm #127 pink silk ribbon, follow the direction of the arrows in the diagram and work a running stitch covering the entire bow and streamers. Pull each stitch through just enough to keep the ribbon from drooping.

3. Using a tapestry needle, follow the arrows on the template given and wrap each stitch twice, keeping the ribbon flat. Carry the ribbon to the wrong side of the fabric and tie off.

4. The loop stitch flower is worked in 4mm #128 pink ribbon. It consists of a circle of 10 loop stitches with a $1/4$" opening in the center of the flower. Work a second circle of 5 loop stitches inside the first, partially filling the $1/4$" opening. The stitches in the second circle should be placed between the stitches in the first circle. Fill the center of the loop stitch flower with a colonial knot worked in 4mm #7 pink silk ribbon.

5. Using 4mm #3 white silk ribbon, work the daisies with a straight stitch. Each daisy contains 6 petals with the center filled with 2-wrap French knots worked in 4mm #13 yellow silk ribbon.

6. Using 2mm #7 pink silk ribbon, create the roses using colonial knots surrounded by outline stitches in 4mm #5 pink silk ribbon. Rosebuds are made with a lazy daisy stitch.

7. Clusters of French knots are worked in 4mm #83 orchid silk ribbon. Use 3 wraps for the knots at the top of the cluster, 2 wrap French knots for the center of the cluster, and 1 wrap for the tip.

8. The small, dark pink buds are worked in 4mm #128 pink silk ribbon. Work 2 short straight stitches with the second stitch covering the first. Using #165 green silk thread, work a straight stitch over the lower half of the bud, a fly stitch surrounding the bud, and a stem stitch to take the stem to the center of the bow. Using #165 green silk thread, work another stem for the leaves.

9. Using the Japanese ribbon stitch and 4mm #18 green silk ribbon, add leaves to fill in where needed.

10. The flowers are worked in between the points on row $12^1/_2$ (see graph for placement). The rosebuds are lazy daisy stitches worked in 2mm #7 pink silk ribbon. The center of each lazy daisy stitch is filled with a straight stitch using 2mm #127 pink silk ribbon. The leaves surrounding the flowers are made with a straight stitch using 4mm #18 green silk ribbon. ✖

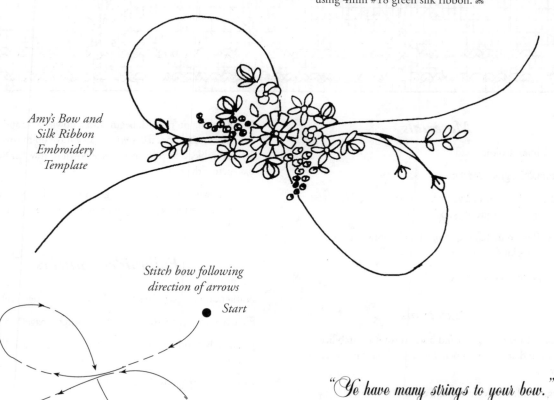

Amy's Bow and Silk Ribbon Embroidery Template

Stitch bow following direction of arrows

● *Start*

"Ye have many strings to your bow."

——John Heywwood

Tulip Garden

In time for spring, this delightful design is smocked and embroidered entirely with silk ribbon. The flower border on the bottom has green cables and leaves with medium pink flowers. These flowers remind me of Monet's garden with its mixture of different colors in the same area. The spray in the middle of the design is a medley of flowers in lavender, white, blue, and pink. Beautiful green in two shades makes the stems and the leaves. The centers of the white and lavender flowers are composed of yellow silk ribbon French knots, and blue French knots are found throughout this design. Yummy! A pretty green border of cables finishes the top of this design. This design seems to say, "Wear me on Easter Sunday morning."

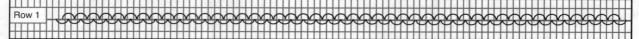

Tulip Garden Silk Ribbon Embroidery Template on next page

Center

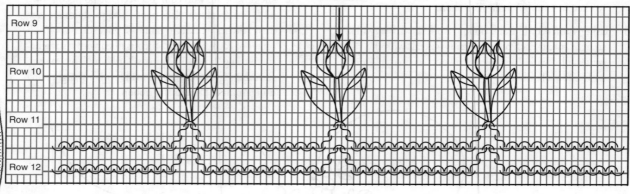

Materials

❋ Silk Ribbon Colors Used:

2mm: #31 green, #18 green

4mm: #3 white, #12 yellow, #44 blue, #125 blue, #68 pink, #31 green, #23 lavender

❋ DMC floss to match the color of your fabric for backsmocking

❋ Color photo - page 40

Directions

1. Pleat 14 rows. The top and bottom rows are stabilizer rows and are not numbered on the graph. Smock 12 rows.

2. Begin with a down cable and cable across row 1 using 2mm #18 green silk ribbon.

3. Backsmock rows 2 through 11 using floss to match the color of your fabric.

4. Working on row 12, begin with a down cable and cable 19 across. Work a 2-step $^{1}/_{2}$ space wave up to row 11$^{1}/_{2}$, 1 up cable, 2-step $^{1}/_{2}$ space wave down to row 12. Repeat across the row.

5. Following the instructions given in step 4, work the same combination beginning on row 11$^{1}/_{2}$, working up to row 11.

Embroidery Stitches

Feather Stitch - page 164

French Knot - page 164

Japanese Ribbon Stitch - page 167

Lazy Daisy - page 167

Pistil Stitch - page 169

Stem Stitch - page 173

Straight Stitch - page 173

1. Work Japanese ribbon stitch tulips in 4mm #68 pink silk ribbon between rows $9^{1}/_{2}$ and 11, starting just above row $9^{1}/_{2}$.

2. Add straight stitch stems with 2mm #31 green silk ribbon.

3. Using 4mm #31 green silk ribbon, work a Japanese ribbon stitch leaf on each side of the stem. The leaves of the tulips are placed above each of the points on row 11.

4. Work the floral spray between rows 4 and 7 following the diagram and chart for flowers and placement. ▨

Tulip Garden Silk Ribbon Embroidery Template

Stitch Guide

Lazy daisy - 4mm #3 white silk ribbon

Center - 3 French knots - 4mm #12 yellow silk ribbon

Pistil stitch - 4mm #44 blue silk ribbon

Fly stitch calyx - 2mm #18 green silk ribbon

Japanese ribbon stitch tulip - 4mm #68 pink silk ribbon

Ribbon stitch leaves - 4mm #31 green silk ribbon

Stem stitch stems - 2mm #31 green silk ribbon

Straight stitch - 4mm #23 lavender silk ribbon

French knot center - 4mm #12 yellow silk ribbon

Lazy daisy leaves - #18 2mm silk ribbon

Feather stitch - #31 green 2mm silk ribbon

French knot - #125 blue 4mm silk ribbon

"I will be the gladdest thing under the sun!
I will touch a hundred flowers and not pick one."

——Edna St. Vincent Millay

Harvest Flowers

Simple and elegant for a round collar or a bishop dress is this flower assortment in beautiful fall colors of rust, gold, green, yellow and brown. Green geometric smocking makes the borders which act as a showcase for the beautiful flowers. The larger flowers are composed of eight lazy daisies; Japanese ribbon stitches make the leaves. Two lazy daisy stitches form the bud and a nine-wrap bullion stitch of embroidery floss cups the base of the buds.

Center

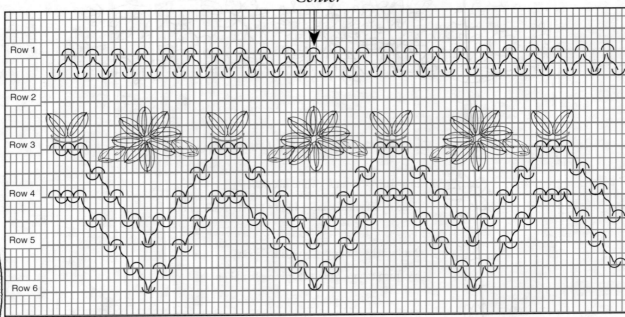

Materials

❧ Silk Ribbon Colors Used:

   4mm: #33 green, #89 red, #55 gold, #12 yellow

❧ DMC Floss: #368 green, #919 brown, #780 brown, #838 brown, white, floss to match color of fabric for backsmocking

❧ Color photo - page 32

Directions

1. Pleat 8 rows. The top and bottom rows are stabilizer rows and are not numbered on the graph. Smock 6 rows.

2. Backsmock row 1, with a cable row, in a color of floss to match fabric.

3. Backsmock between rows 2 and 3 with a 2 step-wave in a color of floss to match the fabric.

4. To center the design, begin with a down cable over the center valley on row 6. Using 3 strands of #368 green floss, work $^1/_2$-step wave up to row $5^1/_2$, up cable, down cable, $^1/_2$-step wave up to row 5, up cable, down cable, repeat to row 4, ending with a 5-cable combination. Repeat following graph across row.

5. Between rows 1 and $1^1/_2$, work $^1/_2$-space baby waves using 3 strands of #368 green floss.

6. Using #919, #780, and #838 brown floss, center a 4-cable flowerette on row 3 over the center valley of each diamond. Alternate the centers of the flowers by using the different shades of brown floss.

Embroidery Stitches

Bullion - page 157

Japanese Ribbon Stitch - page 167

Lazy Daisy - page 167

1. Alternate the colors of the flowers using 4mm #89 red, #55 gold, and #12 yellow silk ribbon. The flowers are created with 8 lazy daisy petals worked around the flowerette center.

2. Work a Japanese ribbon stitch in 4mm #33 green silk ribbon for the leaves on each side of the flower.

3. Small buds are placed in the center of the 5-cable combination on row 3 using 4mm #55 gold silk ribbon. The buds consist of two lazy daisy stitches with a 9-wrap bullion stitch at the base of the bud worked with 1 strand of #368 green floss. ❧

46

Ribbons And Roses

Breathtaking! Heavenly! Magnificent! Treasures of stitching have been taken on this ecru batiste dress smocked entirely in silk ribbons. Two shades of dusty pink, pale green, and pale blue have been combined artfully. The silk ribbon roses in the center are made using two shades of dusty pink, with two rose buds peeking from behind the large roses. Rosebuds top each wave around the bishop trellises with blue silk ribbon French knots peeking from between the pleats on the bottom trellises. Fit for a princess, this dress will be an heirloom to treasure for decades to come.

Center

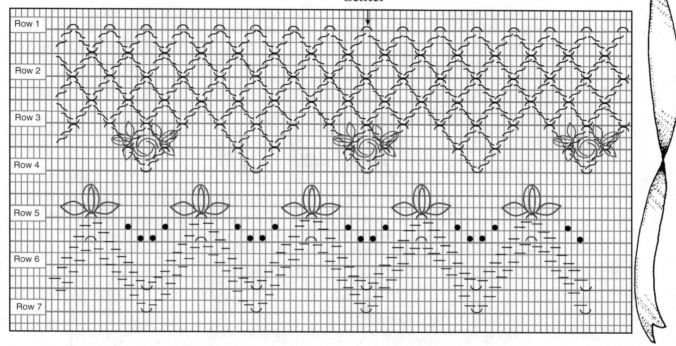

Materials

❀ Silk Ribbon Colors Used:

2mm: #157 and #163 pink

4mm: #157, #163, and #158 pink, #31 green, #125 blue

❀ DMC floss to match color of fabric for backsmocking

❀ Color photo - page 32

Directions

1. Pleat 9 rows. The top and bottom rows are stabilizer rows and are not numbered on the graph. Smock 7 rows.

2. Using floss to match the color of your fabric, backsmock between rows $3^1/_2$ and $5^1/_2$.

3. Using 2mm #157 pink silk ribbon, center the design on row $6^1/_2$. Begin with a down cable and work an 8-step wave from rows $6^1/_2$ to 5. Work 1 up cable, 8-step wave down to row $6^1/_2$. Continue across row. Flip fabric for other side.

4. Following the instructions in step 3, and using 2mm #163 pink silk ribbon, work another row of 8-step waves between rows 7 and $5^1/_2$.

5. Work half space 2-step waves in 2mm #157 pink silk ribbon. Begin in the center of row 1 with 1 up cable and work down to row $1^1/_2$.

6. Repeat instructions in step 5 for rows 2 to $1^1/_2$, rows 2 to $2^1/_2$, and rows 3 to $2^1/_2$ to form diamonds. (When smocking from the bottom and moving up, you will begin with a down cable rather than an up cable.)

7. The points across the bottom of the design are formed by working a 2-step wave between rows 3 and $3^1/_2$, flip fabric and work a one-step wave between rows $3^1/_2$ and 4. Return to row 3, skip 4 pleats and repeat across the design. Refer to graph for placement.

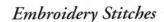

Embroidery Stitches

Bradford Rose - page 156   Lazy Daisy - page 167

Colonial Knot - page 161   Straight Stitch - page 173

French Knot - page 164

1. At the upper point of each 8 - step wave, work a lazy daisy stitch using 4mm #158 pink silk ribbon with a single wrap French knot in 4mm #157 pink silk ribbon at the end.

2. At the base of each bud add two straight stitch leaves in 4mm #31 green silk ribbon. These straight stitch leaves are angled over three pleats.

3. Using 4mm #125 blue silk ribbon, work single-wrap French knots spaced in the pleats between the buds. The French knots should be evenly spaced between rows $5\frac{1}{4}$ and $5\frac{1}{2}$.

4. Work a Bradford rose on the smocked diamonds using the graph for placement. Make a colonial knot in 4mm #158 pink silk ribbon for the center of the Bradford rose. The first row of rose petals is made with three wrapped straight stitches in 4mm #163 pink silk ribbon. The second row of petals is made with six wrapped straight stitches worked in 4mm #157 pink silk ribbon.

5. Add a lazy daisy stitch with a French knot anchor on each side of the rose using 4mm #157 silk ribbon. Make two straight stitch leaves at the base of each bud in 4mm #31 green silk ribbon. ❈

Jack and Jill

For a boy or a girl, this design is smocked with white embroidery floss and has pink or blue satin flowerettes in-between the two step waves. On the bottom half, silk ribbon is woven between the baby waves. Tiny pink roses with green embroidery floss lazy daisies trim the pink side. It is so cute to see that smocking designs can be used for both boys and girls simply by changing the colors. Of course, little girls love to wear blue; however, many little boys' fathers do not love them in pink.

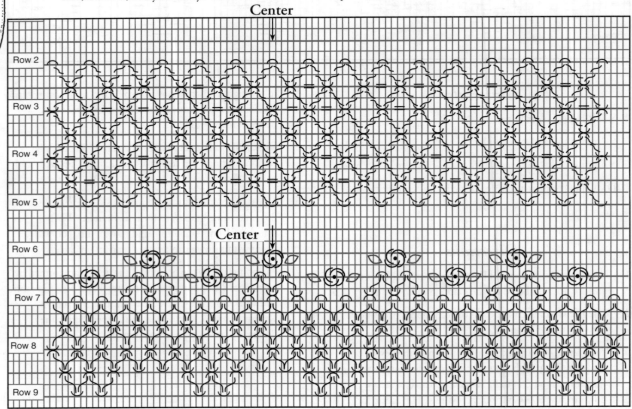

Smocking and embroidery instructions for Jack and Jill located on next page

Materials

❀ Silk Ribbon Colors Used:

   ❀ Girls' Version:

      2mm: #110 pink

      4mm: #7 pink for weaving

      DMC: #564 green, #963 pink, white, color to match fabric for backsmocking

   ❀ Boys' Version:

      Silk Ribbon Colors Used:

      4mm: #82 blue for weaving

      DMC floss: white, #3325 blue, color to match fabric for backsmocking

❀ Color photo - page 38

Directions for Girls and Boys

1. Pleat 11 rows. The top and bottom rows are stabilizer rows and are not numbered on the graph. Smock 9 rows.

2. Backsmock row 6 in a floss color to match fabric.

3. Using white floss, begin on row 2 at the center with an up cable, 2-step wave down to rows $2^1/_2$, 2-step wave up. Repeat across row.

4. Begin row 3 at the center with a down cable, 2-step wave up to row $2^1/_2$, 1 up cable, 2-step wave down to row 3. Repeat across row.

5. Following the instructions in step 3 and 4, repeat between rows 3 and 5.

6. Begin on row 7 with 1 up cable, one-step wave down to row $7^1/_2$, 1 down cable, one-step wave up to row 7. Repeat across row.

7. Begin on row 8 with a down cable, one-step wave up to row $7^1/_2$, 1 up cable, one-step wave down to row 8.

8. Following the instructions in step 7, repeat between rows 8 and $8^1/_2$.

9. Work two one-step waves above row 7 and below row $8^1/_2$, skipping two waves between each. See graph for placement.

10. Pink or blue satin stitches covering two pleats are worked on rows 2 through 5. Follow graph for placement.

11. Using a 2mm silk ribbon color for the version you are working, weave it between rows $7^1/_2$ and 9. Following the graph, weave the ribbon under the smocking. The ribbon will have to be flipped over as you change directions to keep it from twisting.

Embroidery Stitches

French Knot - page 164

Lazy Daisy Stitch - page 167

Straight Stitch - page 173

Girls

1. Using #110 pink 2mm silk ribbon, work silk ribbon roses on rows 6 and $6^1/_2$. Work a straight stitch rose using #110 2mm pink silk ribbon with a French knot in the center made of #110 2mm pink silk ribbon. See chart for placement.

2. Using 2 strands of #564 floss, make lazy daisy leaves beside the roses. ❀

"A sweet child is the sweetest thing in nature."

—— Charles Lamb

Monet's Garden

Springtime with pinks and greens seems to be the theme of this perky smocking design with silk ribbon embellishments. The smocking is done with three shades of green. Silk ribbon flowerettes can be found in the form of three little cables on the upper portion of the plates. Silk ribbon has been threaded through the top rows of green smocking and tied on one side in a perky bow. Beautiful silk ribbon roses embellish the bottom sections of the trellises. Pink and green are such beautiful Easter colors which travel through the summer also.

Center

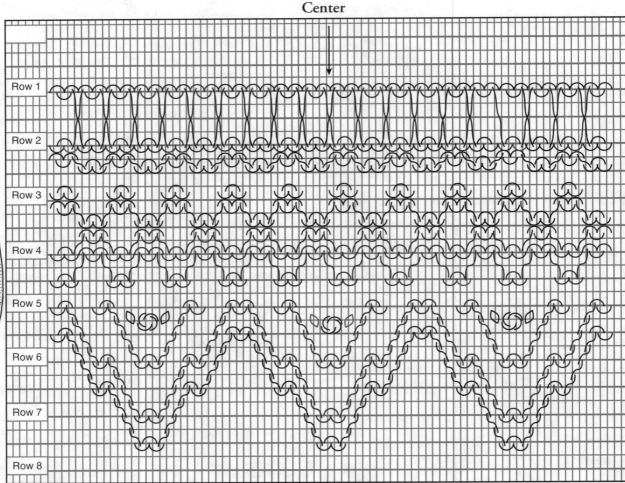

Materials

❈ Silk Ribbon Colors Used:

4mm: #7 and #8 pink

❈ DMC Floss: #503, #504, and 992 green, color to match fabric for backsmocking

❈ Color photo - page 39

Directions

1. Pleat 9 rows. The top and bottom rows are stabilizer rows and are not numbered on the graph. Smock 7 3/4 rows. This design may be used as a bishop or yoke dress.

2. Using 3 strands of #503 green floss, begin on row 1 at center. Work * 1 up cable, 1 down cable, 1 up cable, a full step wave down to row 2, 1 down cable, 1 up cable, 1 down cable, 1 full step wave up to row 1. Repeat from * across the row.

3. Using 3 strands of #504 green floss, begin on row 2 with * 1 down cable, 1 up cable, 1 down cable, 1 full step wave up to row 1,1 up cable, 1 down cable, 1 up cable, 1 full step wave down to row 2. Repeat from * across the row. Note that the full step waves cross between rows 1 and 2.

4. Working directly beneath row 2 in #503 green floss, work * 1 up cable, 1 down cable, 1 up cable, 1 step-wave down to row 2½, 1 down cable, 1 up cable, 1 down cable, 1 step wave up to row 2. Repeat from * across.

5. Following the instructions given in step 4, work from row 3 down to row 3½. Repeat across row.

6. Using 3 strands of #504 green floss, work a mirror image of step 4 beginning on row 4 and working up to row 3½.

7. Using 3 strands of #504 green floss, following instructions in step 3, work from row 4½ up to row 4.

8. Using 3 strands of #504 green floss, beginning on row 5, work * 2 cables (down, up), 4-step wave down to row 6, 1 down cable, 1 up cable, 4-step wave down to row 7, 1 down cable, 1 up cable, 1 down cable, 4-step wave up to row 6, 1 up cable, 1 down cable, 4 step wave up to row 5, Repeat from * across row.

9. Between rows 5½ and 7½, using 3 strands of #503 green floss, repeat the instructions given in step 8.

10. Using 3 strands of #504 green floss, beginning on row 5, 3 pleats from the top edge of the inside valley, (refer to graph for placement) work 1 down cable, 1 up cable, 4-step wave down to row 6, 1 down cable, 1 up cable, 1 down cable, 4 step wave up to row 5. Tie off. Continue working inside valleys across the row. (These waves are worked between the larger connecting waves made in steps 8 and 9.)

11. Above row 3, using 2mm #7 pink silk ribbon, work 1 down cable, 1 up cable, 1 down cable, meeting the cables on row 3, repeat across row. Tie off after each flowerette. Refer to graph for placement.

12. Using 2mm #8 pink silk ribbon, thread the ribbon underneath the smocking between rows 1 and 2.

Embroidery Stitches

Spider Web Rose - page 172

Lazy Daisy - page 167

1. Using 2mm #7 pink silk ribbon, work a spider web rose at each small valley. See graph for placement.

2. Using 3 strands of #992 green floss, work small lazy daisy leaves on each side of the spider web rose.

Sleeves

1. Pleat 4 rows. The top and bottom rows are stabilizer rows and are not numbered on the graph. Tie off to the desired width and smock 2 rows. Refer to "Dress Construction - XII. Sleeve Construction A, Smocked Sleeves, page 107.

2. On row 2 with 3 strands of #503 green floss, work * 1 down cable, 1 up cable, 1 down cable, 1 half step wave up to row 1½, 1 up cable, 1 down cable, 1 up cable, 1 half step wave down to row 2. Repeat from * across row.

3. Working immediately beneath row 2 with 3 strands of #504 green floss, work * 1 down cable, 1 up cable, 1 up cable, 1 full step wave down to row 3, 1 down cable, 1 up cable, 1 down cable, 1 full step wave up to row 2. Repeat from * across the row.

4. Begin stitching on row 3 with 3 strands of #504 green floss. Work * 1 down cable, 1 up cable, 1 down cable, 1 full step wave up to row 2, 1 up cable, 1 down cable, 1 up cable, 1 full step wave down to row 3. Repeat from * across row.

5. Thread 4mm #8 pink silk ribbon underneath the smocking design, tighten to fit arm and tie in a bow. ✼

Sleeve Graph for Monet's Garden

CENTER ↓

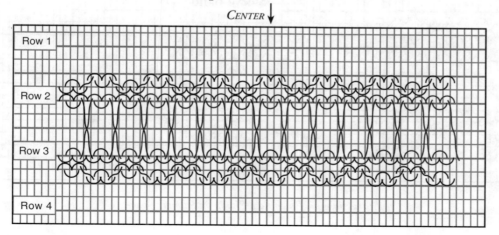

Peach Rose Bishop

What a lucky little girl who receives a bishop dress smocked with this design. The smocking portion of the plate can be smocked with peach embroidery floss or silk ribbon. Beautiful peach waves make the geometric portion of this smocking design. Lovely spider wed roses are in the center of the large hearts; the leaves and stems beneath each rose are worked with a fly stitch in a luscious shade of pale green. Little pearls are stitched on in several places on the upper smocking border. The tiny rosebuds are worked using a one wrap colonial knot. The leaves underneath the tiny rosebuds are fly stitches.

Center

Row 1
Row 2
Row 3
Row 4
Row 5
Row 6
Row 7
Row 8
Row 9

Bonnet

Row 1
Row 2
Row 3
Row 4

Sleeve Band

Instructions for Peach Rose Bishop on following page

Materials

This plate can be worked using 2mm silk ribbon or three strands of floss.

❧ Silk Ribbon Colors Used:

    4mm: #105 Peach, #62 green

❧ DMC Floss: #3779 peach

❧ Color photo - page 36

Bishop Directions

1. Pleat 10 rows. The top and bottom rows are stabilizer rows and are not numbered on the graph. Smock 8 rows.

2. Using white floss, start with a down cable, cable across row 1.

3. Use peach floss or silk ribbon for the remaining rows. Beginning with a down cable, cable across row 2.

4. Working directly above the cables on row 2, *work 1 down cable, 1 up cable, 1 down cable, a $^1/_2$ space one-step wave up to row $1^1/_2$, 1 up cable, 1 down cable, 1 up cable a, $^1/_2$ space one step wave down to row 2. Continue from * across the row.

5. Begin row 3 with a down cable, cable across row 3.

6. Working immediately beneath row 3, *work 1 up cable, 1 down cable, 1 up cable, $^1/_2$ space one-step wave down to row $3^1/_2$, 1 down cable, 1 up cable, 1 down cable, $^1/_2$ space one-step wave up to row 3. Continue from * across the row.

7. To smock row 4, follow the instructions given in step 4 above. The stitches for row 4 will rest on the pleated row rather than directly above the row.

8. Begin row 5 with *1 down cable, 1 up cable, 1 down cable, 5-step wave up to row 4, 1 up cable, l down cable, 1 up cable, 5-step wave down to row 5. Continue from * across the row.

9. Beginning immediately beneath row 5, smock *1 up cable, 1 down cable, 1 up cable, 13-step wave down to row $8^1/_2$, 1 down cable, 1 up cable, 1 down cable, 13-step wave up to row 5, 1 up cable, 1 down cable, 1 up cable. Continue from * across the row.

10 Begin the next row of smocking $^1/_8$" (between rows 5 and 6) below the last row smocked. Follow the instructions given in step 9 above.

Embroidery Stitches

Colonial Knot - page 161

Fly Stitch - page 163

1. Using 4mm #105 peach silk ribbon, work a spider web rose in the center of the large hearts.

2. Using 4mm #62 green silk ribbon, work the leaves and around each rose with a lazy daisy stitch. Refer to graph for placement.

3. Using 4mm #105 peach ribbon, work the rosebuds between rows 2 and 3. The rosebuds are worked with a 1-wrap colonial knot.

4. Using 4mm #62 green silk ribbon, work the leaves and stems for the rosebuds with a fly stitch.

5. Sew $2^1/_2$ mm pearls on the second and third rows. See graph for placement.

Sleeve Band Directions

1. Pleat 4 rows. Rows 1 and 4 are used to help stabilize the pleats while you smock on rows 2 and 3.

2. Following the directions in steps 3 and 4 in the Bishop Directions, smock across row 2.

3. Following the directions in steps 5 and 6 in the Bishop Directions, smock across row 3.

4. Using 4mm #105 peach silk ribbon, work 1-wrap colonial knot buds between rows 2 and 3. See graph for placement.

5. Using 4mm #62 green silk ribbon, work the leaves and stems with a fly stitch.

6. Sew $2^1/_2$ mm pearls on the sleeve band, following the graph for placement.

Bonnet Directions

1. Pleat 6 rows. The top and bottom rows are stabilizer rows and are not numbered on the graph. Smock 4 rows.

2. Smock with peach floss or silk ribbon. Work a row of cables across rows 2 and 3.

3. Following step 4 in Bishop Directions, work from row 2 up to row $1^1/_2$.

4. Following step 6 in Bishop Directions from the *, work from row 1 down to row $1^1/_2$.

5. Following step 6 in Bishop Directions, work from row 3 down to row $3^1/_2$.

6. Following step 4 in Bishop Directions, work from row 4 up to row $3^1/_2$. ▩

Poinsettia Wreath

What little or big girl wouldn't want a Christmas dress smocked and embroidered with this poinsettia? Using several luscious shades of green, burgundy, red, gold and white silk ribbon this wreath is simply magnificent. The design is backsmocked in white to hold the pleats correctly. The borders are smocked with white silk ribbon and almost look pearlized. The little holly berries at the points of the white smocking are composed of French knots and leaves of pale green. There is a berry wreath circle and the poinsettias are tucked away in the corner of the design. The ribbon cascade is elegant and is held in place with embroidery floss French knots.

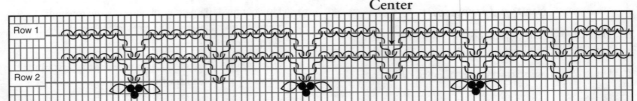

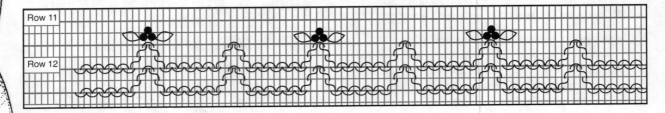

Materials

❋ Silk Ribbon Colors Used:

   2mm: #2 red, #1 white

   4mm: #2 red, #49 red, #50 red, #32 green, #33 green, #75 green, #61 green, #14 gold, #51 gold

❋ DMC Floss: #701 green, floss to match color of fabric

❋ Color photo - page 34

Directions

1. Pleat 14 rows. The top and bottom rows are stabilizer rows and are not numbered on the graph. Smock 12 rows.

2. Backsmock rows 2 - 11, using floss to match the color of your fabric.

3. Working with 2mm #1 white silk ribbon, start on row 1 with an up cable. Work 9 cables, 1/2 space 2-step wave down to row 1 1/2, 1 down cable, 2-step wave up to row 1. Repeat across row.

4. Repeat step 2 working between rows 1 1/2 and 2.

5. Working with 2mm #1 white silk ribbon, start on row 12. Begin with a down cable, cable 9 across, a 2-step wave up to row 11 1/2, 1 up cable, 2-step wave down to row 12. Repeat across row.

6. Repeat step 5 stitching on rows 12 1/2 up to 12.

7. The berries are worked using 2mm #2 red silk ribbon. Make three 2-wrap French knots at the point of every other two-step wave. See graph for placement. Add 2 straight stitch leaves in 4mm #32 green silk ribbon to each group of berries. Repeat for the bottom design.

Embroidery Stitches

Colonial Knot - page 161   Straight Stitch - page 173

Fly Stitch - page 163   Twisted Straight Stitch - page 177

French Knot - page 164

Lazy Daisy Stitch - page 167

1. Using a washout marker, trace a 2-inch circle on the pleated fabric centering the circle between rows 3 1/2 and 8 1/2.

2. Using 4mm #49 red silk ribbon, work two-wrap French knots 1/2" apart around the circle, tying off each French knot on the back of the fabric. See diagram for placement.

3. Using 4mm #75 green silk ribbon, join the berries with a twisted straight stitch.

4. The leaves for the berries are made using a straight stitch in 4mm #75 green silk ribbon.

5. Using 4mm #61 green silk ribbon, cut a piece of the ribbon 18" long and tie into a bow.

6. Stitch the center of the bow to the lower left side of the circle. The flowers will be worked around the loops with some of the stitches done over the ribbon.

7. Arrange the bow loops and streamers. Attach them to the pleats using single-wrapped French knots with 2 strands of #701 green floss.

8. Working with 4mm #14 gold silk ribbon, work 3 single-wrap French knots for the poinsettia center. Refer to the diagram for placement.

9. Using 4mm #50 red silk ribbon, work six Japanese ribbon stitches around the center French knots.

10. Using 4mm #49 red silk ribbon, add a second row of slightly shorter Japanese ribbon stitches between those worked in the first row.

11. Using 4mm #33 green silk ribbon, work straight stitch leaves around the poinsettia flowers.

12. Using 4mm #51 gold silk ribbon, work the gold stalks in a series of fly stitches. Refer to the diagram for placement.

13. The berries are made with a colonial knot in 4mm #2 red silk ribbon. Scatter the berries around the flowers.

14. The straight stitch leaves are made with 4mm #32 green silk ribbon.

15. If filler is needed, work lazy daisy stitches in 4mm #49 red silk ribbon. ▨

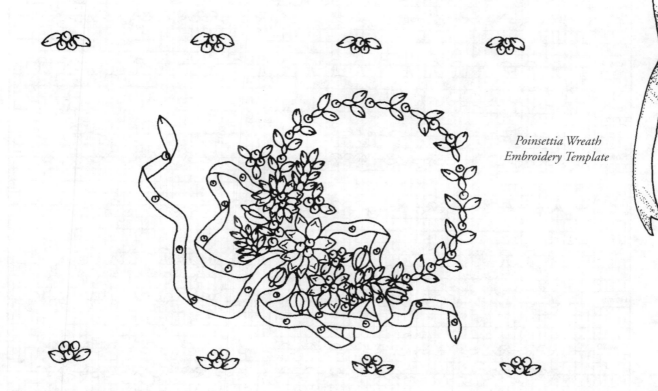

Poinsettia Wreath
Embroidery Template

Robin's Egg Renaissance

Just too beautiful for words is this smocking design plate is smocked on white fabric with robin's egg blue embroidery floss. Silk ribbon in robin's egg blue is woven through certain sections of one-step waves. Pink roses with green floss lazy daisy leaves finish one row. I certainly think of the older girl's dress when looking at this design. It is so very sophisticated and elegant, and not very babyish.

Center

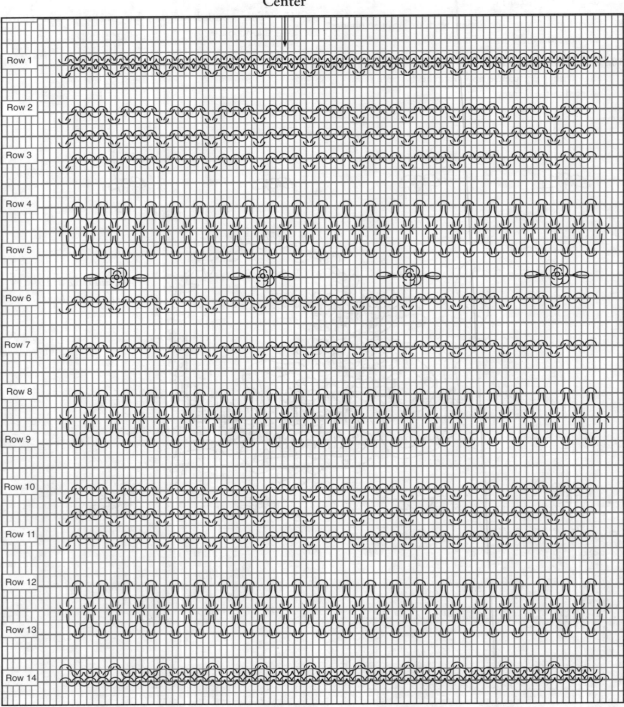

Instructions for Robin's Egg Renaissance on following page

Materials

❀ Silk Ribbon Colors Used:

  2mm: #115 blue, #157 pink

❀ DMC floss: #775 blue, #3318 green, floss to match color of fabric.

❀ Color photo - page 38

Directions

1. Pleat 16 rows. The top and bottom rows are stabilizer rows and are not numbered on the graph. Smock 14 rows.

2. Beginning with a down cable, cable across row 1 using 3 strands of #775 blue floss.

3. Beginning with an up cable 3 pleats to the left of center, work a 5 cable, $^1/_4$ space baby wave combination, meeting the cables of row 1. Continue across the row. Flip the fabric and repeat for other side. Refer to graph.

4. Using the instructions given in step 3, smock rows 2, $2^1/_2$, and 3.

5. Begin working between rows 4 and $4^1/_2$ with a down cable on row $4^1/_2$, work a one-step $^1/_2$ space wave up to row 4, up cable, $^1/_2$ space 1-step wave combination across row. Flip fabric and repeat for other side.

6. Using the instructions given in step 5, smock between row $4^1/_2$ and 5, forming diamonds. Begin with an up cable just below row $4^1/_2$.

7. Repeat step 3 between rows 6 and $6^1/_4$; 7 and $7^1/_4$.

8. Between rows 8 and 9, refer to steps 5 and 6.

9. Between rows 10 and $11^1/_4$, refer to steps 3 and 4.

10. Between rows 12 and 13, refer to steps 5 and 6,

11. Row 14 is a mirror image of row 1. Follow directions in steps 2 and 3.

12. Using 2mm #115 blue silk ribbon, weave ribbon under rows 4 and 5, 8 and 9, and 12 and 13.

Embroidery Stitches

Spider Web Rose - page 172

Lazy Daisy - page 167

1. Using 2mm #157 pink silk ribbon, work spider web roses between rows 5 and 6. See graph for placement.

2. The leaves are made with a lazy daisy stitch using 2 strands of #3318 green floss. Place the leaves on each side of the roses. ❀

The bird of paradise alights only upon the

hand that does not grasp.

John Berry

Woven Elegance

Beautiful for a boy or a girl is this woven ribbon elegant smocking design plate. Pale yellow and pale blue ribbons are woven in-between the bottom portion of one-step waves smocked in pale blue. The top geometric smocking in pale yellow and blue is very beautiful and unique. The smocking is done with embroidery floss and the ribbon is silk.

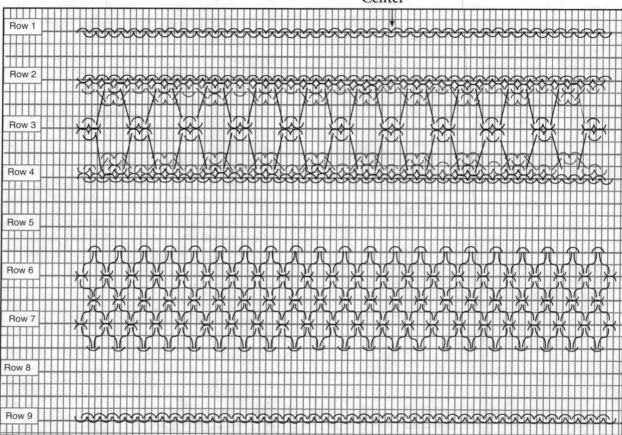

Materials

❧ Silk Ribbon Colors Used:

   2mm: #34 beige, #44 blue

❧ DMC Floss: #3325 blue, #746 yellow, floss to match color of fabric

❧ Color photo - page 37

Directions

1. Pleat 11 rows. The top and bottom rows are stabilizer rows and are not numbered on the graph. Smock 9 rows.

2. Row 9 can be left unsmocked to release the pleats, if desired.

3. Backsmock rows 5 and 8 using a floss to match the color of your fabric.

4. Beginning with a down cable worked in with three strands of #3325 blue floss, cable across row 2.

5. Beginning on row 3 with three strands of #7325 blue floss, * cable 3,)down, up, down) one full step wave up to row 2, cable 3, (up, down, up) one full step wave down to row 3 and repeat from * across row.

6. Beginning on row 3 with three strands of #7325 blue floss, work * an up, down, up cable, 1 full step wave down to row 4, down, up, down cable, 1 full step wave up to row 3 and repeat from * across row.

7. Beginning immediately below row 4 with an up cable using three strands of #3325 blue floss, cable across the row.

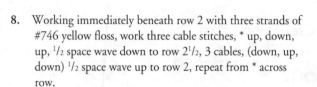

8. Working immediately beneath row 2 with three strands of #746 yellow floss, work three cable stitches, * up, down, up, $^1/_2$ space wave down to row $2^1/_2$, 3 cables, (down, up, down) $^1/_2$ space wave up to row 2, repeat from * across row.

9. Following the instructions * given in step 8, mirror image the design, stitching from row 4 up to row $3^1/_2$.

10. Beginning on row 6 with three strands of #3325 blue floss, work * 1 down cable down, $^1/_2$ step wave up to row $5^1/_2$, 1 up cable, $^1/_2$ step wave down to row 6. Repeat from * across row.

11. Using three strands of #3325 blue floss, begin immediately beneath row 6 with * 1 up cable, $^1/_2$ step wave down to row $6^1/_2$, down cable, $^1/_2$ step wave up to row 6.

12. Beginning on row 7, follow the instructions given in step 10, working from row 7 to row $6^1/_2$.

13. Beginning on row 7, follow the instructions given in step 11, working from row 7 to row $7^1/_2$.

14. Thread 2mm #44 blue silk ribbon #34 beige and beneath the smocking on rows 6 and 7. Make sure to flip the ribbon to keep it flat. Refer to photo on page 37. ❈

Donna's Crest

The background of two-step waves forms the perfect pallet for the silk ribbon painting in the middle. The blue waving ribbons are actually smocked in and the roses in the design are pink with a pearl tucked in each center. Blue flowers with yellow French knots add to the beauty of this design. Little blue French knots are scattered over the design also. Being a sophisticated design, this masterpiece could be used for many different occasions.

Materials

❈ Silk Ribbon Colors Used:

2mm: #125 and #126 blue, #8 pink, #31 green, #13 yellow

❈ DMC Floss: white

❈ Color photo - page 36

Directions

1. Pleat 12 rows. The top and bottom rows are stabilizer rows and are not numbered on the graph. Smock 10 rows.

2. Border Rows: Beginning with an up cable, cable across rows 1 and 10, using three strands of white floss.

3. Beginning on row 3 with three strands of white floss, start with a *down cable, 2 step wave up to row 2, 1 up cable, 2-step wave down to row 3. Repeat from * across the row.

4. Beginning on row 3, work an * up cable, 2-step wave down to row 4, 1 down cable, 2-step wave up to row 3. Repeat from * across the row forming diamonds.

5. Following instructions given in steps 3 and 4, continue stitching from rows 4 through 9, creating diamonds.

6. Knot and bow: Begin 1 pleat to the left of center. Starting on row 3, work 3 cables in 2mm #126 blue silk ribbon, beginning with a down cable. Work a 1-step wave up to row 2, 3 cables (up, down, up), 1-step wave down to row 3, ending with a down cable on row 3. Flip the fabric and following the directions given above, work the bottom half of the right side of the bow. Repeat for left side of bow. Refer to the graph.

7. Streamers: Using 2mm #126 blue silk ribbon, begin the streamers on row 4, see graph for placement. Work 4 steps down to row 6. Beginning with a down cable, work 5 cables on row 6. Work a 5-step wave up to row 5. Beginning with an up cable, work 5 cables across row 5. Work a $^1/_2$ space wave down to row $5^1/_2$. Work a down cable on row $5^1/_2$ and a 5-step wave up to row $4^1/_2$, ending with an up cable. This will complete the streamer for the right side of the bow.

8. Repeat instructions given in step 7 for the left streamer, reversing the stitches according to the graph..

Embroidery Stitches

French Knot - page 164   Pullen Knot - page 168

Lazy Daisy - page 167   Spider Web Rose - page 172

1. Following the diagram for placement, work the large spider web rose in 2mm #8 pink silk ribbon on row 5.

2. Work the two remaining spider web roses on row 4 using 2mm #8 pink silk ribbon. See diagram for placement.

3. Fill in around the roses with lazy daisy stitch leaves made with 2mm #31 green silk ribbon.

4. The forget-me-knots are made with 1-wrap French knots using 2mm #126 blue silk ribbon.

5. Stitch a single pearl in the center of each rose. ❈

Donna's Crest

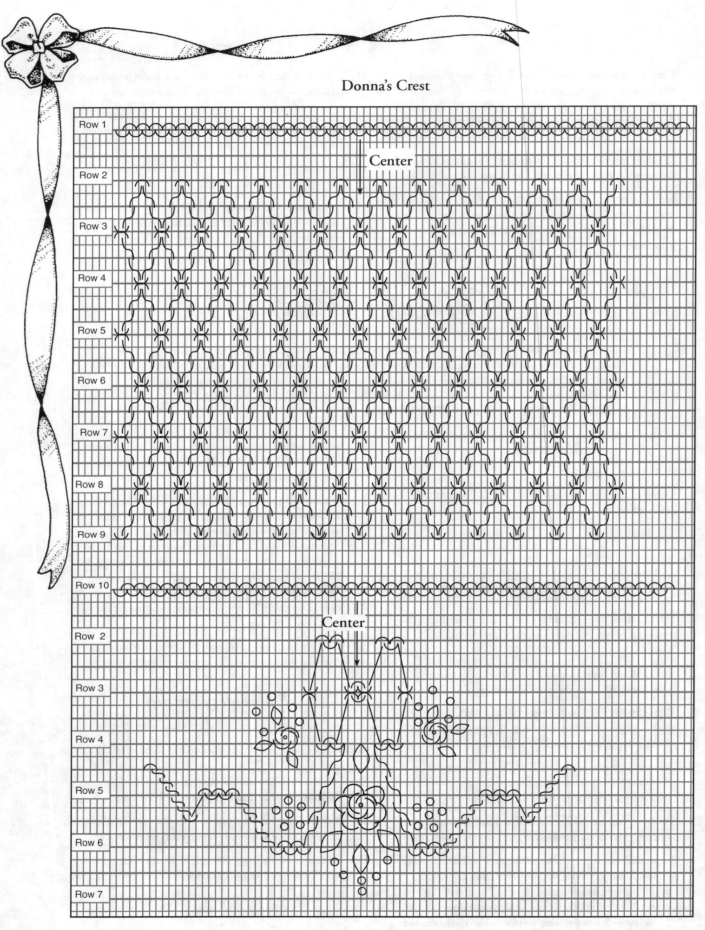

Row 1

Center

Row 2

Row 3

Row 4

Row 5

Row 6

Row 7

Row 8

Row 9

Row 10

Center

Row 2

Row 3

Row 4

Row 5

Row 6

Row 7

Sarah's Wreath

Borders of green and rose floss pick up the beautiful colors in the three wreaths on this white broadcloth fabric. The colors of the delightful flowers in these wreaths are rose, pale green, yellow, robin's egg blue and pale blue. Perky would be the word to describe the cascaded blue silk ribbon bows which are attached to the smocking fabric with blue silk ribbon French knots. This smocking design would be beautiful not only on little girl's clothing but also on a bedroom pillow. It could be used for a ring bearer's pillow since the ring (circular) theme is carried out in the wreaths.

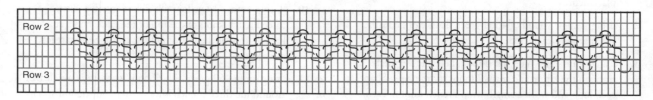

Silk Ribbon Embroidery Template

Materials

☙ Silk Ribbon Colors Used:

4mm: #125 blue, #62 green, #14 yellow, #158 rose, #115 blue

☙ DMC Floss: #3373 rose, #504 green, floss to match color of fabric

☙ Color photo - page 37

Directions

1. Pleat 10 rows. The top and bottom rows are stabilizer rows and are not numbered on the graph. Smock 8 rows.

2. Backsmock rows 3 - 8 using a color of floss to match the fabric.

3. Using three strands of #504 green floss, begin smocking on row 2. Smock * 1 up cable, 2-step $^1/_2$ space wave down to row $2^1/_2$, 1 down cable, 2-step $^1/_2$ space wave up to row 2.

4. Using #3373 rose floss, begin stitching on row $2^1/_4$. Stitch down to row $2^3/_4$, following the instructions given in step 3.

5. Using #504 green floss, work a 2-step $^1/_2$ space wave between rows 8 and $8^1/_2$, following instructions given in step 3.

6. Using #3373 rose floss, begin stitching on row $8^1/_4$, stitching down to row $8^3/_4$, following instructions given in step 3.

Embroidery Stitches

Feather Stitch - page 164   Lazy Daisy - page 167

French Knot - page 164   Straight Stitch - page 173

Japanese Ribbon Stitch - page 167

1. Using a washout marker, draw three circles on the surface of the pleated fabric 1¼" in diameter. See chart for placement.

2. Using a single strand of #504 green floss, work a feather stitch around each circle.

3. Using 4mm #125 blue silk ribbon, take a loose stitch through the fabric and form 2 loops for the bow. Shape each loop and work a single-wrap French knot in each loop to anchor the loops to the fabric.

4. Using 4mm #125 blue silk ribbon, make the streamers for the bow. Work a single-wrap French knot on the streamers to anchor them to the fabric. See chart for placement.

5. Work a single straight stitch over the center of the bow for the knot.

6. Using 4mm #158 rose silk ribbon, work straight stitch flowers around the circle. See chart for placement.

7. Using 4mm #62 green silk ribbon, work straight stitch leaves around the rose colored flowers.

8. Using 4mm #14 yellow silk ribbon, work single Japanese ribbon stitch flowers.

9. Using 4mm #62 green silk ribbon, work straight stitch leaves around the Japanese ribbon stitch flowers.

10. Using 4mm #14 yellow silk ribbon, work a cluster of three French knots at the top of the circle and a single French knot at the bottom of the circle. See chart for placement.

11. Using 4mm #62 green silk ribbon, work lazy daisy leaves around the three French knot cluster and straight stitch leaves around the single French knot.

12. Using 4mm #115 blue silk ribbon, work single French knots with blue 4mm silk ribbon straight stitches around the French knots. See graph for placement. ▩

Cathedral Windows

Perhaps from the windows of Notre Dame this silk ribbon smocking plate was inspired. Smocked on an ecru dress, the colors in the windows are teal, white, aqua and burgundy. The smocked windows are teal silk ribbon and the flowers and leaves are of burgundy and teal. Little white French knots further embellish the window designs.

Center

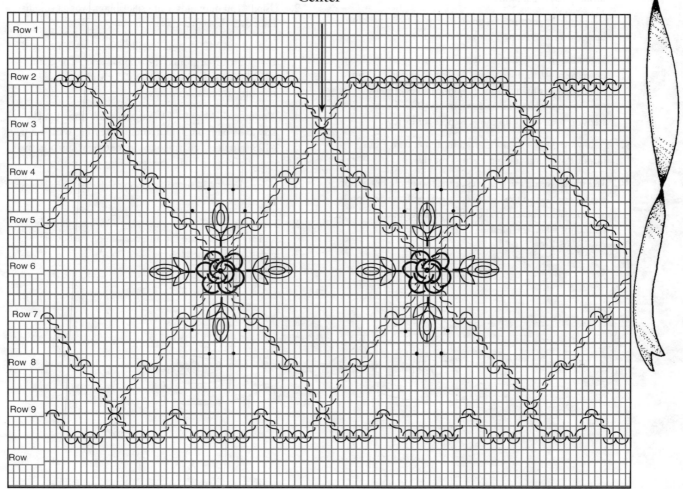

Materials

❧ Silk Ribbon Colors Used:

   4mm: #129 and #130 burgundy, #134 teal, #3 white, #132 aqua

❧ DMC: Floss to match the color of fabric

❧ Color photo - page 35

Directions

1. Pleat 10 rows. Smock 8¹/₂ rows.

2. Starting in the <u>center</u> of row 3 working with 4mm #132 aqua silk ribbon, work 1 down cable, 4 steps up to row 2, 25 cables across, 4 steps down to row 3, 1 down cable. Continue across row repeating wave and cable combination.

3. Following instructions given in step 2, turn fabric upside down and repeat across the row for other side.

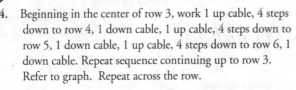

4. Beginning in the center of row 3, work 1 up cable, 4 steps down to row 4, 1 down cable, 1 up cable, 4 steps down to row 5, 1 down cable, 1 up cable, 4 steps down to row 6, 1 down cable. Repeat sequence continuing up to row 3. Refer to graph. Repeat across the row.

5. Following the instructions given in step 4, turn the fabric upside down and repeat across the row.

6. Between rows 6 and 9, repeat a mirror image of step 4, forming large diamonds.

7. Following the instructions given in step 4, turn the fabric upside down and repeat across the row.

8. Beginning in the center on row 9, work 1 up cable, 2 steps down to row $9^1/_2$, five cables, 2 steps up to row 9, 1 up cable, 2 steps down to row $9^1/_2$, nine cables, 2 steps up to row 9, 1 up cable, 2 steps down to row $9^1/_2$, 5 cables, 2 steps up to row 9, 1 up cable. Repeat across row.

9. Following the instructions given in step 8, turn fabric upside down and complete across the row.

10. Backsmock inside the triangles at the top of the design, on rows 3 and 4, and rows $7^1/_2$ and $8^1/_2$. The large diamonds are not backsmocked to allow for "puffing" of the diamonds when the pleating threads are removed.

Embroidery Stitches

Colonial Knot - page 161

Twisted Chain Stitch Rose - page 178

Lazy Daisy Stitch - page 167

Straight Stitch - page 173

Fly Stitch - page 163

1. The flowers are worked at the junctions of the diamonds. See graph for placement.

2. Using #130 burgundy 4mm silk ribbon, work a colonial knot over the center cable.

3. Using 4mm #129 burgundy silk ribbon, work a twisted chain stitch rose around the colonial knot. The chain stitch rose should contain 10 to 12 chain stitches and circle the colonial knot twice.

4. Working with 4mm #130 burgundy silk ribbon, make lazy daisy buds on all four sides of the rose. With 4mm #129 burgundy silk ribbon work a straight stitch in the center of the lazy daisy. See graph for placement.

5. Using 4mm #134 teal silk ribbon, make fly stitch leaves at the base of each bud.

6. French knots are made with 4mm #3 white silk ribbon and are added at the top and bottom of the flowers. See graph for placement. ▨

Footfalls echo in the memory

Down the passage which we did not take

Towards the door we never opened

Into the Rose Garden

— T. S. Eliot

Round Yoke Christening Gown

Using a round yoke design with smocking below the yoke, this dress is fit for a museum. Silk ribbon embroidery, white on white, is gorgeous on the round yoke. White embroidery floss is used for the stems and white 4mm silk ribbon is used for the lazy daisy stitch flowers and the Japanese ribbon stitch leaves. A pearl is at the end of each leaf and at the base of the silk ribbon flowers. Geometric smocking using white silk ribbon is found around the neckline and on the sleeves. White silk ribbon flowers are nestled in certain spots in the smocking and once again, little pearls are stitched in place. The scalloped hem is stitched in place with double needle pintucks. A second row of double needle pintucks is placed above the previous row. White silk ribbon flowers are stitched at the point of the scallops forming the hem. A pearl is stitch at the point of each flower group. Using this design for your baby's christening or your doll's new dress would be sure to take prizes in any competition.

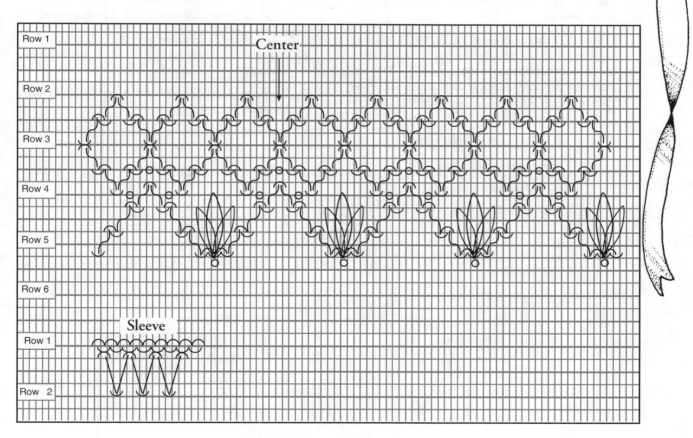

Materials

❋ Silk Ribbon Color Used:

    4mm: #3 white

❋ DMC Floss to match the color of your fabric for backsmocking

❋ 1 package of seed pearls or glass beads

❋ Color photo - page 22

❋ Pattern used for christening dress: Chery Williams Round Yoke

Directions

1. Pleat 6 rows. Smock 4$^1/_2$ rows.

2. Backsmock row 1 with 2 strands of floss to match your fabric.

3. Using 4mm #3 white silk ribbon, begin in the center front on row 3 with a down cable. Work a $^1/_2$ space baby wave up to row 2$^1/_2$. Working on row 2$^1/_2$, work 1 up cable, 1 down cable, $^1/_2$ space baby wave up to row 2. On row 2, work an up cable, $^1/_2$ space baby wave down to row 2$^1/_2$, 1

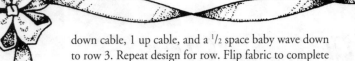

down cable, 1 up cable, and a $^1/_2$ space baby wave down to row 3. Repeat design for row. Flip fabric to complete row.

4. Repeat directions in step 3 for rows 3 and 4, forming diamonds. Refer to graph.

5. The last row of the design is worked $^1/_4$ space above row 4 (row $3^3/_4$) and $^1/_4$ space below row 5 (row $5^1/_4$). Beginning in the <u>center</u> on row $3^3/_4$ with an up cable, *$^1/_2$ space baby wave down to row $4^1/_4$, down cable, up cable, $^1/_2$ space down to row $4^3/_4$, an up cable, $^1/_2$ space down to row $5^1/_4$, 5 cable combination beginning with a down cable. Work a $^1/_2$ space wave up to row $4^3/_4$, up-down cable combination, $^1/_2$ space wave up to row $4^1/_4$, $^1/_2$ space wave up to row $3^3/_4$, 1 up cable, repeat from * across row. Flip fabric to complete row.

6. Tiny pearls or glass beads are stitched to the fabric using a single strand of floss. See graph for placement. The silk lilies are centered over the 5 cables on row $5^1/_4$. They are made with lazy daisy stitches. A single pearl is stitched to the base of each lily. See graph for placement.

Embroidery Stitches

Japanese Ribbon Stitch - page 167

Lazy Daisy Stitch - page 167

Stem Stitch - page 173

All embroidery stitches are worked with white floss and 4mm white silk ribbon.

1. Using a washout marker or #2 pencil, trace the round yoke embroidery design on the fabric. This design is traced on the yoke of the dress.

2. Using a single strand of floss, stitch the vine in a stem stitch.

3. Stitch the leaves for the vine using a lazy daisy stitch.

4. The silk lilies are stitched using the instructions given in Step 6 above.

5. The buds are Japanese ribbon stitches with a pearl stitched at the tip of each bud.

Sleeves

Refer to "Dress Construction - XII, Construction A, Smocked Sleeves" on page 107.

1. Pleat 4 rows. The top and bottom rows are stabilizer rows and are not numbered on the graph. Smock 2 rows.

2. Beginning on row 1, cable across the row beginning with a down cable.

3. Beginning underneath the cables on row 1, work a 1-step baby wave down to row 2. ▨

Yoke Embroidery Template
for Christening Dress

Rose Garland

Just gorgeous is this garland of silk ribbon embroidery. This garland would be just as beautiful stitched as a flat design as it is on this wonderful smocked fabric. Two shades of pink roses, blue roses, dark blue flowers, and pale blue flowers, with green leaves and green embroidery work together to present this most elegant swag of flowers. Two perky blue silk ribbon bows are tied on each side at the top of the swag. Two shades of pink silk ribbon are used to smock the borders on the top and the bottom. One might envision this smocking design on a flower girl dress with the colors in the swag matching the colors in the bouquets of the bridesmaids. This design would be magnificent on a pillow for a sun porch, a living room or a bedroom.

Center

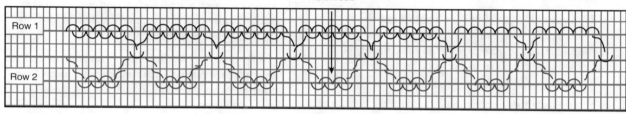

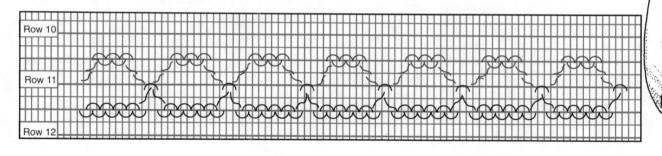

Materials

🍀 Silk Ribbon Colors Used:

  4mm: #122, #123 and #153 pink, #101, and #117 purple, #18 and #154 green, #13 yellow, and #10 blue

  7mm: #10 blue

🍀 DMC Floss: #913 green, color to match fabric

🍀 Color photo - page 34

Directions

1. Pleat 13 rows. The top and bottom rows are stabilizer rows and are not numbered on the graph. Smock 11 rows.

2. Backsmock rows 4 through 10.

3. Begin five pleats to the left of the center valley, on row 1 with 4mm #123 pink silk ribbon. Work 9 cables beginning with an up cable, 1 step wave between rows 1 and $1^1/2$. Repeat across.

4. To add contrast colored scallops use 4mm #122 pink silk ribbon. Begin at the end of row $1^1/2$ in the valley beside the right pleat of the bottom cable of the 1 step wave.

5. Trellis 2 steps down to row 2, cable 5, trellis 2 steps up to row $1^1/2$. Carry the ribbon to the wrong side across the back of the fabric to the other side of the l step wave. Repeat across.

6. Following the instructions given in step 3 above, work the cable-wave combination in #123 pink 4mm silk ribbon between rows $11^1/2$ and 11 with the cables on row $11^1/2$. This row is a mirror image of rows 1 to $1^1/2$.

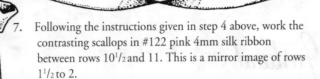

7. Following the instructions given in step 4 above, work the contrasting scallops in #122 pink 4mm silk ribbon between rows 10^1/$_2$ and 11. This is a mirror image of rows 1^1/$_2$ to 2.

Embroidery Stitches

Bradford Rose - page 156

French Knot - page 164

Spider Web Rose - page 172

Straight Stitch - page 173

Japanese Ribbon Stitch - page 167

Loop Stitch - page 168

1. Using a washout marker, draw a curve centered between rows 5 and 9. The lower center of the curve will rest on row 8, curving up at each end to row 6. The width of the curve is 3 inches.

2. Using 4mm #123 and #153 pink silk ribbon threaded in the same needle, work a large spider web rose in the center of the scallop. Make sure that an equal amount of each color of ribbon shows as you work. See graph for placement.

3. Work two slightly smaller roses on each side of the large center rose, using the same color combination as the large rose. When working the two smaller roses, allow the ribbon to twist for a more ruffled look.

4. Using 4mm #123 pink silk ribbon, work two sizes of Bradford roses. See graph for placement.

5. Using 4mm #122 pink silk ribbon, surround the Bradford roses with three to five wrapped straight stitches.

6. Using 4mm #113 purple silk ribbon, work three single wrap French knots for the center of the purple roses.

7. Using 4mm #101 purple silk ribbon, for the purple complete the backstitch roses.

8. The purple forget-me-knots are worked as follows: A single wrap French knot in 4mm #13 yellow silk ribbon for the center surrounded by five single wrap French knots in 4mm #117 purple silk ribbon.

9. Blue daisies are worked with one 4mm #13 yellow silk ribbon French knot for the center, five straight stitch petals worked in 4mm #10 blue silk ribbon.

10. Using 4mm #122 and 123 pink silk ribbon, fill in the design with straight stitch buds.

11. Japanese ribbon stitch leaves are worked in 4mm #18 and #154 green silk ribbon. If needed, use the leaves to fill in and balance your design.

12. Using 4mm #10 blue 7mm silk ribbon, work the bows at the end of the garland. Each bow is worked with 4 loop stitches, with a loose straight stitch to fill in the center and form a knot.

13. Using #913 green floss, connect the buds and leaves with straight stitches. ❈

Rose Garland Silk Ribbon Template

Heritage Baskets

Since smocking has been around for several hundred years, it seemed appropriate to call these beautiful baskets heritage baskets. The pink borders, baskets, flowers, leaves and bow are worked in silk ribbon. This dress reminds one of a wonderful spring day with a young girl in a meadow picking flowers in a handmade basket from her grandfather.

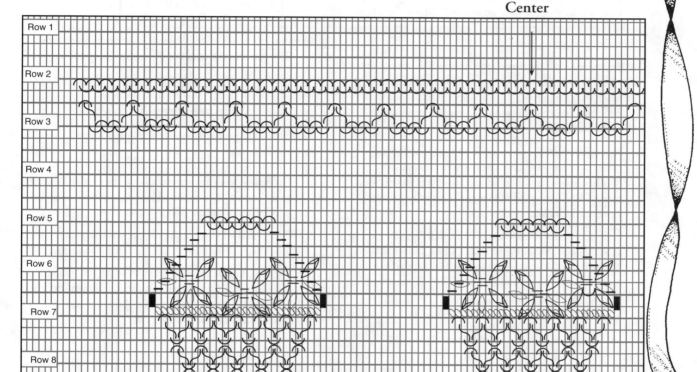

Materials

 Silk Colors Used:

    7mm: #128 rose

    4mm: #165 brown, #68 pink, #32 green, #3 white

 DMC: #839 brown, floss to match color of fabric for backsmocking

 Color photo - page 33

Directions

1. Pleat 12 rows. Smock rows 2-11.

2. Using floss to match the color of the fabric, backsmock rows 1, 4, 5, 6, 7, 8, and 9.

3. Beginning with a down cable in 4mm #68 pink ilk ribbon, cable across rows 2 and 11.

4. Beginning at the center of row $2^1/2$, work an up cable, $^1/2$ space wave down to row 3, cable 5, $^1/2$ space wave up to row $2^1/2$. Repeat to end of row. Return to center, turn fabric upside down and complete the design.

69

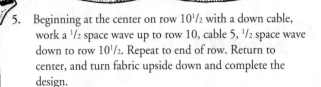

5. Beginning at the center on row 10^{1}/$_{2}$ with a down cable, work a ^{1}/$_{2}$ space wave up to row 10, cable 5, ^{1}/$_{2}$ space wave down to row 10^{1}/$_{2}$. Repeat to end of row. Return to center, and turn fabric upside down and complete the design.

6. Using 4mm #165 brown silk ribbon, begin the center basket 15 pleats to the left of center on row 7. Work an up cable on row 7, a ^{1}/$_{2}$ space wave down to row 7^{1}/$_{2}$, down cable, ^{1}/$_{2}$ space wave up to row 7. Repeat for a total of 6 cable wave combinations. This forms the top or widest part of the basket.

7. Beginning under the down cable on row 7^{1}/$_{2}$, work 1 up cable, ^{1}/$_{2}$ space wave down to row 8, 1 down cable, ^{1}/$_{2}$ space wave up to row 7^{1}/$_{2}$, 1 up cable. Repeat for a total of 5 cable wave combinations. This will complete row 2 of the basket.

8. Beginning under the down cable on row 8, work 1 up cable, ^{1}/$_{2}$ space wave, down to row 8^{1}/$_{2}$, 1 down cable. Work ^{1}/$_{2}$ space wave, 1 up cable up to row 8. Repeat for a total of 4 cable wave combinations. This will complete row 3 of the basket.

9. Beginning under the down cable on row 8^{1}/$_{2}$, work 1 up cable, ^{1}/$_{2}$ space wave, 1 down cable, down to row 9. Work ^{1}/$_{2}$ space wave, 1 up cable up to row 8^{1}/$_{2}$. Repeat for a total of 3 cable wave combinations. This will complete the last row of the basket.

10. The base of the basket and the top edge of the basket are completed with a stem stitch. Work 30 stitches on the top edge of the basket and 14 stitches at the base.

11. The base of the basket handle is made by satin stitching over 2 pleats between rows 6^{1}/$_{2}$ and 7. Refer to graph for placement.

12. The basket handle is made with 8 trellis stitches worked between row 6^{1}/$_{2}$ and 5, cable 11, and 8 trellis stitches down to row 6^{1}/$_{2}$. Refer to graph for placement.

13. Using 4 strands of #829 brown floss, work three 4-cable flowerettes in the center of the basket. See graph for placement.

Embroidery Stitches

Japanese Ribbon Stitch - page 167

Lazy Daisy Stitch - page 167

1. The flower petals are worked around the 4-cable flowerette using 7mm #128 rose silk ribbon. Work four flower petals with a Japanese ribbon stitch.

2. Using 4mm #332 green silk ribbon, work lazy daisy stitch leaves around the flowers. See graph for placement.

3. The bow is made by using 4mm #3 white silk ribbon. Take a deep stitch between two pleats and then "tie" the bow on the front. Trim ends to make a neat bow. See diagram for placement of bow. ▨

Kate Irene

Another cover dress smocking plate that is beyond beautiful. This dress is made of a dusty pink silk dupioni and the smocking takes my breath away. The Peter Pan collar is covered with ecru French lace which matches the wide ecru French edging lace on the sleeves. The smocking is done with Marlitt rayon floss which gives a beautiful shine on the silk dupioni. Regular embroidery floss would be beautiful also. The smocking design is done with two-step waves into a point for the high section and into two points for the bottom section. The center has been left unsmocked for a beautiful puffing effect. I think the silk dupioni makes a more beautiful puffing effect. A continuous garland of silk ribbon embroidery done in pale green, two shades of pink, ecru, dusty lavender, pale gold and deep gold is found at the bottom of the top section. A similar strip of silk ribbon work travels on the bottom section of smocking also. The sleeves are gorgeous with ecru French round thread lace's being stitched on flat. Several rows of two step waves done in ecru Marlitt stitch the background, and a matching garland of silk ribbon flowers are found in the center. There is a lazy daisy silk ribbon flower on the sash done in ecru, green and gold.

Materials

❀ Marlitt Rayon Floss: #1034

❀ Silk Ribbon:

   4mm: #31 green, #178 dark purple, #157 peach, #163 dusty rose, #34 beige, #54 gold, #35 tan

   7mm: #31 green

❀ DMC Floss: #503 green

❀ Color photo - pages 9,13

❀ Silk ribbon embroidery template page 74

❀ Smocking graph on page 73

Directions

Upper Design

1. Beginning on row $1^1/2$ with a down cable, work a $1/2$ space 2-step wave across the row between rows $1^1/2$ and $1/2$. Continue waves to row 4.

2. Following the graph closely, begin working on row 4 to 4 $1/2$ and decrease $1^1/2$ waves on the end of rows 5, 6, 7, 8, 9, and the half rows between them.

Lower Design

3. Beginning on row $7^1/2$ with an up cable, work $1^1/2$ waves, down to row 8.

4. Beginning on row 8, increase the right side of the design by $1^1/2$ waves on rows 8, 9, 10, 11,12, and their $1/2$ space rows. Refer to the graph..

5. Working from row 12 to $12^1/2$, decrease the left side of the design, skip $1^1/2$ waves and work to the right, increasing $1^1/2$ waves on the right side.

6. Working on row $12^1/2$ to 13, decrease $1^1/2$ waves on the left side. Work 25 complete waves.

7. Working on rows 13-17, complete the bottom part of the design, decreasing $1^1/2$ waves on each side of each row.

8. Beginning on row $12^1/2$, working from the center of the design, skip 1 wave from the previous work. Beginning with a down cable on row $12^1/2$, work waves on the right side of the design to the edge.

9. Working on rows 12 - $7^1/2$, decrease on the left and work waves to the end of the row.

Sleeves

1. Cable across row 1.

2. Begin on row $1^1/2$ with a down cable, work a two-step wave up to row 1, up cable. Repeat across the row.

3. Begin on row $1^1/2$, underneath the row just completed, with an up cable, two-step wave down to row 2, down cable, 2-step waves up to row $1^1/2$. Repeat across row.

4. Follow the instructions given in step 2 and 3 above until you have smocked rows 2, 3, and 4.

5. Cable across row 4.

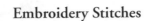

Embroidery Stitches

French Knot - page 164

Lazy Daisy Stitch - page 167

Wrapped Running Stitch - page 176

Template on page 74

1. Lightly mark the vine guidelines on the fabric using a washout marker.

2. Using 3 strands of DMC #503, work $^1/_4$ inch running stitches on the line.

3. Using 4mm #31 green silk ribbon, loosely wrap the running stitches allowing the silk ribbon to twist (wrapped running stitch).

4. Stitch a five petal lazy daisy flower in 4mm #34 beige as indicated on the drawing.

5. Work one wrap French knots using 4mm #54 gold silk ribbon in the center of the lazy daisy flowers.

6. Work spider web roses along vines alternating the colors of 4mm #163 dusty rose, #178 purple, #157 peach, #54 gold silk ribbon.

7. Work the leaves for the spider web roses with ribbon stitches using 7mm #031 green silk ribbon.

Sleeve Embroidery

Refer to embroidery stitches given for the dress.

Tempalte on page 74.

1. Using a washout marker, draw the line over the smocking stitch to represent the stem.

2. Using #503 green floss, work $^1/_4$-inch running stitches on the drawn line.

3. Using 4mm #31 green silk ribbon, loosely wrap the running stitches allowing the silk ribbon to twist (wrapped running stitch).

4. Work a single spider web rose in 4mm #178 dark purple, #54 gold, and #157 peach silk ribbon. See graph for placement.

5. Using 4mm #34 beige silk ribbon, work two lazy daisy stitch flowers

6. Using 4mm #54 gold silk ribbon, work single wrap French knots in the center of each lazy daisy flower.

7. Using 7mm #31 green silk ribbon, work Japanese ribbon stitch leaves along the vine. ▧

Kate Irene Sleeve Graph

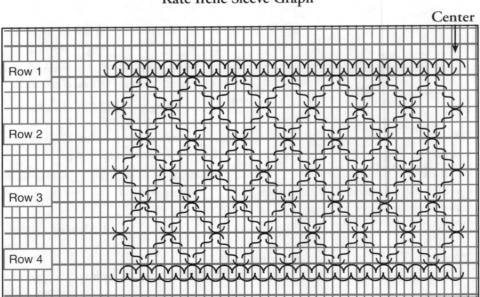

Kate Irene Smocking Graph

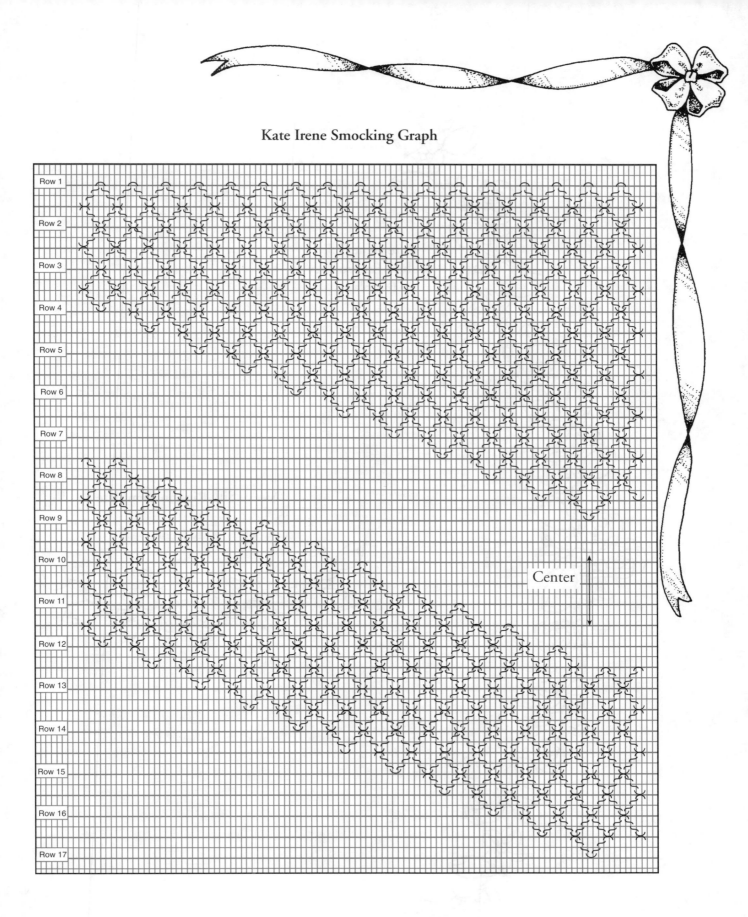

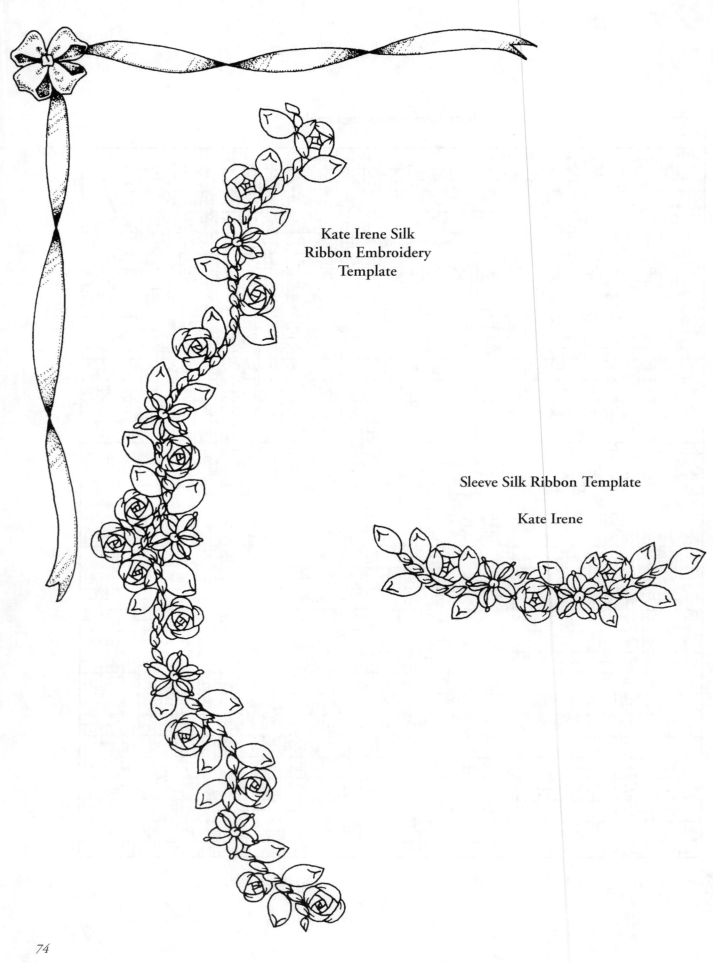

Kate Irene Silk
Ribbon Embroidery
Template

Sleeve Silk Ribbon Template

Kate Irene

74

Misty

The pattern for Misty, a cover dress, is an example of the use of the pattern included in *Silk Ribbon Treasures*. Misty is worked in gorgeous ecru silk dupioni fabric. The Peter Pan collar is finished with tiny piping of the ecru silk with gathered French edging around the collar. The bodice of the dress is smocked with ecru silk ribbon. It would be just as pretty smocked with embroidery floss. A two inch square of beautiful silk ribbon flowers is found in the center of the bodice. The silk ribbon flowers are made using a lazy daisy stitch, French knots and Japanese ribbon stitch for the leaves. Gold beads are stitched at random through out the silk flower. The same lazy daisy flowers and leaves are found on the bottom of the design which dips down in the center front.

The sleeves fall in the "to die for" category with four rows of two-step waves smocked in ecru with three pink lazy daisy flowers that match the flowers in the center of the dress with gold beads tucked away in the flowers. The bottom of the sleeves are edged in ecru French lace. Each sash tail has a dusty pink lazy daisy flower with green leaves and a gold French knot in the center.

Materials

❧ Silk Ribbon Colors Used:

    4mm: #160 light mauve, #15 yellow, #155 light green, #163 mauve

❧ Marlitt: #1036 rayon floss

❧ Gold Seed Beads

❧ Color photo - pages 16-17

❧ Smocking graph on page 76

Directions

1. Pleat 22 rows. The top row and bottom two rows are stabilizer rows and are not numbered on the graph. Smock 19 rows.

2. Begin on row $1^1/_2$ with an up cable. Work a 2-step $^1/_2$ space wave up to row 1, down cable, 2-step $^1/_2$ space wave down to row $1^1/_2$. Repeat across row.

3. Begin on row $1^1/_2$ with a down cable. Work a 2-step $^1/_2$ space wave down to row 2, up cable, 2-step $^1/_2$ space wave up to row $1^1/_2$. Repeat Across row.

4. Repeat instructions given in steps 2 and 3 until you have smocked $14^1/_2$ rows.

5. Follow the graph closely. Continue to work the waves as instructed in step 2 and 3 above, decreasing $1^1/_2$ waves on each row.

6. Working $^1/_8$ space below row 14 and following the shape of the preceding rows, work a 2-step wave, 5-step trellis combination along the row to the center. Repeat for remaining side of design.

Sleeves

1. Using the instructions given in step 2 and 3, smock 3 rows for the sleeves.

Embroidery Stitches

Lazy Daisy - page 167   Straight Stitch - page 173

French Knot - page 164   Pullen Knot - page 168

1. Following the graph for placement, for 5-petal lazy daisy flowers in 4mm #160 light mauve silk ribbon.

2. Work 4mm #15 yellow silk ribbon French knots for the center of the flowers.

3. Using 4mm #155 pale green silk ribbon work 3 - 4 straight stitch leaves around each flowers.

4. Scatter Pullen knot buds using 4mm #163 dusty rose silk ribbon.

5. Fill in the balance of the design with gold beads. ❧

Misty Smocking Graph

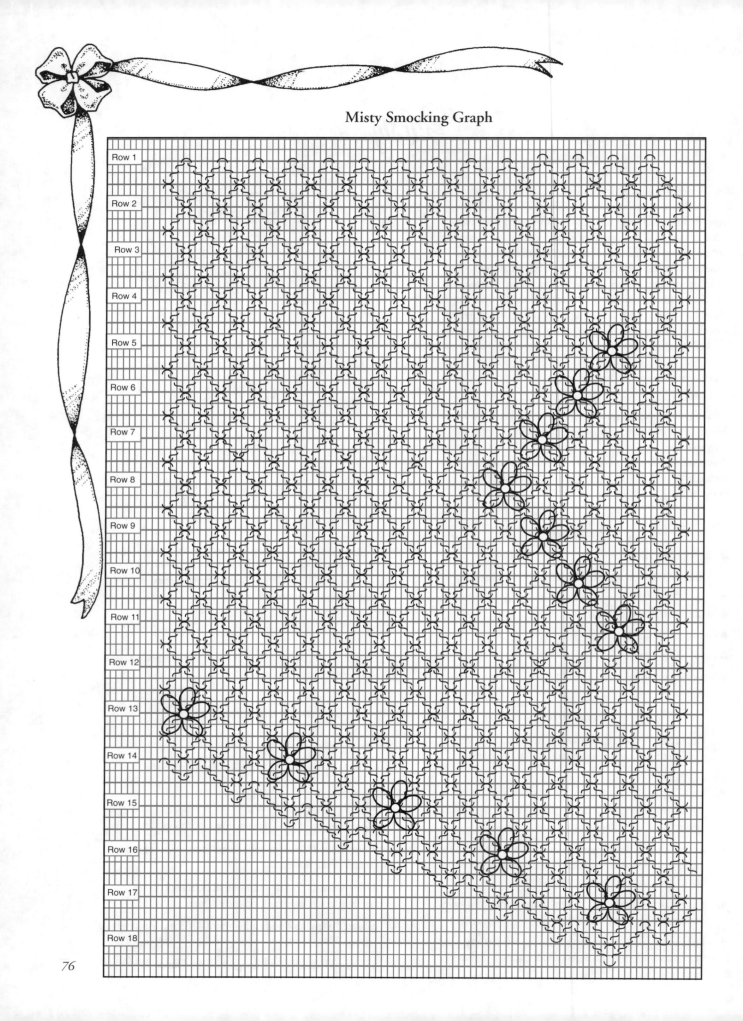

Row 1
Row 2
Row 3
Row 4
Row 5
Row 6
Row 7
Row 8
Row 9
Row 10
Row 11
Row 12
Row 13
Row 14
Row 15
Row 16
Row 17
Row 18

Kelly Michelle

Using the pattern in this book, this dress is fit for a coronation ball. The whole back of this smocking design is backsmocked in white floss. Made of white silk dupioni, the smocking is done with a blue Marlitt floss. Eight-step waves make the diamonds which have pink and white lazy daisy flowers at the points. Pale green silk ribbon lazy daisies make the leaves and bright yellow French knots finish the centers of the flowers. The sleeves have a beautiful smocked design with blue floss and more of the pink and white lazy daisies. The English netting lace around the collar and the sleeves is carried out on the bottom of the dress. English netting insertion is found in two places on the skirt, also.

Materials

❀ Floss: Marlitt rayon floss #1059; DMC cotton floss, white

❀ Silk Ribbon Colors Used:

4mm: #1 white, #14 yellow, #5 pink, #154 green

❀ Color photo pages 9-10,11-12

Directions

Smock with two strands of blue Marlitt unless otherwise indicated.

1. Pleat 26 rows. The top and bottom rows are stabilizer rows and are not numbered on the graph. Smock 24^1/$_2$ rows. If your pleater does not pleat 26 rows, it is possible to do this design on 24 rows. You will have no holding row at the top. You must make sure that you leave a seam allowance above the top pleating row. When you reach the bottom of the design, pull the fabric into pleats below the last row of stitching.

2. Begin smocking on row 1 with an up cable at center front. Work two-step ^{1}/$_2$ space waves between rows 1 and 1^1/$_2$ across the row. Turn the fabric and complete the other end of the row.

3. Follow the graph closely. Begin with an up cable on row 1^1/$_2$ directly under the third bottom cable to the left of center on row 1^1/$_2$. *Work two steps down to row 2, down cable, two steps up to row 1^1/$_2$, up cable, eight steps down to row 3, down cable, eight steps up to row 1^1/$_2$, up cable. Repeat from * across the row. Turn and complete the other end of the row.

4. Beginning on row 2, directly below the first down cable to the left of center on row 2, *up cable, eight steps down to row 3^1/$_2$, down cable, two steps up to row 3, up cable, two steps down to row 3^1/$_2$, down cable, eight steps up to row 2, Repeat from * across the row. Turn and complete the other end of the row.

5. Continue following the instructions in steps 3 and 4 down to and including rows 18 to 19^1/$_2$.

6. To shape the bottom of the design, begin with a down cable on the center two pleats of row 24^1/$_2$. Work a five-step ^{3}/$_4$ space trellis up to row 23^1/$_2$, up cable, two-step trellis down to row 23^3/$_4$, down cable, five-step trellis up to row 23, up cable, two step trellis down to row 23^1/$_4$. Continue the (five-step trellis ^{3}/$_4$ space, two-step trellis ^{1}/$_4$ space) combination to the end of the row. Follow the graph carefully. Tun the fabric and complete the other end of the row.

7. Work another row of the (five-step trellis ^{3}/$_4$ space, two-step trellis ^{1}/$_4$ space) combination directly under the row worked in step 6.

8. The next several rows will form the shaped bottom area of the design and will not be full diamonds. Where the diamond design runs into the bottom boundary rows, take the needle to the back of the smocking and tie off the floss. Turn the work and begin at the center to complete the design for the other end of the row.

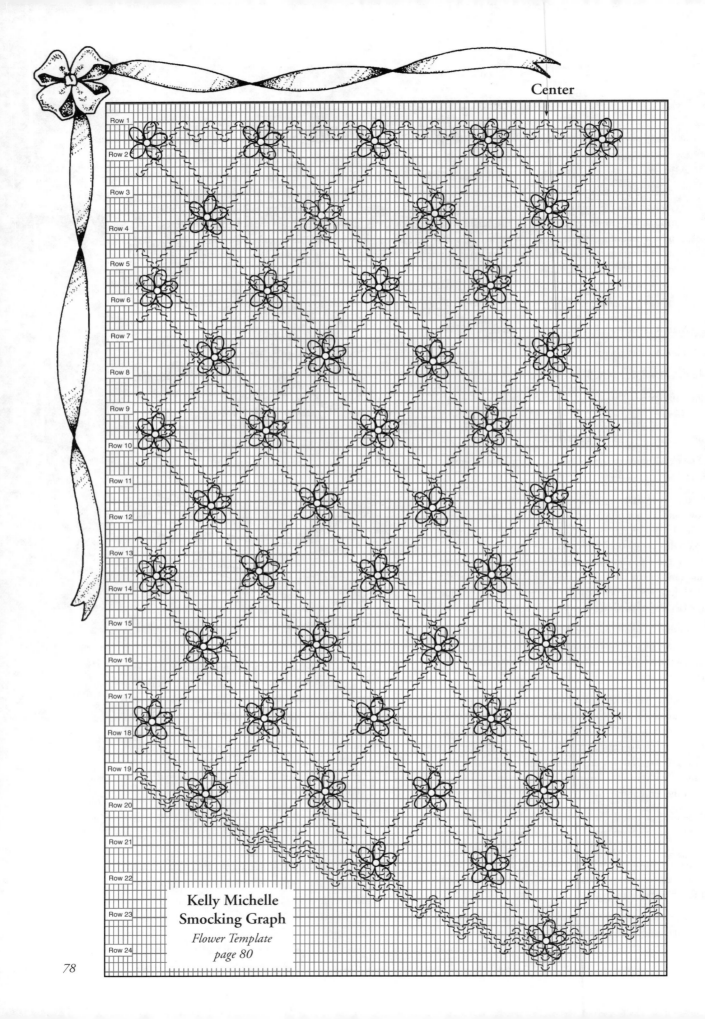

Center

Row 1
Row 2
Row 3
Row 4
Row 5
Row 6
Row 7
Row 8
Row 9
Row 10
Row 11
Row 12
Row 13
Row 14
Row 15
Row 16
Row 17
Row 18
Row 19
Row 20
Row 21
Row 22
Row 23
Row 24

Kelly Michelle Smocking Graph
*Flower Template
page 80*

78

9. To finish filling in the design, begin on row 19$^{1}/_{2}$, directly under the first down cable to the left of center. Work an up cable, *two steps down to row 20, down cable, two steps up to row 19$^{1}/_{2}$, up cable, eight steps down to row 21, down cable, eight steps up to row 19$^{1}/_{2}$, up cable. Repeat from * across the row, turn and complete the other end of the row.

10. Working between rows 20 and 21$^{1}/_{2}$, begin at center, directly below the down cable on row 20. Work an *up cable, eight steps down to row 21$^{1}/_{2}$, down cable, two steps up to row 21, up cable, two steps down to row 21$^{1}/_{2}$, down cable, eight steps up to row 20, Repeat from * across the row. Turn and complete the other end of the row.

11. Working between rows 21$^{1}/_{2}$ and 23, begin directly under the second down cable to the left of center on row 21$^{1}/_{2}$ with an up cable. Repeat step 8 from *.

12. Working between rows 22 and 23$^{1}/_{2}$, begin directly below the first down cable to the left of center on row 22 with an up cable. Repeat step 9 from *.

13. With two strands of white DMC floss, backsmock the design area on the wrong side.

Sleeves

Refer to "Dress Construction- Xll. Sleeve Construction - A. Smocked Sleeves" before smocking the sleeves.

1. Pleat 5 rows, smock 3$^{1}/_{2}$ rows. The top row is a stabilizer row and is not numbered on the graph. The first row of pleating should be $^{1}/_{2}$" from the cut edge of the sleeve bottom. The lace should be attached just below the bottom pleating row.

2. Backsmock rows 1 - 4 with two strands of white DMC floss.

3. Begin on row 1 with an up cable at center. Work two-step waves between rows 1 and 1$^{1}/_{2}$, to the end of the pleats. Turn the fabric and work the other end of the row.

4. Begin on row 1$^{1}/_{2}$ with an up cable directly below the third bottom cable to the left of center on row 1$^{1}/_{2}$. Work *two steps down to row 2, down cable, two steps up to row 1$^{1}/_{2}$, up cable, eight steps down to row 2$^{1}/_{2}$, down cable, eight steps up to row 1$^{1}/_{2}$, up cable. Repeat from * to the end of the pleats, turn and complete the other end of the pleats.

5. Begin on row 2 with an up cable, directly below the first down cable to the left of center on row 2. Work *eight steps down to row 3, down cable, two steps up to row 2$^{1}/_{2}$, up cable, two steps down to row 3, down cable, eight steps up to row 2, up cable. Repeat from * across, turn and complete the other end of the row.

Embroidery Stitches

Lazy Daisy Stitch page 167

French Knot page 164

1. Work five-petal lazy daisy flowers using 4mm #1 and #5 silk ribbons. Place the flowers and alternate the colors as indicated on the graphs and template. Also refer to the color photos.

2. Using 4mm #14 yellow silk ribbon, work a single-wrap French knot in the center of each flower.

3. Use 4mm #154 green silk ribbon to work lazy daisy leaves on each side of the flowers. ❈

Kelly Michelle Sleeve Smocking Graph

Center

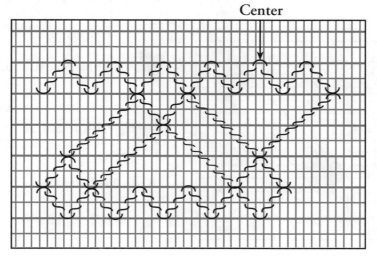

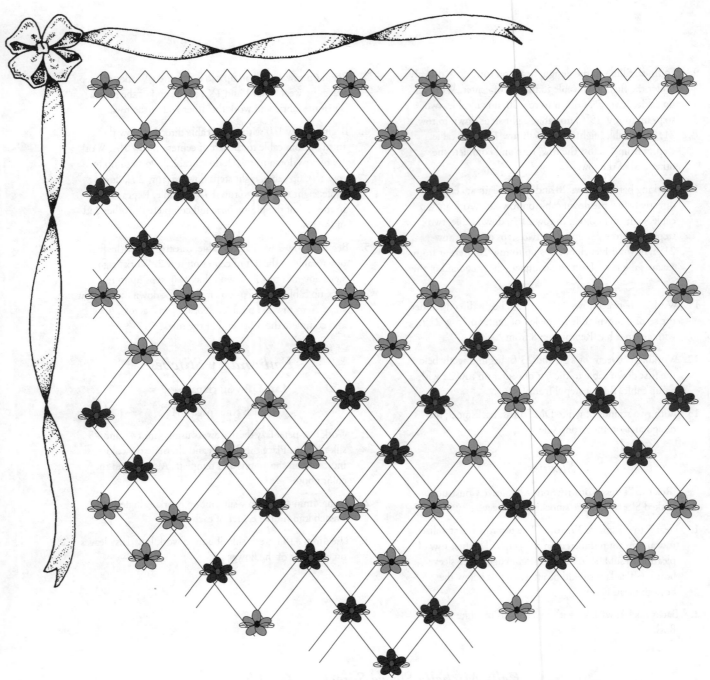

Kelly Michelle Floral Template

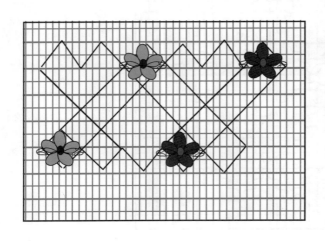

 - Pink Silk Ribbon Flower

 - White Silk Ribbon Flowers

Kelly Michelle Sleeve

Floral Template

Summer Delight

This beautiful dress is on the cover of this book. Using the dress pattern in this book out of Imperial blue batiste, this smocking plate combines geometric smocking with embroidery floss and silk ribbon embroidery. Several rows are backsmocked below the front yoke of the dress. The main smocking of the dress is two step waves smocked in white floss. On the top and bottom of this plate is a row of waves smocked in darker blue. The bouquet in the center has flowers in pink, blue and yellow, and leaves in green. The cascaded bow is of white silk ribbon. Each stitching point is held in place with a pearlized white bead. White beads are also found in the centers of the yellow silk roses on the bouquet.

Materials

❧ Silk Ribbon Colors Used:

  2mm: #18 green

  4mm: #111 pink, #154 green, #119 yellow, #23 lavender, #98 blue

  7mm: #3 white

❧ DMC floss: white, #3753 pale blue, #3755 blue

❧ Glass beads: pearl white

❧ Color photo - page 15

Directions

Smock with three strands of white floss unless otherwise indicated.

1. Pleat 20 rows. The top and bottom rows are holding rows and are not numbered on the graph.

2. Backsmock rows 1 - 4, using two strands of #3753 pale blue floss.

3. Beginning at center front on row 9 with a down cable, smock 2-step $^1/_2$ space waves between rows 9 and $8^1/_2$, to the end of the row. Turn the fabric and work across the other end of the row.

4. Beginning at center front on row 9 with an up cable, smock 2-step $^1/_2$ space waves between rows 9 and $9^1/_2$, to the end of the row. Turn the fabric and work across the other end of the row. The smocking will form diamonds.

5. Working between $^1/_2$ space rows as before, repeat steps 3 and 4 to smock diamonds from rows ($9^1/_2$ to 10) to rows (12 to $12^1/_2$). Refer to the graph

6. To begin shaping the top of the design, begin on row $8^1/_2$, with a down cable over the point of the first diamond to the right of center. Work the 2-step $^1/_2$ space waves as before, between rows $8^1/_2$ and 8, to the end of the row.

Turn the fabric and work across the other end of the row, beginning at the point of the first diamond to the left of center.

7. Beginning on row 8 with a down cable at the point of the second diamond, work the 2-step $^1/_2$ space waves to the end of the row, turn and begin smocking at the point of the second diamond to finish the row as before.

8. On subsequent rows, moving up the rows, begin the smocking with a down cable at the point of the second diamond, work the waves across, turn the fabric and work the remainder of the row, beginning at the point of the second diamond each time and working to the edge of the fabric.

9. Continue working up the rows, working fewer diamonds each time. Stop the smocking at the armhole lines. Work the rows until only one diamond is worked at the edge. Refer to the graph and photograph.

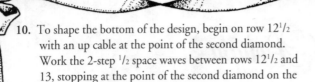

10. To shape the bottom of the design, begin on row 12¹/₂ with an up cable at the point of the second diamond. Work the 2-step ¹/₂ space waves between rows 12¹/₂ and 13, stopping at the point of the second diamond on the other end of the row.

11. Work the next diamonds between rows 13 and 13¹/₂, starting and stopping at the points of the second diamonds on each end of the row.

12. Continue working down the rows in the same pattern, until there is only one diamond worked in the center of the bottom row.

13. Using three strands of #3755 blue floss, begin at center front on the top edge of the design, at the point where the "V" begins to shape. Leave a long tail on the back of the smocking to be worked in later. Come to the front of the fabric in the first valley to the left of the center valley.

14. This row of smocking will be placed directly above the top row of the design and will form an outline for the smocked shape. *Work a down cable, then five steps up, top cable, and two steps down. Refer to the graph. Repeat from * across the row, turn the fabric and continue the pattern across the other end of the row, using the long tail at the back to work the first stitches.

15. Beginning at center front on the bottom edge of the design, using #3755 blue floss, come up in the first valley to the left of the center valley and leave a long tail as before.

16. Working directly below the bottom edge of the smocked design, repeat the instructions from * in step 14 and work across the row, turn the fabric and continue the pattern across the other end of the row as before. Refer to the graph.

17. Backsmock all rows of the un-smocked area in the upper "V" shape made by the design.

Embroidery Stitches

Colonial Knot - page 161

Fly Stitch - page 163

French Knot - page 164

Lazy Daisy Stitch - page 167

Spider Web Rose - page 172

Straight Stitch - page 173

1. Refer to the diagram for placement and lightly draw the stems onto the pleated fabric. Add dots to indicate placement for the pink lazy daisy flowers and the two yellow spider web roses.

2. Using 4mm #111 pink silk ribbon, work three five-petal lazy daisy flowers as indicated on the diagram. Use 4mm #119 yellow silk ribbon to add French knot centers to the flowers.

3. Use 4mm #119 yellow silk ribbon to work the two spider web roses. Add a pearl bead to the center of each rose.

4. At the top of the bouquet, work three 4mm #119 yellow silk ribbon French knots for flower centers, above and between the four flowers in the center of the bouquet. Refer to the diagram for placement. Use 4mm #98 blue to add six colonial knot "petals" around each center.

5. Use 4mm #154 green to add a fly stitch to each blue flower, forming leaves.

6. Add two lazy daisy leaves to each of the pink flowers, using 2mm #18 green silk ribbon. Refer to the diagram for placement.

7. Work two lazy daisy buds between the three pink flowers with 4mm #23 lavender silk ribbon. Refer to the diagram and photo for placement.

8. Fill in the empty spaces around the yellow spider web roses, using colonial knots worked in 4mm #154 green silk ribbon.

9. Use 2mm #18 green silk ribbon to add straight stitch stems at the bottom of the bouquet, letting the ribbon weave under the smocking stitches to anchor it in a few places. Refer to the color photograph.

10. Use a 15" piece of 7mm #3 white silk ribbon to tie a hand-tied bow. Attach the center of the bow to the embroidery with a straight stitch over the knot at the point where the flowers join the stems. Shape the bow streamers, following the diagram. Tack the streamers in place by sewing pearls at the folds and curves, and on each end. Trim the ends. ▨

Silk Ribbon Embroidery Template

Summer Delight Smocking Graph

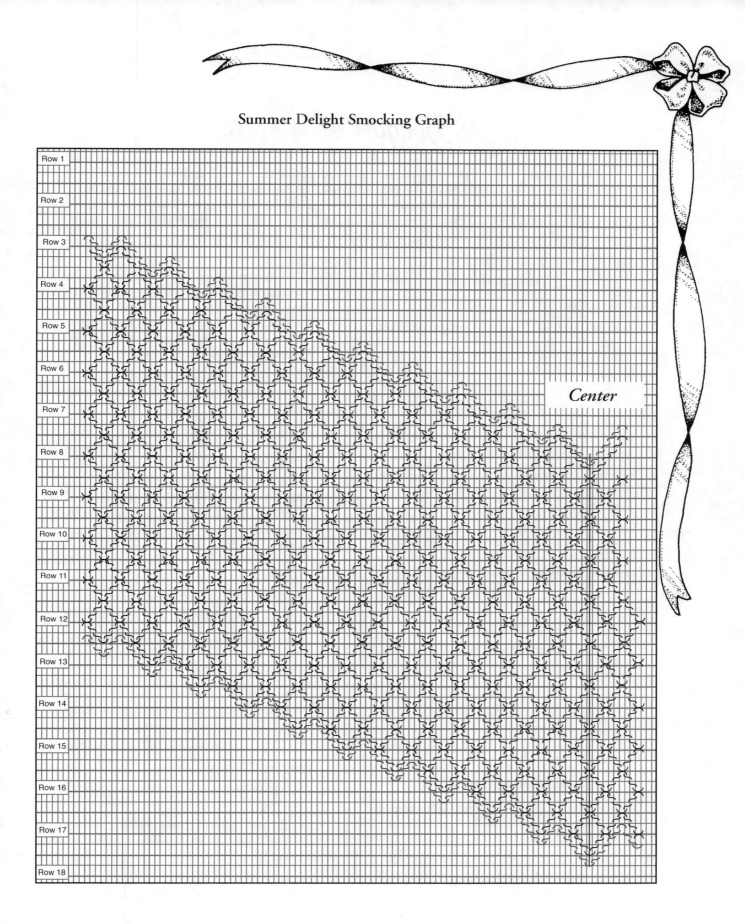

Center

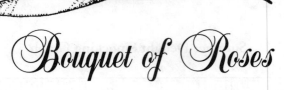

Bouquet of Roses

The opulence of ecru silk dupioni is further enhanced by five bouquets placed on elegantly smocked two-step waves. Embroidery floss is used for the smocking; silk ribbon makes the bouquets. Four small bouquets surround the larger bouquet. The roses on each bouquet are from three shades of pink silk ribbon; green embroidery floss makes the leaves and the stems. A lovely teal blue silk ribbon is cascaded for the bows that hold each flower bouquet. Any of these bouquets would be just as lovely stitched on a flat fabric as they are stitched on top of the smocking.

Materials

❧ Silk Ribbon Colors Used:

    4mm: #111 pink, #112 rose, #114 dark rose, #134 teal

❧ DMC Floss: #937 green

❧ Color photo - page 39

Directions

1. Pleat 16 rows. Rows 1 and 16 are stabilizer rows and are not numbered on the graph. Smock rows 2 - 15.

2. Begin with an up cable on row 2, work a two step wave down to row $2^1/_2$, down cable, two step wave up to row 1. Repeat across row.

3. Repeat instructions given in step 2, beginning with a down cable on row 3. Alternate the rows beginning with up cables and down cables to form the diamonds of the design. Repeat these instructions until you have completed 14 rows.

Embroidery
Embroidery Stitches

Couching - page 162	Spider Web Rose - page 172
French Knot - page 164	Stem Stitch - page 173
Japanese Ribbon Stitch - page 167	Straight Stitch Rose - page 177
Lazy Daisy Stitch - page 167	

Center Bouquet

1. Referring to the diagram for placement, lightly draw stems and mark larger flower positions on the pleated piece, using a washout marker.

2. Using # 937 green floss, work the stems in stem stitch and work the leaves using a lazy daisy stitch.

3. Using 4mm #112 dark rose, work five spider web roses. See template for the placement.

4. Using 4mm #114 dark rose, work two Japanese ribbon stitch flowers with a 4mm #111 pink silk ribbon French knot worked in the center.

5. Work three straight stitch roses. Use 4mm #114 dark rose silk ribbon and work a French knot for the center of each rose. Using 4mm #112 rose silk ribbon, work one row of straight stitches around each French knot. Using 4mm #111 pink silk ribbon, work another row of straight stitches surrounding each dark rose row.

6. Using 4mm #114 dark rose silk ribbon, work lazy daisy buds scattered throughout the design. See template for placement.

7. Using 4mm #111 pink silk ribbon, work a series of Japanese ribbon stitches to fill in the blank spaces left in the design.

8. The bow at the base of the bouquet is hand tied using 4mm #134 dark teal silk ribbon. Leave long tails on each side of the bow. Couch the bow to the smocked fabric with matching floss by stitching across the ribbon, pinching the ribbon together. The tails of the bow are carried through the smocked fabric to the wrong side and tied off.

Small Bouquets

1. Referring to the diagram for placement, lightly draw stems and mark larger flower positions on the pleated piece, using a washout marker.

2. Using two strands of #937 green floss, work the stems with the stem stitch and add a few lazy daisy leaves to form a background for the flowers.

3. Refer to the individual instructions for each bouquet to embroider the flowers.

4. With two strands of #937 green floss, work lazy daisy leaves to fill in the bare spots in the designs.

5. Tie the bows and attach them to the fabric the same as the large bow, but make them smaller to match the size of the bouquets.

Upper Left Bouquet

1. Refer to steps 1 and 2 under "Small Bouquets".

2. Use 4mm #112 rose silk ribbon to work the three larger spider web roses as indicated on the template.

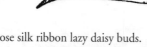

3. Add six 4mm #114 dark rose silk ribbon lazy daisy buds. Refer to the template and the color photograph for placement.

4. Fill in with four 4mm #111 pink silk ribbon buds, using the Japanese ribbon stitch.

5. Refer to steps 4 and 5 under "Small Bouquets" to finish the embroidery.

Lower Left Bouquet

1. Refer to steps 1 and 2 under "Small Bouquets".

2. Work three Japanese ribbon stitch flowers, using 4mm #112 rose silk ribbon. Add French knot centers to the flowers with 4mm #114 dark rose silk ribbon.

3. Scatter Japanese ribbon stitch buds throughout the design, randomly using 4mm #111, #112 and #114 silk ribbon. Refer to the color photograph for color placement.

4. Refer to steps 4 and 5 under "Small Bouquets" to finish the embroidery.

Upper Right Bouquet

1. Refer to steps 1 and 2 under "Small Bouquets".

2. Work three straight stitch roses in the positions for the larger flowers. Use 4mm #114 dark rose silk ribbon French knots for the centers, 4mm #112 rose silk ribbon for the first row of stitches, and 4mm #111 pink silk ribbon for the outer row of stitches.

3. Scatter seven 4mm #112 rose silk ribbon lazy daisy buds throughout the design. Refer to the template and the color photograph for placement.

4. Add a few Japanese ribbon stitch buds to fill in the design, using 4mm #111 pink and #114 dark rose silk ribbons.

5. Refer to steps 4 and 5 under "Small Bouquets" to finish the embroidery.

Lower Right Bouquet

1. Refer to steps 1 and 2 under "Small Bouquets".

2. Work 4mm #112 rose silk ribbon spider web roses in the positions for the three larger flowers.

3. Scatter five Japanese ribbon stitch buds throughout the design, working with 4mm #112 rose silk ribbon. Refer to the template and the color photograph.

4. Add five 4mm #114 dark rose silk ribbon buds and three 4mm #111 pink silk ribbon buds, using the Japanese ribbon stitch. Refer to the template and the color photograph.

5. Refer to steps 4 and 5 under "Small Bouquets" to finish the embroidery. ▨

UPPER LEFT BOUQUET

LOWER LEFT BOUQUET

CENTER BOUQUET

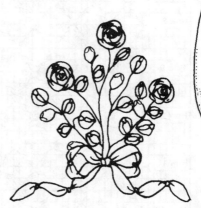

UPPER RIGHT BOUQUET

LOWER RIGHT BOUQUET

Bouquet of Roses Smocking Graph

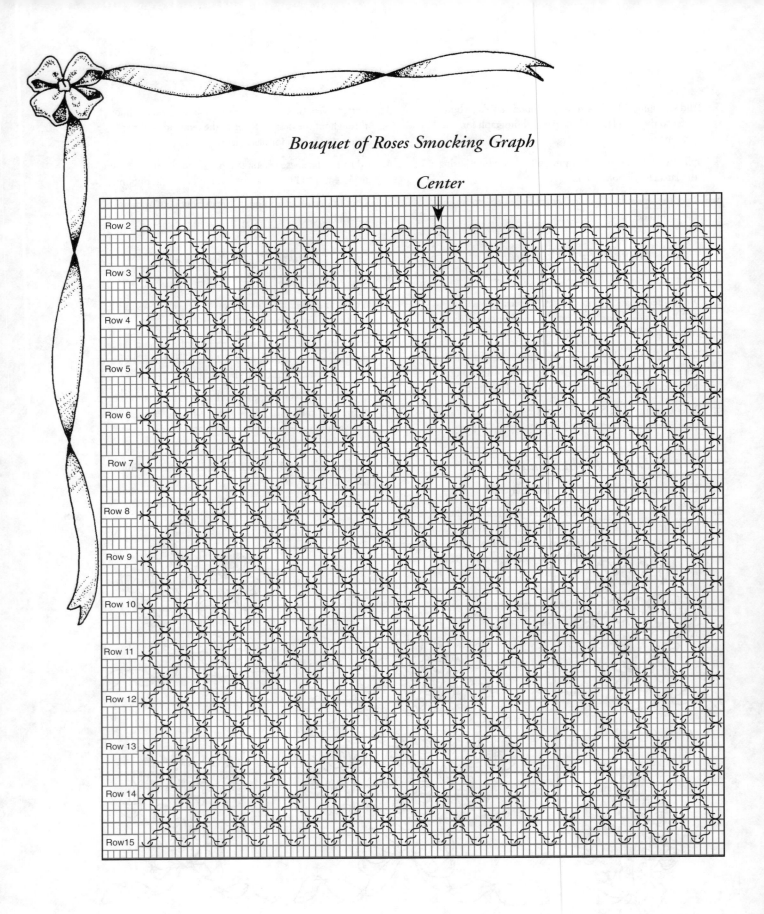

Victorian Garden

Burgundy silk dupioni, silk ribbon smocking and silk ribbon embroidery combine unusual colors and fabulous stitches. Smocking is found on both sides of the center section which is embroidered with green floss, yellow silk ribbon flowers, gold French knots and green silk ribbon leaves. Two bouquets are found on either side perched on top of the smocking. Gray silk ribbon borders are found at the top and the bottom of the smocking designs. Gray cascading ribbons form a bow at the bottom of the bouquet which is pale pink, gray, gold and green. The smocked double portions are back smocked with burgundy floss.

Center

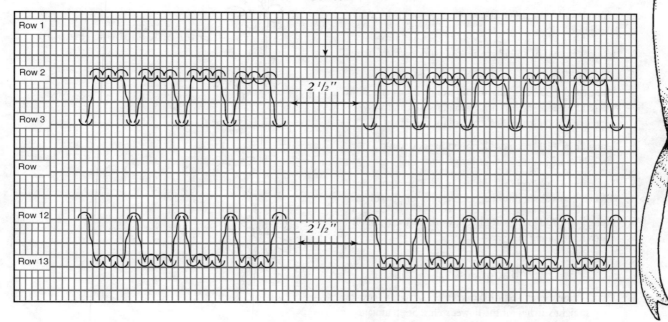

Materials

✿ Silk Ribbon Colors Used:

2mm: # 100 orchid

4mm: #65 taupe, #147 gold, #111 pink, #141 tan, #35 beige

7mm: #20 green

✿ DMC floss: #783 gold, #3052 green, floss to match the fabric

✿ Color photo - page 40

Directions

1. Mark the center of the fabric. Pleat 15 rows. The top and bottom rows are stabilizer rows and are not numbered on the graph. Smock 13 rows.

2. Working from the center of the pleated fabric, remove the pleating threads 1¹/₄ inches on each side of the center mark, giving 2¹/₂ inches of flat fabric. Tie off pleating threads creating two sections of pleats.

3. Backsmock all pleated rows in each panel with floss to match the color of the fabric.

4. The smocking design for this plate should <u>always</u> be started on the inside pleat nearest the center of the flat fabric and worked to the outside. This will enable you to make the design equal in both panels. Each of the smocked panels will be smocked beginning on row 2 with 2mm #162 orchid silk ribbon, work * 1 down cable, 1 full step wave up to row 1, 5 cable combination beginning with an up cable, 1 full step wave down to row 2. Repeat from * across the row. Repeat design for other panel.

5. Between rows 12 and 13 work a mirror image of the instructions given in step 4.

Embroidery

Embroidery Stitches

French Knot - page 164

Japanese Ribbon Stitch - page 167

Loop Stitch - page 168

Stem Stitch - page 173

Straight Stitch - page 173

Center Panel Design

1. Using a washout marker, trace the center panel vine on to the fabric.

2. Using 4 strands of #3052 green floss, work a stem stitch for the vine.

3. Using 4mm #35 beige silk ribbon, work the flowers on the stems alternating petals with a straight stitch and a Japanese ribbon stitch. See diagram for placement.

4. Using 2mm #100 orchid silk ribbon, work one wrap French knots in the center of each flower.

5. Using 4mm #147 gold silk ribbon, work clusters of three French knots along the vine. See diagram for placement.

6. Using 7mm #20 green silk ribbon, work Japanese ribbon stitch leaves along the vine.

Bouquets

1. Using 1 single strand of #3052 green floss, work a series of long straight stitches for the flower stems. See template for placement.

2. Using 4mm #65 taupe silk ribbon, work three Japanese ribbon stitch flowers with a single wrap French knot in the center of each flower. See template for placement.

3. Using 4mm #147 gold silk ribbon, work the salvia on the two outside stems using short straight stitches. See template for placement.

4. Using 4mm #111 pink silk ribbon, work the larkspur with a loop stitch. Begin the flower at the base with several loop stitches, gradually decreasing until you have single loop stitches at the top. See template for placement.

5. Using two strands of #783 gold floss, work single wrap French knots in the center of each loop stitch.

6. Using 7mm #20 green silk ribbon, scatter Japanese ribbon stitch leaves in the design.

7. Working where the long straight stitches intersect, use 4mm #141 tan silk ribbon to make a bow. Take a straight stitch into the fabric. Shape the ribbon into bow loops, pin in place. Using the same color ribbon, work single-

wrap French knots to anchor the bow to the fabric. Shape the streamers, work single-wrap French knots to anchor the streamers, carry the ribbon to the back of the fabric and tie off. Repeat design for other side. ▨

Center Silk Ribbon Template

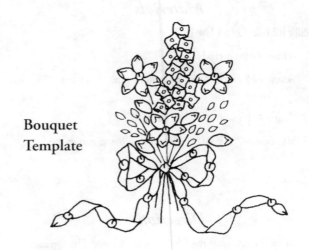

Bouquet Template

Morgan Ross
The Silk Ribbon Dress

Including a garment pattern in our books has been a long standing tradition. When we were thinking about a wonderful pattern for this silk ribbon book, we began to list requirements. First, we wanted a dress for little girls and big girls. That meant a "to the waist" style with sizing from 2-10. Secondly, we wanted an easy to make dress. Third, we wanted lots of collar variations for embellishment if the seamstress desired. Fourth, we wanted a spectacular sleeve which was very full and very pretty. Fifth, we decided that with all of these collar variations, we would cut a high yoke, high back version also. It would have been a shame to have these gorgeous collars only fit on a smocked dress! Sixth, we wanted a beautiful sash option which you can use or not use. We love sashes; however, some might prefer a dress without a sash. I think it would be interesting to count the possible combinations of this pattern. Finally, the pattern design was chosen and we believe you will be extremely excited about it.

Silk dupioni is one of our favorite fabrics to use for smocking. We have featured our dresses made up, primarily, in this fabric. Since this pattern is completely traditional, we can vision it's being made of batiste, broadcloth, calico prints, silk batiste, small prints, large prints, Italian cotton, pique, light weight corduroy, flannel, challis, light weight denim, and chambray. The fabric choice is entirely up to you and you are the designer!

The collars are varied and many. First, there is the traditional Peter Pan collar which can be made plain or trimmed in lace. If you wish, a tiny bit of silk ribbon embroidery can be added to the collar. The traditional scalloped collar is next with the uniform scallop sections. Then, there is a variation of this scalloped collar where the collar isn't divided evenly but has a larger scallop in the front with smaller ones on the sides. There is a round collar which lends itself beautifully to lace trim, silk ribbon embroidery or both. Next there is a square collar with all of its possibilities for trim. The pointed collar has long been a favorite in this industry for people who love to embellish collars.

With all of these collars, we think this will be the favorite yoke pattern for many people mothers and daughters and granddaughters. Our models have loved the to the waist back treatment with the beautiful sash. By the way, the sash is a wonderful place to stitch a little silk ribbon embroidery.

Enjoy this pattern which we believe to be a classic choice in little girl's dressing. We would love to see some of your variations so don't forget to send us a snapshot after you make your special dress. ▒

Morgan Ross Dress

(see page 114 for more illustrations.)

Fabric and Lace Requirements for the Dress

Size	Fabric
2 and 4	$2\frac{1}{2}$ yds.
6	$2\frac{3}{4}$ yds.
8	3 yds.
10, 12 and 14	$3\frac{1}{2}$ yds.

Dress Front

Dress Back

For all sizes: $1\frac{1}{4}$ yds. of $\frac{5}{8}$" wide lace edging for smocked sleeves and sleeves with elastic

Fabric and Trim Requirements for the Collars

Use the flat trim measurements for piping, entredeux, flat lace and tatting.
To use gathered lace, double the amount needed for flat trim.

Collar Types	Sizes	Fabric	Flat Trim
Scalloped I and II,	2 and 4	$\frac{1}{3}$ yd.	$1\frac{1}{4}$ yds.
Round and Square	6	$\frac{3}{8}$ yd.	$1\frac{3}{8}$ yds.
	8 and 10	$\frac{1}{2}$ yd.	$1\frac{1}{2}$ yds.
	12 and 14	$\frac{1}{2}$ yd.	$1\frac{3}{4}$ yds.
Pointed	2	$\frac{3}{8}$ yd.	$1\frac{1}{2}$ yds.
	4	$\frac{1}{2}$ yd.	$1\frac{1}{2}$ yds.
	6	$\frac{1}{2}$ yd.	$1\frac{3}{4}$ yds.
	8 and 10	$\frac{5}{8}$ yd.	$2\frac{1}{4}$ yds.
	12 and 14	$\frac{5}{8}$ yd.	$2\frac{3}{8}$ yds.
Peter Pan	2, 4 and 6	$\frac{1}{4}$ yd.	1 yd.
	8, 10, 12 and 14	$\frac{1}{4}$ yd.	$1\frac{1}{4}$ yds.

Smocked

Dress Back with Sash

Embroidered Edging for Smocked or Ruffled Collars

Sizes 2, 4 and 6: $1\frac{1}{4}$ yds. of edging, $3\frac{1}{2}$" to 4" wide

Sizes 8, 10, 12 and 14: $1\frac{1}{2}$ yds. of edging, $4\frac{1}{2}$" to 5" wide

Notions: purchased or self-made piping, buttons, 1 yd. of $\frac{1}{4}$" elastic (optional for sleeves), thread, floss and ribbon for embroidery and smocking, double-sided wash-away basting tape, washout marking pen

— *Special Note* —

Making Baby Piping

If self-made piping will be used, measure all of the places it will be applied and use these instructions for making it:

*Cut a bias strip $1\frac{1}{4}$" wide by the length needed. Bias may be pieced so that the piping will be made in one long strip. Place tiny cording along the center of the strip on the wrong side and fold the fabric over the cording, meeting the long edges of the fabric. Use a zipper foot to stitch close to the cording (**fig. a**).*

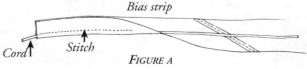

Bias strip

Cord   Stitch

FIGURE A

90

General Dress Directions

Important: Read through all of the instructions before beginning to cut and sew, because there are many variations and options to be considered. Any sleeve and collar variation may be used for any dress, therefore no specific pattern pieces have been listed with the smocking plates. In order to duplicate a specific dress, please refer to the color photographs (page 9-40) and detailed line drawings (page 114).

I. General Directions

All pattern pieces are found on the pattern pull-out. Seam allowances are included in all pattern pieces. Adjustments to pattern pieces will not change the seam allowances.

All seams are ¹/₄" unless otherwise noted. Overcast the seam allowances using a zigzag or serger, or make French seams.

A. Layout and Cutting

(Refer to the Layout Guide)

1. Follow the layout guide to cut two front yokes on the fold, two waisted bodice backs or short back yokes on the fold, and two sleeves on the fold. Collars will be cut later. It may be necessary to adjust the waisted back bodice length if the smocking rows given for a specific graph are fewer or more than the suggested number for the skirt (**refer to the chart in part B of this section for suggested number of smocking rows**). Make changes to the back bodice as follows:

   a. If the plate calls for fewer smocking rows, shorten the back bodice by ³/₈" for each omitted row.

   b. If the plate calls for more smocking rows, lengthen the back bodice by ³/₈" for each additional row. There is not much room for adding smocking rows, and only one or two should be considered. Be sure to check that the new back waistline will not extend lower than the child's natural waistline.

2. Sashes are optional, to be used with the waisted back bodice only.

3. Bias strips will be cut for smocked, ruffled or detached collars and bound sleeves only, or for piping. Add the amounts of piping needed for each section (yokes, collar, sleeves) to determine the total amount of bias that will be required.

4. Trace the armhole template onto a piece of stiff paper.

5. Cut a front and a back skirt piece to the measurements given in the chart. Since a 45" wide skirt is not wide enough to smock for larger sizes, side panels will be added to sizes 10 - 14 after smocking is completed. Measurements for the side panels are included in the skirt chart. Skirt length may be adjusted by using a deeper or narrower hem, or by adding to or subtracting from the cut length of the skirt pieces. If cutting lengths are adjusted, be sure to change the front and back skirt pieces by equal amounts. If a fancy band will be used, refer to the specific directions in section XV.B for information on adjusting the skirt length, as well as the materials needed for the fancy band.

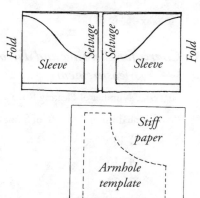

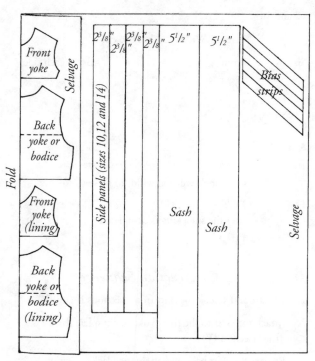

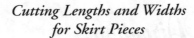

Cutting Lengths and Widths for Skirt Pieces

For larger sizes, the numbers in parentheses indicate the width to cut the two side panels for each smocked skirt section, and the length is the same as the main skirt piece for that size.

A 4" hem allowance and ¹/₂" waistline seam allowance are included in the given measurements.

size	yoke front and high back yoke	waisted back bodice
2	21¹/₂" x 40"	17³/₈" x 40"
4	24¹/₈" x 40"	18⁵/₈" x 40"
6	29⁷/₈" x 40"	23³/₈" x 40"
8	34³/₄" X 45"	28¹/₈" x 45"
10	36¹/₈" x 45" (2³/₈")	29" x 45"
12	39" x 45" (2³/₈")	31¹/₄" x 45"
14	40³/₈" x 45" (2³/₈")	3³/₄" x 45"

B. Charts for Pleating and Tie-off Measurements

Suggested Number of Pleating Rows

Size	# of Pleated Rows	# of Smocked Rows
2	11-13	9 - 11
4	14 - 16	12 - 14
6 and 8	17 - 19	15 - 17
10	19 - 21	17 - 19
12 and 14	21 - 23	19 - 21

Tie-off Width, cut edge to cut edge

Size	Front	Back (each side)
2	13¹/₂"	7"
4	13³/₄"	7¹/₄"
6	14¹/₂"	7³/₄"
8	16"	8-3/8"
10	13¹/₄"	7"
	side panels will add width to these sizes	
12	14¹/₂"	7³/₄"
	after the smocking is completed	
14	15¹/₂"	8¹/₄"

C. Construction Sequence

1. Prepare and smock the skirt front (sections II and III).

2. Attach the skirt to the front yoke to complete the dress front (section IV).

3. Prepare the skirt back and apply the placket (section V).

4. Attach the skirt back to the high back yoke or waisted bodice, and attach optional sashes (section VI).

5. Sew the dress back to the front, right sides together, at the shoulder seams (section VII).

6. Adapt the collar pattern if necessary (section VIII.B).

7. Embellish and construct the collar (section VIII.C, sections IX and X).

8. Attach the collar to the dress, or finish the collar and neck edge for a detachable collar (section XI).

9. Hand -whip the lining in place (section XI).

10. Construct the sleeves (section XII) and attach the sleeves to the dress (section XIII).

11. Sew the side seams (section XIV).

12. Turn up the hem, or make and attach a fancy band (section XV).

13. Finish the dress by adding buttonholes and buttons, and a sash loop (section XVI).

II. Preparing the Skirt Front

To add side panels to the skirt for sizes 10, 12 and 14, refer to the Special Note at the end of this section before pleating the skirt piece.

1. Fold the skirt piece in half and mark the center front with a washable pen or a small thread loop. Roll the skirt piece on a dowel and pleat the number of rows required for the smocking design (refer to the chart in section I.B). The first pleating thread should be ¹/₄" from the top edge of the fabric. If the number of rows for the graph is different from the number suggested for the skirt, the waisted back bodice must be adjusted so that the waistline seam will meet the bottom smocked row of the front skirt (refer to the instructions given in section I.A step 1) .

2. Remove the pleating threads from the ¹/₄" seam allowance at each side of the skirt piece. Tie-off the skirt piece to the measurements given in the chart (section I.B) (**fig. 1**).

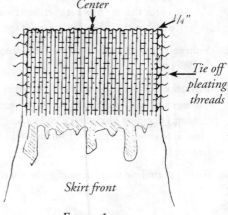

Center

¹/₄"

Tie off pleating threads

Skirt front

FIGURE 1

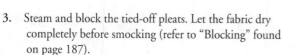

3. Steam and block the tied-off pleats. Let the fabric dry completely before smocking (refer to "Blocking" found on page 187).

4. Use the armhole template guide to mark the armhole curves. Do not cut out the armholes (**fig. 2**).

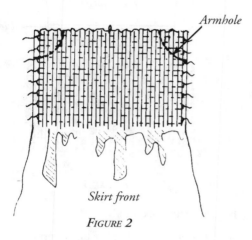

Armhole

Skirt front

FIGURE 2

── *Special Note* ──

Adding Side Panels to Larger Sizes

In order to have enough fullness in the pleats for sizes 10 - 14, side panels must be added to the skirt piece. The following modifications to the instructions in sections II and III will be necessary:

1. *Pleat the center skirt piece as directed, and tie-off to the given measurement. Do not draw the armholes. The skirt will be smocked all the way across, since there are no armholes at this point.*

2. *After smocking, attach the extra pieces to each side of the center piece with a ¹/₄" seam, using a zipper foot to stitch close to the pleats (**fig. a**).*

3. *Use the template to draw armholes on the side panels. Stay-stitching is not necessary (**fig. a**).*

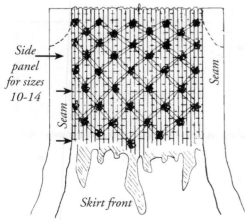

Side panel for sizes 10-14

Seam

Seam

Seam

Skirt front

FIGURE A

III. Smocking the Skirt Front

1. Remember that the top and bottom pleating rows are the stabilizer rows. They are not part of the smocking design. The top row may be smocked with cables or stem stitch, on the right or wrong side, to make construction easier.

2. Refer to the individual graphs for specific smocking instructions. Refer to the Special Note above for smocking sizes 10 - 14. For sizes 2 - 8, stop the smocking at the armhole guide lines (**fig. 1**).

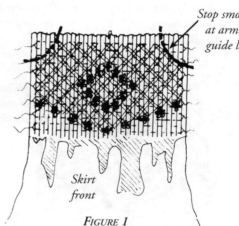

Stop smocking at armhole guide lines

Skirt front

FIGURE 1

3. Refer to the graphs and stitch keys for embroidery placement.

4. Stay-stitch along the armhole guide lines with a tiny zigzag or straight stitch to hold the pleats (**fig. 2**).

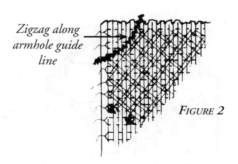

Zigzag along armhole guide line

FIGURE 2

5. Re-block the smocking if needed before constructing the dress.

6. Do not remove the pleating threads until the dress is constructed.

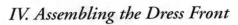

IV. Assembling the Dress Front

1. Cut out the armholes on the skirt front piece, being careful not to cut through the stay-stitching, and do not cut off the knots of the smocking.

2. For a piped yoke:

   a. Cut a piece of piping the length of the bottom edge of the front yoke pattern.

   b. To attach the piping, place double-sided wash-away basting tape along the seam allowance of purchased or self-made piping. Stick the piping to the smocked skirt piece, just above the top row of smocking (the seam allowance is 1/2"). Be sure to keep the piping straight (**fig. 1**).

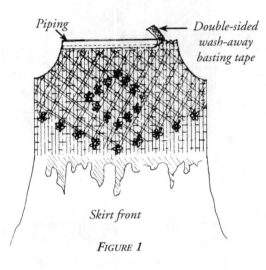

Piping — *Double-sided wash-away basting tape*

Skirt front

FIGURE 1

   c. Place one front yoke piece to the skirt piece, right sides together, and pin in place (**fig. 2**).

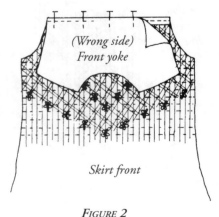

(Wrong side) Front yoke

Skirt front

FIGURE 2

   d. Use a zipper foot or cording foot to stitch through all the layers, close to the piping (refer to fig. 2).

   e. Press the seam toward the yoke, exposing the piping (**fig. 3**).

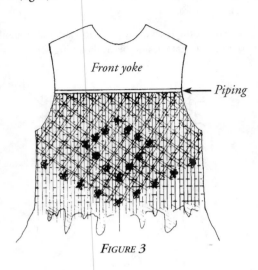

Front yoke — *Piping*

FIGURE 3

3. For a decorative yoke overlay:

   a. Place one front yoke piece to the skirt piece, right sides together, and pin in place. Stitch the yoke to the skirt with a 1/2" seam (**fig. 4**).

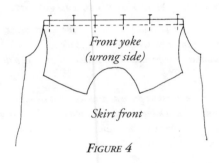

Front yoke (wrong side)

Skirt front

FIGURE 4

   b. Press the seam toward the yoke (refer to fig. 3).

   c. Place the bottom cutting line of the front yoke pattern along the decorative edge of the overlay fabric and cut out one front yoke overlay (**fig. 5**).

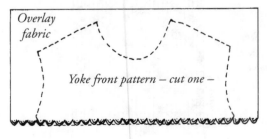

Overlay fabric

Yoke front pattern – cut one –

FIGURE 5

d. Place the wrong side of the overlay to the right side of the yoke, matching side and shoulder seams. Baste the overlay in place along the armholes, shoulder and neck edges (**fig. 6**).

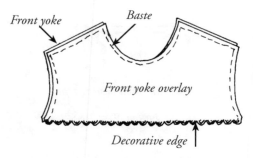

Front yoke   *Baste*

Front yoke overlay

Decorative edge

FIGURE 6

V. Preparing the Skirt Back

If the dress back will be smocked, refer to the Special Note at the end of this section before completing section A below.

A. Applying a Placket and Piping to a High Back Yoke

1. For an unsmocked back skirt, trace and cut out the armholes (if the skirt will be smocked, refer to the Special Note at the end of this section). Fold the back skirt piece in half and make a light crease along the center back. Cut a 4" slit along the crease at the top of the skirt. Run two rows of gathering stitches, $1/4$" and $1/2$" from the top edges of the back skirt piece, stopping the stitches $1/4$" from the slit and the side edges (**fig. 1**).

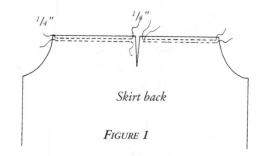

$1/4$" $1/4$"

Skirt back

FIGURE 1

2. Cut two pieces of piping, each 1" longer than the bottom edge of the back yoke pattern (**fig. 2**).

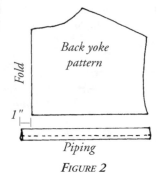

Fold   *Back yoke pattern*

1"

Piping

FIGURE 2

3. Pull the gathering threads (or pleating threads) out of the way and place the piping to the right side of the skirt piece, with the stitching of the piping lined up on the $1/2$" seam allowance of the skirt. Pin the piping in place for 2" on each side of the slit, but do not stitch (**fig. 3**).

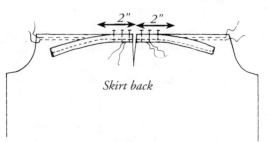

2"   2"

Skirt back

FIGURE 3

4. Cut a piece of fabric for the placket, 1" x 8" with one long side on the selvage. Open the slit in the skirt out to form a straight line and place the raw edge of the slit along the long cut edge of the placket piece, right sides together. There will be a small "V" shape at the bottom of the slit, this is normal. Use a $1/4$" seam to stitch the skirt to the placket, with the skirt on top. The ends of the piping will be caught in the seam. *Do not* catch the gathering threads in the seam. The seam will catch only a few threads of the skirt slit at the "V" (**fig. 4**).

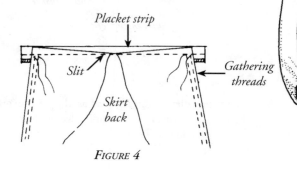

Placket strip

Slit   *Gathering threads*

Skirt back

FIGURE 4

5. Press the seam toward the placket piece. Fold the selvage edge of the placket to the inside and whip the selvage edge to the stitching line (**fig. 5**).

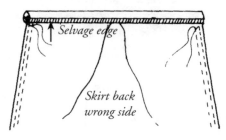

Selvage edge

Skirt back wrong side

FIGURE 5

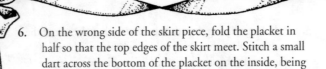

6. On the wrong side of the skirt piece, fold the placket in half so that the top edges of the skirt meet. Stitch a small dart across the bottom of the placket on the inside, being careful not to catch the skirt in the stitching (**fig. 6**).

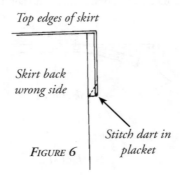

Top edges of skirt

Skirt back wrong side

Stitch dart in placket

FIGURE 6

7. Fold the right placket to the inside and leave the left placket extended. The finished dress will lap right over left (**fig. 7**).

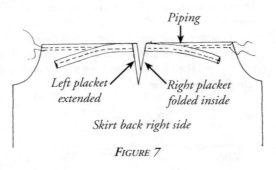

Piping

Left placket extended

Right placket folded inside

Skirt back right side

FIGURE 7

8. Pull up the gathering threads or adjust the pleats to make the skirt fit the yokes, matching the edges of the placket to the back fold line (**fig. 8**).

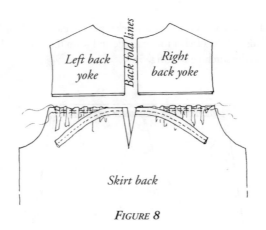

Left back yoke

Back fold lines

Right back yoke

Skirt back

FIGURE 8

9. Apply washout basting tape to the side of the piping seam allowance that will be against the skirt. Stick the piping to the skirt, matching the stitching line of the piping to the ¹/₂" seam allowance. Use a zipper foot to baste close to the piping (**fig. 9**).

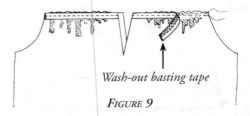

Wash-out basting tape

FIGURE 9

B. Applying a Placket to an Unpiped High Back Yoke or Waisted Back Bodice

1. For an unsmocked high-yoke skirt, trace and cut out the armholes.

2. Fold the back skirt piece in half and make a light crease along the center back. Cut a 4" slit along the crease at the top of the skirt. Run two rows of gathering stitches, ¹/₄" and ¹/₂" from the top edges of the back skirt piece, stopping the stitches ¹/₄" from the slit (refer to fig. 1 in part A of this section).

3. Cut a piece of fabric for the placket, 1" x 8" with one long side on the selvage. Open the slit out to form a straight line and place the raw edge of the slit along the long cut edge of the placket piece, right sides together. There will be a small "V" shape at the bottom of the slit, this is normal. Use a ¹/₄" seam to stitch the skirt to the placket, with the skirt on top. The seam will catch only a few threads of the skirt slit at the "V" (refer to fig. 4 in part A of this section).

4. Press the seam toward the placket piece. Fold the selvage edge of the placket to the inside and whip the selvage edge to the stitching line (refer to fig. 5 in part A of this section).

5. On the wrong side of the skirt piece, fold the placket in half so that the top edges of the skirt meet. Stitch a small dart across the bottom of the placket on the inside, being careful not to catch the skirt in the stitching (refer to fig. 6 in part A of this section).

6. Fold the right placket to the inside and leave the left placket extended. The finished dress will lap right over left (**fig. 10**).

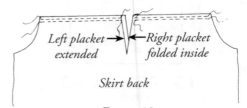

Left placket extended

Right placket folded inside

Skirt back

FIGURE 10

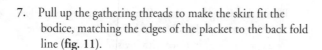

7. Pull up the gathering threads to make the skirt fit the bodice, matching the edges of the placket to the back fold line (**fig. 11**).

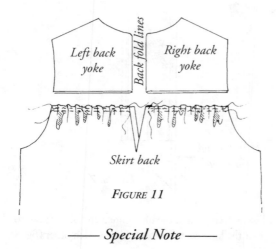

FIGURE 11

—— *Special Note* ——

Smocked Back Skirt

If the dress back will be smocked, use the high back yoke option with piping. It will be necessary to make the following modifications to the instructions given in section V.A:

1. *For sizes 10 - 14, refer to the Special Note at the end of section II, then continue with these instructions.*

2. *After cutting the slit (section V.A, step 1), pleat the top of the skirt with the same number of rows as the skirt front. Be sure that the second edge of the slit goes into the pleater straight.*

3. *After pleating, separate the edges of the slit, pull some slack into the pleating threads and cut them to allow the slit to open. Remove the pleating threads from ¹/₄" at the slit edges and the sides (**fig. a**).*

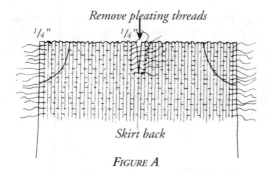

FIGURE A

4. *Apply the placket as directed in section V.A, steps 2 - 7. Line up the corded edge of the piping just above the top row of smocking.*

5. *Pull up the pleating threads and tie-off to the measurements given in the chart (section I.B). Mark the armholes for sizes 2 - 8. Smock according to the directions in section III.*

6. *Continue with section V.A, step 9, placing the piping just above the top row of smocking.*

VI. Assembling the Dress Back

A. Bodice to Skirt

1. Press a crease in the bodice back pieces along the foldline. This creates a lining for each bodice piece. Make sure that one piece is the right bodice and the other is the left bodice. Mark the pieces so that the bodice section will not be confused with the lining section (**fig. 1**).

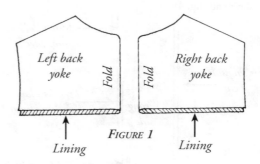

FIGURE 1

2. Pin one bodice section to the skirt, right sides together. The crease in the bodice will meet the edge of the placket (remember that the right placket is folded to the inside, the crease will meet the foldline). Adjust the skirt gathers to fit the bodice and baste the bodice to the skirt (**fig. 2**).

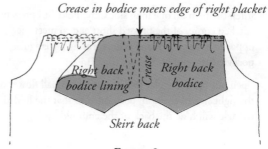

FIGURE 2

3. Stitch in place with a ¹/₂" seam. If piping is used, the seam should be stitched close to the piping with a zipper foot. Trim the seam and press the bodice up (**fig. 3**).

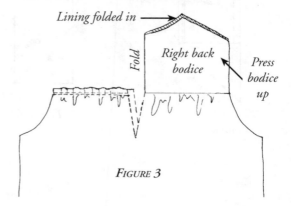

FIGURE 3

4. Repeat steps 1 - 3 for the remaining bodice piece.

B. Sashes for Waisted Back Bodice

1. Cut sash pieces to the following sizes:

    Sizes 2 - 6: $4^{1}/_{2}$" by 36"

    Sizes 8 - 14: $5^{1}/_{2}$" by 45"

2. Stitch $^{1}/_{8}$" from the edge on each long side, using a short straight stitch. Press the long edges to the wrong side along the stitching lines. Press another $^{1}/_{8}$" on each long side to create a $^{1}/_{8}$" double hem. Also press $^{1}/_{4}$" along one short end (**fig. 4**).

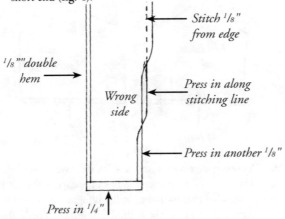

$^{1}/_{8}$""double hem →

← Stitch $^{1}/_{8}$" from edge

Wrong side

← Press in along stitching line

← Press in another $^{1}/_{8}$"

Press in $^{1}/_{4}$" ↑

FIGURE 4

3. Stitch the hem on one long side only. Fold and press the stitched corner of the pressed short end to meet the opposite unhemmed long edge, forming a triangular pocket at the end of the sash (**fig. 5**).

4. Open out the triangular fold and stitch a small flower on the right side of the sash, positioned so that the folded triangle will hide the back of the embroidery (**fig. 6**).

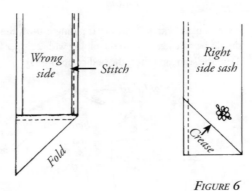

Wrong side — Stitch

Fold

FIGURE 5

Right side sash

Crease

FIGURE 6

5. Refold the triangular piece. Hem the remaining long edge, stitching through the folded end. Tack the center of the open pocket edge in place with invisible stitches (**fig. 7**).

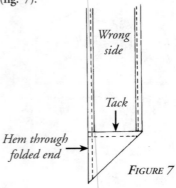

Wrong side

Tack ↓

Hem through folded end →

FIGURE 7

6. Fold a deep pleat at the unhemmed end of the sash, so that the long edges almost fold over each other (**fig. 8**).

Deep pleat

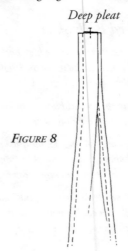

FIGURE 8

7. Place the raw ends of the sash pieces at the sides of the bodice back, with the bottom edge of the sash overlapping the waistline seam by $^{1}/_{4}$". Baste the sash pieces in place (**fig. 9**).

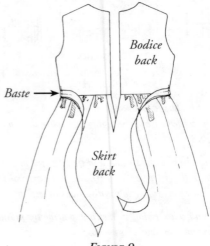

Bodice back

Baste →

Skirt back

FIGURE 9

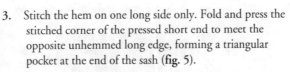

VII. Shoulder Seams

1. Open out the back bodice linings. Pin the dress front to the dress back at the shoulder seams, right sides together. Stitch the seams. Do not stitch the lining in this seam (**fig. 1**).

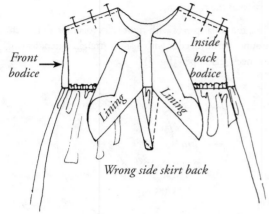

Front bodice

Inside back bodice

Lining *Lining*

Wrong side skirt back

FIGURE 1

2. With right sides together, stitch the remaining front yoke piece to the bodice back lining sections at the shoulder seams. Press all of the shoulder seams open (**fig. 2**).

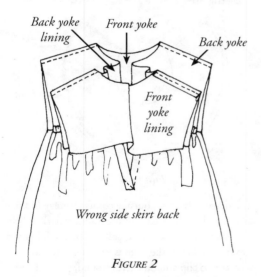

Back yoke lining *Front yoke* *Back yoke*

Front yoke lining

Wrong side skirt back

FIGURE 2

VIII. Peter Pan and Flat Collar Variations and Construction

A. Variations

There are several collar variations presented here. Smocked or ruffled collars are described, as well as shaped flat collars: Round, Square, Pointed and Scalloped I and II. The trimming methods described are embroidery, lace overlay, piping, piping with gathered lace, entredeux with flat lace or tatting and entredeux with gathered lace. The pattern piece for each collar will show which trim method it was designed to use. There is also a section explaining how to adapt a pattern for different trims.

After the pattern is adapted (if necessary) for the chosen trims, refer to the section describing that particular trim. Application of that trim to the various collar types will be discussed. References may also be made to other sections which contain general information that will be helpful.

B. Adapting Collar Patterns for Different Trims

When adapting a pattern for trims, adjustments will be made to only those edges where the trim is applied. The neck seam will not be changed on any pattern. The trim may not extend up the center back edges of some shaped collars; in that case, the center back edge will not be adjusted. For some large flat collars, the width of the trim will not affect the look of the collar enough to make any adjustment necessary. In all cases, the seam allowance will remain the same as indicated on the pattern.

In figures 1 - 4, the solid line is the original cutting line, and the dotted line is the new cutting line.

1. If a collar is designed for no trim and trim will be added, subtract the finished width of the trim from only the outer edge of the pattern piece. The change may be as little as $1/8$" for baby piping, or as much as $5/8$" for entredeux and lace edging. Do not change the neck seam (**fig. 1**).

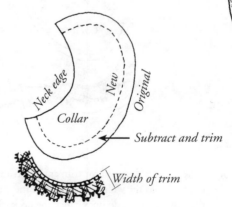

Neck edge *New* *Original*

Collar

Subtract and trim

Width of trim

FIGURE 1

2. If the collar is designed for trim (the size will be specified on the pattern), a different size trim may be used by making the following adjustments:

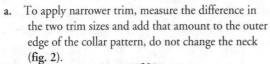

a. To apply narrower trim, measure the difference in the two trim sizes and add that amount to the outer edge of the collar pattern, do not change the neck (**fig. 2**).

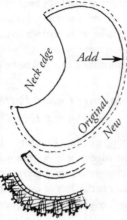

Neck edge *Add* → *Original* *New*

FIGURE 2

b. To apply wider trim, measure the difference in the two trim sizes and subtract that amount from the outer edge of the collar pattern, do not change the neck (**fig. 3**).

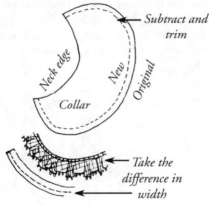

Subtract and trim →

Neck edge *New* *Original*

Collar

Take the difference in width →

FIGURE 3

3. If the collar is designed for trim and the trim will be omitted, add the width of the trim to the outer edge of the collar pattern, do not change the neck (**fig. 4**).

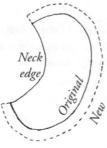

Neck edge

Original *New*

FIGURE 4

C. General Instructions for Peter Pan or Flat Collar Construction

Some trim applications will be done before construction and some will be applied after construction. The specific instructions for each trim method will refer to this construction section at the right time.

1. Place the collar pieces with right sides together and stitch around the outer edge with a short straight stitch, leaving the neck seam open (**fig. 5**).

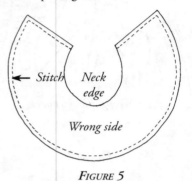

← *Stitch* *Neck edge*

Wrong side

FIGURE 5

2. Set the machine for a tiny zigzag and stitch again, just outside the previous stitching. Trim the seam close to the zigzag (**fig. 6**).

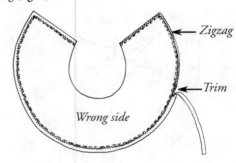

Zigzag ←

Trim ←

Wrong side

FIGURE 6

3. Trim diagonally across outside corners (square lfid pointed collars, and the back edge of the round collar) and clip into inside points (scalloped collars). Be careful not to clip into the stitches. If the seam is very small, it may not be necessary to clip around curves (round, pointed and scalloped collars) (**fig. 7**).

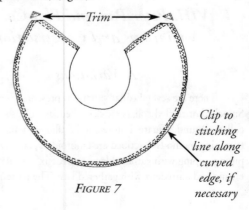

← *Trim* →

Clip to stitching line along curved edge, if necessary

FIGURE 7

4. Turn the collar to the right side and press the edges well. Baste the neck edges together (**fig. 8**).

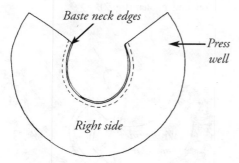

Baste neck edges

Press well

Right side

FIGURE 8

IX. Collar Embellishment for Peter Pan and Flat Collars

A. Embroidery

1. Embroidery should be the first embellishment added to a collar. When adding embroidery to a plain collar, be sure that the design fits in the required space with a little space between the design and the seam line. Allow a little extra room at the neck edge to allow for the fold of the collar to the outside (**fig. 1**).

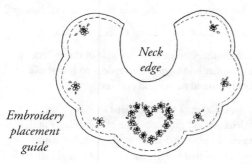

Neck edge

Embroidery placement guide

FIGURE 1

2. Trace the pattern onto fabric that is at least 1" larger than the pattern on all sides and stay-stitch around the collar outline, but do not cut out the collar. This prevents the collar from stretching as the embroidery work is done, and it also allows more room to work close to the seam lines (**fig. 2**).

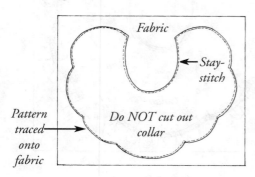

Fabric

Stay-stitch

Pattern traced onto fabric

Do NOT cut out collar

FIGURE 2

3. Refer to general embroidery instructions for information on design transfer, hoops, supplies and stitching.

4. Embroidered pieces should be pressed facedown on a padded surface.

5. Cut out the collar pieces and refer to the specific instructions in section IX for any other trims to be added, then construct the collar according to section VIII.C.

B. Lace Overlay

1. To add or omit an overlay, no pattern adjustments are needed.

2. Cut the collar piece from the lace (cut two lace pieces for Peter Pan collars). Also cut two collar pieces from fabric (cut four for Peter Pan collars).

3. Place the wrong side of the lace collar against the right side of the fabric collar. Baste the two layers together and treat as one piece of fabric (**fig. 3**).

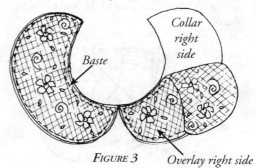

Collar right side

Baste

FIGURE 3

Overlay right side

4. Refer to the specific instructions in section IX for any other trims to be added, then construct the collar according to section VIII.C.

C. Baby Piping

1. Pattern Adjustments:

   a. To add baby piping to a plain collar, refer to section VIII.B, step 1.

   b. To use baby piping on a collar designed for wider trim, refer to section VIII.B, step 2a.

   c. To omit piping, refer to section VIII.B, step 3.

2. Cut the collars from the fabric.

3. Trim the seam allowance of the piping to $1/4$". Clip the seam allowance of the piping so that it will lie smoothly around the collar curves (**fig. 4**).

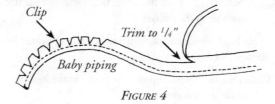

Clip

Trim to $1/4$"

Baby piping

FIGURE 4

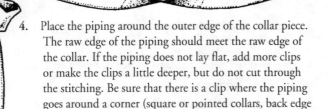

4. Place the piping around the outer edge of the collar piece. The raw edge of the piping should meet the raw edge of the collar. If the piping does not lay flat, add more clips or make the clips a little deeper, but do not cut through the stitching. Be sure that there is a clip where the piping goes around a corner (square or pointed collars, back edge of round collars) or into a point (scalloped collars) (**fig.** 5).

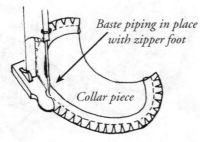

Piping

Collar piece

FIGURE 5

5. Use a cording foot or zipper foot to baste the piping in place, with the stitches close to the cord of the piping (**fig.** 6).

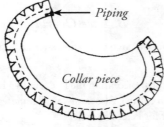

Baste piping in place with zipper foot

Collar piece

FIGURE 6

6. Refer to section VIII.C to construct the collar. Use a zipper foot and work with the piped pieces on top so that you can stitch right on top of the previous stitching line.

D. Baby Piping with Gathered Lace

1. Pattern adjustments:

   a. To add gathered lace and piping to a plain collar, refer to section VIII.B, step 1. The actual width of the lace will be used as the finished width, because this method does not take up a seam allowance in the lace. Since the piping will overlap the lace, no other adjustments are needed.

   b. To add gathered lace to a collar already designed for baby piping, refer to section VIII.B, step 2b. Subtract ¹/₈" from the actual lace width and use this number as the difference.

2. Apply baby piping and construct the collar as directed in section IX.C.

3. Gather the lace by pulling the top thread of the heading. Adjust the gathers evenly.

4. Working on the wrong side of the collar, place the right side of the lace heading over the piping and whip the lace to the under collar (**fig.** 7).

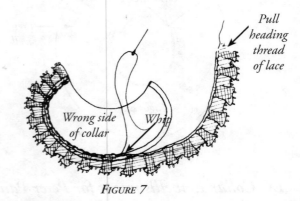

Pull heading thread of lace

Wrong side of collar   *Whip*

FIGURE 7

E. Entredeux with Lace

1. Pattern Adjustments:

   a. To add entredeux and lace to a plain collar, refer to section VIII.B, step 1 and use the combined widths of the lace and trimmed entredeux as the finished width.

   b. To change the width of the trim on a collar designed for a specific size trim, refer to section VIII.B, step 2.

2. Construct the collar according to section VIII.C.

3. Trim the batiste border from one side of the entredeux. Clip the other border of the entredeux so that it will lie smoothly around curves and corners.

4. Place the collar on a pinning board and shape the entredeux around the outer edge of the collar. Pin the entredeux in place and steam to shape it. For corners (square or pointed collars, back edge of round collars) or points (scalloped collars), the entredeux may be cut and overlapped by one hole to give sharp points (**fig.** 8).

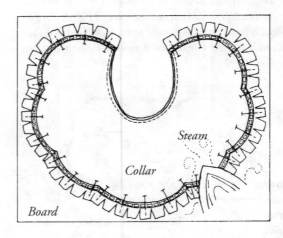

Steam

Collar

Board

FIGURE 8

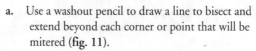

5. After the entredeux has dried completely, butt it to the edge of the collar and hand-whip or zigzag it in place. If a zigzag is used, make sure that the needle goes into each hole of the entredeux. Trim the remaining border from the edge of the entredeux (**fig. 9**).

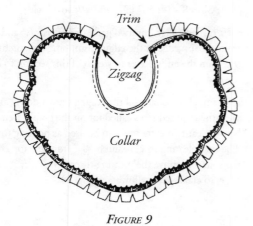

FIGURE 9

6. To shape flat lace around curves (round, pointed and scalloped collars):

   a. Place the collar on a pinning board and butt the lace to the edge of the entredeux, following the shape of the collar.

   b. To go around curves, pin the outer edge of the lace flat, then use a pin to pull the heading thread just enough to make the heading lie flat around the curve. Steam the lace to shape it, then let it dry completely before attaching it to the entredeux (refer to step 9 in this section) (**fig. 10**).

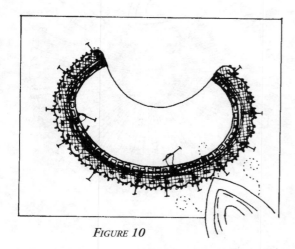

FIGURE 10

7. To miter flat lace around corners and points (square, pointed and scalloped collars):

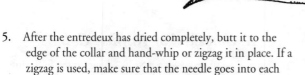

a. Use a washout pencil to draw a line to bisect and extend beyond each corner or point that will be mitered (**fig. 11**).

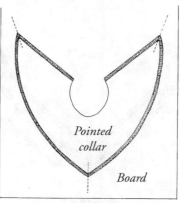

Pointed collar

Board

FIGURE 11

b. Butt the lace heading to the entredeux and pin, following the collar shape until a corner or point is reached. Place pins through the lace at both points where the bisecting line crosses the lace edges (**fig. 12**).

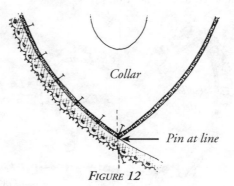

Collar

Pin at line

FIGURE 12

c. Fold the lace back on itself, in the direction it just came from. Remove the pin at the wide edge of the miter and replace it on the line, through both layers of lace (**fig. 13**).

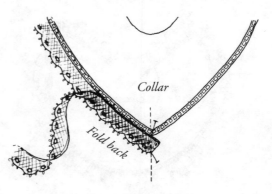

Collar

Fold back

FIGURE 13

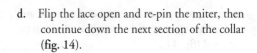

d. Flip the lace open and re-pin the miter, then continue down the next section of the collar (**fig. 14**).

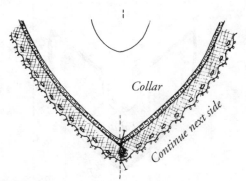

Collar

Continue next side

FIGURE 14

e. Refer to step 9 in this section to attach the lace.

8. To gather lace, pull the gathering threads in the lace heading and adjust the gathers evenly. When going around an outside corner, readjust the gathers so that there is a little extra fullness at the corner. When going into an inside point, readjust the gathers so that there is a little less fullness (**fig. 15**).

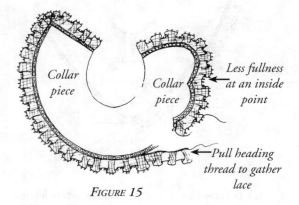

Collar piece

Collar piece

Less fullness at an inside point

Pull heading thread to gather lace

FIGURE 15

9. To attach the lace, butt the edge of the lace heading to the entredeux and whip by hand or zigzag, making sure that the needle goes into every hole of the entredeux (**fig. 16**).

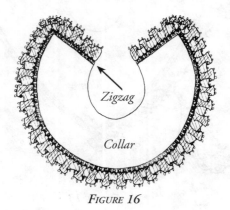

Zigzag

Collar

FIGURE 16

X. Smocked or Ruffled Collars

1. Cut a piece of embroidered Swiss edging to the following sizes, with one long side along the decorative edge:

    Sizes 2 - 6: 40" long and 3^1/$_2$" to 4" wide

    Sizes 8 - 14: 50" long and 4^1/$_2$" to 5" wide

2. For a ruffled collar, run two gathering rows, ^{1}/$_4$" and ^{1}/$_2$" from the top edge of the edging, stopping the stitching ^{1}/$_2$" from the ends. Refer to step 6 of this section to hem the ends.

3. For a smocked collar, roll the edging onto a dowel and pleat the required rows called for on the graph. Remember to pleat two extra rows, to be used as holding rows. The first pleating row should be ^{1}/$_4$" from the top edge of the collar. Remove the pleating threads from ^{1}/$_2$" at each edge, to create seam allowances (**fig. 1**).

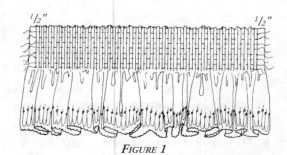

^{1}/$_2$" ^{1}/$_2$"

FIGURE 1

4. Shape and block the collar, using steam to set the pleats. Let the collar dry completely before smocking (**fig. 2**).

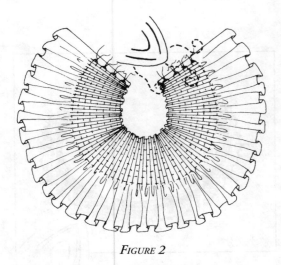

FIGURE 2

5. Smock the top holding row with a stem stitch; this replaces backsmocking and will make construction easier. Smock the collar according to the specific instructions with the graph. Re-block after smocking, if necessary.

6. Turn under ¼" and then ¼" again at the collar back edges, to form a hem. Stitch the folded edge of the hem to the back side of the collar (**fig. 3**).

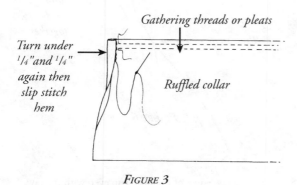

Gathering threads or pleats

Turn under ¼" and ¼" again then slip stitch hem

Ruffled collar

FIGURE 3

XI. Completing the Collar and Neck Edge

A. Attaching Peter Pan and Wide Flat Collars to the Dress

1. Push the yoke lining out of the way and pin the completed collar to the neck edge of the dress, matching the center fronts and center backs. The wrong side of the collar will be against the right side of the dress. The center back edges of all collars should meet the center back line of the dress back. The two sections of Peter Pan collars should just meet each other at the center front as they cross the ¼" seam allowance line. Baste the collar in place (**fig. 1**).

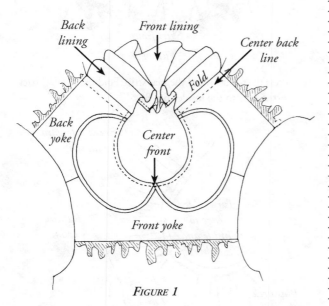

Back lining

Front lining

Center back line

Back yoke

Fold

Center front

Front yoke

FIGURE 1

2. Fold the lining over the bodice (right sides will be together, with the collar in between the layers) and pin along the neck edge. Make sure that center fronts and shoulder seams are matched, and the back edge is turned to the outside along the fold. Stitch through all layers with a ¼" seam (**fig. 2**).

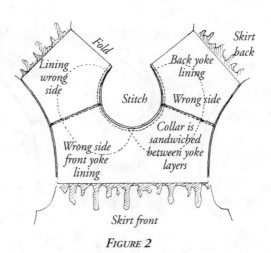

Fold

Skirt back

Lining wrong side

Back yoke lining

Stitch

Wrong side

Collar is sandwiched between yoke layers

Wrong side front yoke lining

Skirt front

FIGURE 2

3. Trim and clip the neck seam. Turn the lining to the inside and press well.

4. Turn under the ½" seam allowance at the bottom lining edges and whip the lining to the waistline seams of the dress back and the dress front (**fig. 3**).

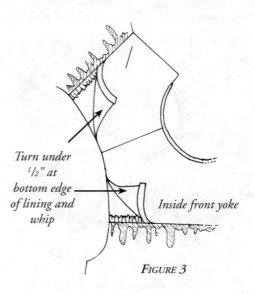

Turn under ½" at bottom edge of lining and whip

Inside front yoke

FIGURE 3

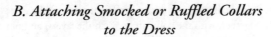

B. Attaching Smocked or Ruffled Collars to the Dress

1. Fold the bodice lining to the wrong side of the dress, wrong sides together, matching the center fronts and shoulder seams. Baste the two layers together along the neck edge (**fig. 4**).

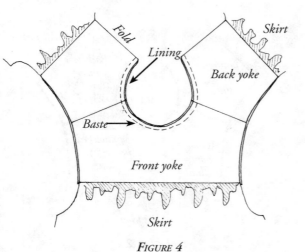

FIGURE 4

2. Pin the completed collar to the dress at the neck edge, with the center fronts matched. The left back collar edge should stop 1" from the back fold. The right back collar edge should meet the back fold. Adjust the pleats or gathers to fit. The wrong side of the collar will be against the right side of the dress. Baste the collar to the dress (**fig. 5**).

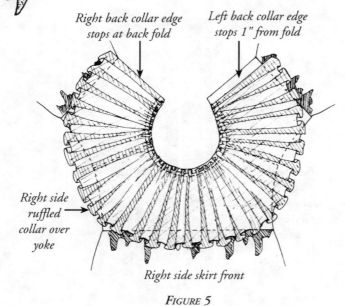

FIGURE 5

3. Cut a bias strip 2" wide and $^1/_2$" longer than the neck edge of the dress.

4. Fold the bias strip with wrong sides together and long edges meeting. Press the folded strip (**fig. 6**).

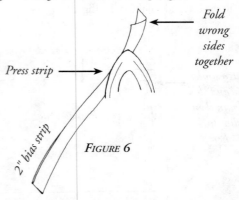

FIGURE 6

5. Place the raw edges of the bias strip even with the raw neck edge of the dress. Let the bias strip extend $^1/_4$" past the folded back edges of the dress. Stitch the bias strip in place with a $^1/_2$" seam. Trim the seam to a neat $^1/_4$" (**fig. 7**).

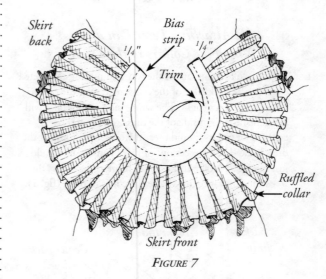

FIGURE 7

6. Press the seam toward the bias strip. Fold the two $^1/_4$" back extensions to the inside (**fig. 8**).

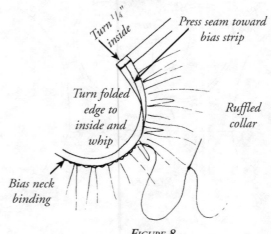

FIGURE 8

106

7. Turn the folded edge of the bias strip to the inside to meet the stitching line, and whip the bias strip to the seam by hand (refer to fig. 8).

8. Turn under the $^1/_2$" seam allowance at the bottom lining edges and whip the lining to the waistline seams of the dress back and the dress front (refer to fig. 3 in part A of this section).

C. Detached Collars

1. Fold the lining over the bodice, right sides together, and pin along the neck edge. Make sure that center fronts and shoulder seams are matched, and the back edge is turned to the outside along the fold. Stitch through all layers with a $^1/_4$" seam (refer to fig. 2 in part A of this section, omitting the reference to the collar).

2. Trim and clip the neck seam. Turn the lining to the inside and press well.

3. Turn under the $^1/_2$" seam allowance at the bottom lining edges and whip the lining to the waistline seams of the dress back and the dress front (refer to fig. 3 in part A of this section).

4. Attach a bias binding to the collar neck edge:

   a. Cut a bias strip $1^5/_8$" by the length of the dress neck edge from center back to center back, plus $^1/_2$".

   b. Fold the bias strip with wrong sides together and long edges meeting. Press the folded strip (refer to fig. 6 in section B).

   c. Place the raw edges of the bias strip even with the top pleating thread or top gathering thread at the neck edge of the collar. Let the bias strip extend $^1/_4$" past the back edge of the collar. Stitch the bias strip in place with a $^1/_4$" seam. Trim the seam allowance to a neat $^1/_4$" (**fig. 9**).

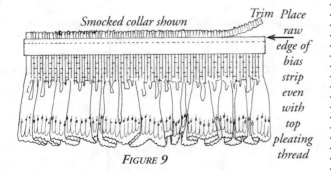

Smocked collar shown   Trim   Place raw edge of bias strip even with top pleating thread

FIGURE 9

   d. Press the seam toward the bias strip. Fold the two $^1/_4$" back extensions to the inside (refer to fig. 8 in part B of this section).

   e. Turn the folded edge of the bias strip to the inside to meet the stitching line, and whip the bias strip to the seam by hand (refer to fig. 8 in part B of this section).

   f. Attach a button and loop to the neck edges of the collar (**fig. 10**).

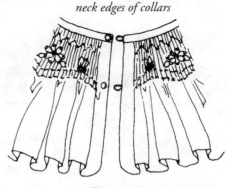

Attach button and loop to neck edges of collars

FIGURE 10

XII. Sleeve Construction

To add a sleeve cap ruffle to a sleeve, refer to the Special Note at the end of this section.

Sleeve Band Measurements

Use the following measurements for cutting elastic or bias binding, or for tying-off smocked sleeves:

Size	Each Sleeve
2	$8^1/_4$"
4	$9^1/_4$"
6	$9^7/_8$"
8	$10^1/_4$"
10	$10^1/_2$"
12	$10^3/_4$"
14	11"

A. Smocked Sleeves

1. Mark the center top and bottom of the sleeve before pleating. Roll the sleeves onto a dowel and pleat the required number of rows. Remember to pleat two extra rows to be used as stabilizer rows. Let the bottom edge of the sleeve run through the pleater groove that is two away from the last threaded needle, or as directed in the instructions for a specific sleeve. Leave long pleating threads so that the sleeve can be flattened after pleating.

2. Flatten the sleeve and finish the bottom edge with lace:

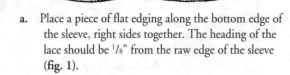

a. Place a piece of flat edging along the bottom edge of the sleeve, right sides together. The heading of the lace should be ¹/₈" from the raw edge of the sleeve (**fig. 1**).

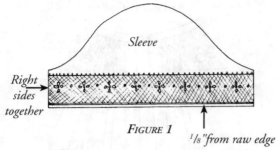

Right sides together

Sleeve

¹/₈" from raw edge

FIGURE 1

b. Set the machine for a zigzag stitch. The stitch should be wide enough that the left "zig" goes over the heading of the lace and the right "zag" goes all the way off the edge of the fabric. Tighten the upper thread tension to make the fabric roll over the heading of the lace (**fig. 2**).

Sleeve

FIGURE 2

Zigzag

c. Press the lace open.

3. Remove the pleating threads from 1" of fabric at each side of the sleeve and run two gathering rows across the top of the sleeve, ¹/₄" and ¹/₂" from the edge (**fig. 3**).

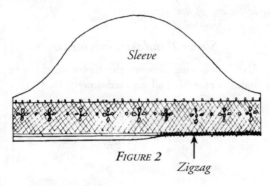

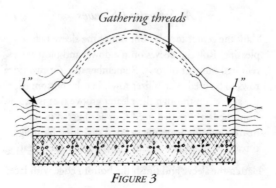

Gathering threads

1"   1"

FIGURE 3

4. Pull up the pleats and tie-off to the measurements in the chart, from cut edge to cut edge. Steam the pleats and let dry completely before smocking.

108

5. Smock the sleeves according to the chosen graph. If the sleeves are too loose after smocking, they may be backsmocked, or a ribbon of the correct length may be hand-whipped to the back side of the smocking (**fig. 4**).

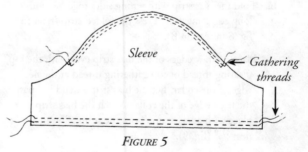

Wrong side of sleeve

Ribbon hand-whipped to back side of smocking

FIGURE 4

6. Refer to section XIII to attach the sleeves to the dress.

B. Sleeves with Bias Binding

For this sleeve option, cut the sleeve along the "Short Puffed Sleeve" line.

1. Run two gathering rows across the top and bottom of the sleeves, ¹/₄" and ¹/₂" from the edges (**fig. 5**).

Sleeve

Gathering threads

FIGURE 5

2. Cut two bias strips 1⁵/₈" wide by the measurement given in the chart, or measure the child's arm and add ¹/₂". Fold the bias strips with wrong sides together and long edges meeting. Press the folded strips (**fig. 6**).

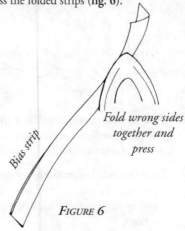

Bias strip

Fold wrong sides together and press

FIGURE 6

3. Place the raw edges of the bias strips even with the bottom edge of the sleeves. Pull up the gathers to make the bottom of the sleeves fit the bias strips, stopping the gathers 1" from each edge. Pin and stitch the bias strips in place with a $1/4$" seam. Trim the seam to a neat $1/4$" (**fig. 7**).

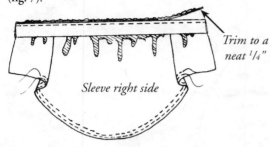

Trim to a neat $1/4$"

Sleeve right side

FIGURE 7

4. Press the seam toward the bias strip and attach the sleeves to the dress (refer to section XIII). Sew the side seams of the dress (refer to section XIV).

5. Turn the folded edge of the bias strips to the inside of the sleeves, letting the edges meet the stitching lines that attached the bindings. Whip the bindings to the seam by hand (**fig. 8**).

Wrong side

Folded edge of bias strip to inside of sleeve

FIGURE 8

C. Elastic in the Sleeves with Bullion Loops and Ribbon

1. Mark the elastic placement line on the wrong side of the sleeves with a washable pen or pencil, $1 1/2$" from the bottom edge (**fig. 9**).

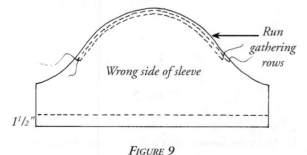

Run gathering rows

Wrong side of sleeve

$1 1/2$"

FIGURE 9

2. Mark placement dots for the bullion loops: Divide the length of the sleeve bottom edge by five. Use that number to place six dots just above the elastic placement line, beginning and ending at the underarm seams, marking on the right side of the fabric with a washout pen or pencil. Also mark six dots $1/4$" below the first row of dots (**fig. 10**).

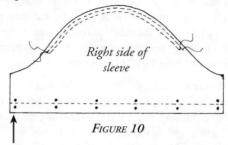

Right side of sleeve

FIGURE 10

Placement dots for bullion loops

3. Attach flat edging to the bottom edge of the sleeve according to section XII.A, step 2.

4. Cut a piece of elastic to the size of the upper arm of the child plus $1/4$". Use the lengths given in the chart if the child is not available to be measured. Lay the elastic over the placement line and straight stitch down the middle of the elastic at one edge of the sleeve for $5/8$" (**fig. 11**).

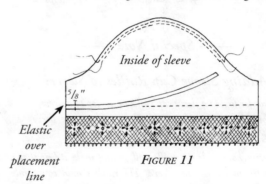

Inside of sleeve

$5/8$"

Elastic over placement line

FIGURE 11

5. Raise the needle and set the machine for a zigzag stitch wide enough to clear both edges of the elastic. Stretch the elastic along the placement line and zigzag over it to within $5/8$" of the other edge of the sleeve. Set the machine back to a straight stitch and stitch down the middle of the elastic to the edge of the sleeve (**fig. 12**).

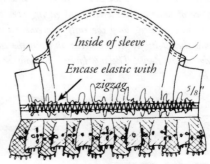

Inside of sleeve

Encase elastic with zigzag

$5/8$"

FIGURE 12

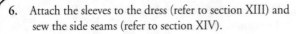

6. Attach the sleeves to the dress (refer to section XIII) and sew the side seams (refer to section XIV).

7. After the sleeve underarm seam is sewn, make five bullion loops (only one loop will be made at the underarm seam where two dots meet). Refer to the instructions for making a bullion rose on page 157. Only one bullion stitch will be made for each loop. The stitch must be long enough to span across the elastic stitching, and there must be enough wraps on the needle to cover the stitch. Be sure to use a long milliner's (straw) needle in order to have room on the needle for all of the wraps.

8. After the dress is finished, ribbon may be threaded through bullion loops on the outside of the sleeve to hide the elastic stitching. Begin and end threading the ribbon at the center front of the sleeve, so that the bow will be on the front (**fig. 13**).

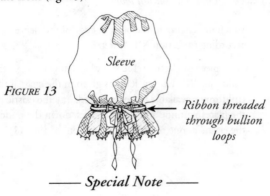

Sleeve

FIGURE 13

Ribbon threaded through bullion loops ←

—— **Special Note** ——

Adding Sleeve Cap Ruffles to Sleeves

In order to add a sleeve cap ruffle to the top of a sleeve, follow these instructions first and then construct the sleeve according to the instructions in the above section.

*Decide how wide the ruffle will be and make a line that far from the top, across the sleeve. The ruffle should cover only the cap of the sleeve and not extend into the underarm curve. If there is a yoke overlay, the bottom edge of the ruffle should be placed so that it will meet the bottom edge of the overlay after the sleeve cap is gathered. An easy way to place the line, especially for an overlay, is to place the armhole template on the sleeve pattern, matching the side edge and the curve. Make a dot at the seamline of the template. Mark both sides of the sleeve this way and connect the dots to form the line (**fig. a**). Place a piece of wide embroidered Swiss edging over the sleeve, with the decorative edge along the ruffle placement line of the sleeve. Trim the edging to fit the sleeve and pin the edging to the top edge of the sleeve. The two layers will now be treated as one (**fig. b**).*

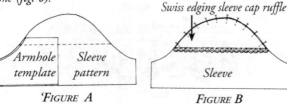

Swiss edging sleeve cap ruffle

| Armhole template | Sleeve pattern |

Sleeve

'FIGURE A   **FIGURE B**

XIII. Attaching the Sleeves to the Dress

1. Baste the bodice and the lining together at the armhole edge (**fig. 1**).

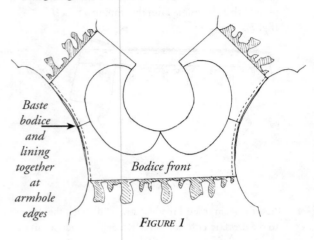

Baste bodice and lining together at armhole edges

Bodice front

FIGURE 1

2. Pull up the gathers at the top of the sleeves to fit the armhole. Pin the sleeves to the dress, matching the center of the sleeve top edge to the shoulder seam of the dress. Adjust the gathers to stop at the yoke line in front and in the back. If a sleeve cap ruffle and yoke overlay are used, the bottom edge of the ruffle should meet the bottom edge of the overlay (**fig. 2**).

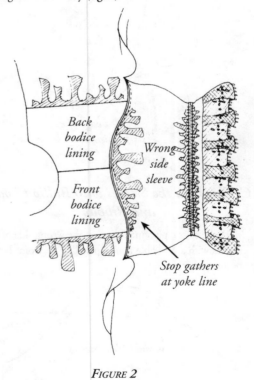

Back bodice lining

Front bodice lining

Wrong side sleeve

Stop gathers at yoke line

FIGURE 2

3. Stitch the sleeves in place with a ¹/₄" seam. Remove the extra gathering thread and pleating threads.

XIV. Side Seams

If a fancy band will replace the hem, sew only one side seam, attach the fancy band (refer to section XV.B) and then sew the remaining side seam.

1. Pin the side seams from the bottom of the sleeves all the way to the bottom edge of the dress. The sleeve seams should meet at the bottom edge and the underarm seam. The bottom edge of the smocking should meet the back waist seam if a waisted back bodice is used. If sashes are used, they will be sewn into the seam (**fig. 1**).

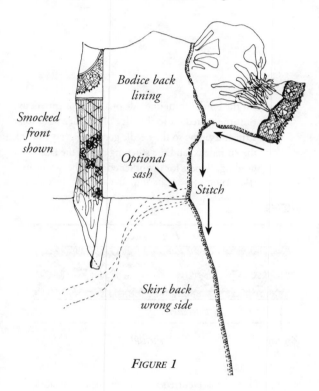

Smocked front shown

Bodice back lining

Optional sash

Stitch

Skirt back wrong side

FIGURE 1

2. Stitch with a $^1/_4$" seam, treating the bodice and lining as one layer. Press the seams toward the dress back.

XV. Hems

A. Turned-up Hem

1. Press $^1/_4$"to the wrong side around the bottom edge of the dress (**fig. 1**).

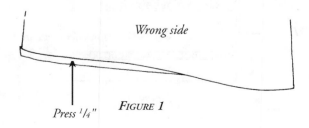

Wrong side

Press $^1/_4$"   **FIGURE 1**

2. Press the hem to the wrong side of the dress at the hem line and pin or baste (**fig. 2**).

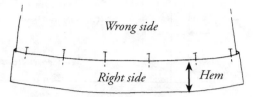

Wrong side

Right side   Hem

FIGURE 2

3. Slip-stitch or blind-hem the dress.

B. Fancy Band

1. To make the fancy band as pictured, use English cotton netting lace, entredeux and fabric strips. Fabric strips are cut 2$^1/_4$" wide. The insertion used is 1$^1/_2$" wide and the edging is 2" to 4" wide. For smaller sizes, use narrower widths of fabric and lace or use fewer rows, to keep the band width proportional to the skirt length. The following amounts will be needed:

   Insertion lace: 2 pieces as long as the skirt width
   sizes 2 - 6: 5 yds.; size 8: 5$^1/_4$ yds.; sizes 10 - 14: 6 yds.

   Edging lace: 1 piece for the bottom ruffle, 2 to 3 times the skirt width
   sizes 2 - 6: 4$^1/_2$ - 7 yds.; size 8: 5 - 7$^1/_2$ yds. sizes 10 - 14: 6 - 9 yds.

   Entredeux: 5 pieces as long as the skirt width
   sizes 2 - 4: 11$^1/_2$ yds.; size 8: 12$^1/_2$ yds.; sizes 10 - 14: 15 yds.

   Fabric: 4 strips, 45" long for sizes 2 - 8; 5 strips for sizes 10 - 14

2. Sew the fabric strips into two long strips to be used in the band, following step 3 for sizes 2 - 8, and following step 4 for sizes 10 - 14.

3. Sizes 2 - 8: Sew two strips of fabric together at the ends to make a long strip. Match the seam to the dress side seam and trim each end of the strip to make the strip fit the skirt. Repeat for the other two strips (**fig. 1**).

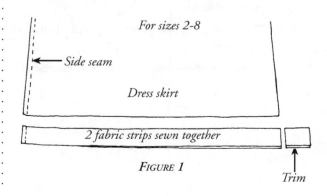

For sizes 2-8

Side seam

Dress skirt

2 fabric strips sewn together

FIGURE 1

Trim

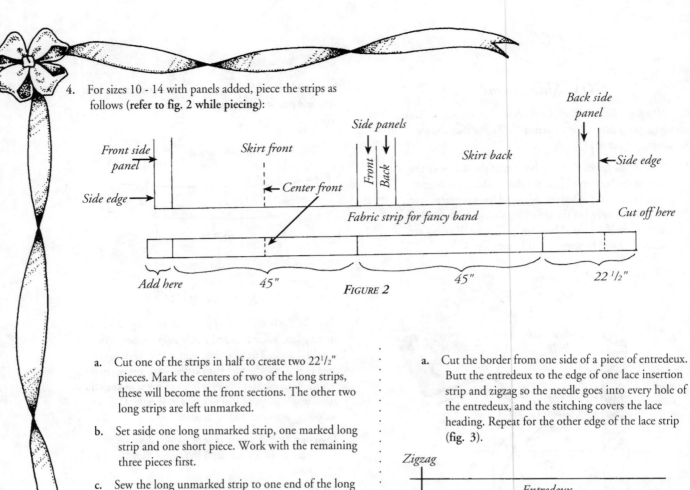

4. For sizes 10 - 14 with panels added, piece the strips as follows (**refer to fig. 2 while piecing**):

Front side panel

Side edge

Skirt front

Center front

Side panels

Front *Back*

Skirt back

Back side panel

Side edge

Cut off here

Fabric strip for fancy band

Add here   45"   *Figure 2*   45"   22 1/2"

a. Cut one of the strips in half to create two 22¹/₂" pieces. Mark the centers of two of the long strips, these will become the front sections. The other two long strips are left unmarked.

b. Set aside one long unmarked strip, one marked long strip and one short piece. Work with the remaining three pieces first.

c. Sew the long unmarked strip to one end of the long marked strip, right sides together, creating a strip approximately 90" long. Sew the 22¹/₂" piece to one end of this long strip.

d. Match the center mark on the strip to the center of the front skirt bottom edge.

e. The strip will extend past the edge of the skirt on one side, and will not reach the edge on the other side. Trim the long end so that it extends only 1" past the edge of the skirt.

f. On the end that does not reach the edge of the skirt, sew the piece that was cut off of the long end, placing the pieces with right sides together. This end will now extend beyond the skirt edge and should be trimmed the same as the other end, with 1" left extending past the skirt edge.

g. Refer to fig. 2 and repeat steps a - f to create a second fabric strip.

h. The two strips are now ready to be pieced into the fancy band.

5. Piece the band as follows, referring to fig. 5 for placement:

a. Cut the border from one side of a piece of entredeux. Butt the entredeux to the edge of one lace insertion strip and zigzag so the needle goes into every hole of the entredeux, and the stitching covers the lace heading. Repeat for the other edge of the lace strip (**fig. 3**).

Zigzag

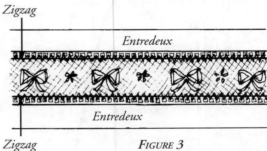

Entredeux

Entredeux

Zigzag   *Figure 3*

b. Place the lace/entredeux strip to one of the fabric strips, right sides together. Stitch "in-the-ditch" of the entredeux. Trim the seam to ¹/₈", then overcast the edge with a wide, short zigzag and tightened upper thread tension to roll the edge neatly. Attach entredeux to the other side of the fabric strip (**fig. 4**).

Stitch–in–the–ditch

Trim to ¹/₈" and zigzag

Fabric strip

Wrong side

Entredeux lace strip

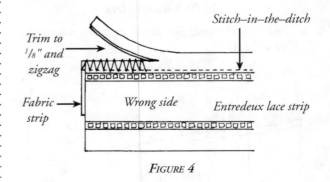

Figure 4

112

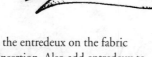

c. Trim the border from the entredeux on the fabric strip and attach lace insertion. Also add entredeux to the other edge of the insertion (refer to step a in this section).

d. Add another fabric strip to the band and attach entredeux to the edge (refer to step b in this section).

e. Run two gathering rows across the top edge of the lace edging or pull the heading thread and adjust the gathers evenly. Pin the ruffle to the entredeux below the fabric. The gathering thread should lie along the "ditch" of the entredeux. "Stitch-in-the-ditch" and press the gathers in the seam allowance to flatten them. Trim the seams and roll the edges as described in step b above.

6. Different combinations of lace, fabric or embroidered insertions may be used to create an original fancy band.

7. Measure from the top "ditch" of the entredeux to the bottom edge of the ruffle. Add that width to the 4" hem allowance and shorten the skirt pieces by the total (**fig. 5**).

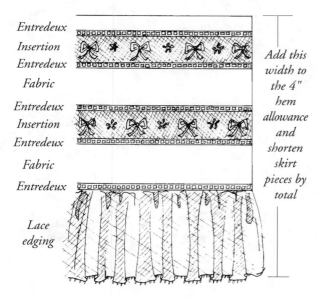

Entredeux
Insertion
Entredeux
Fabric
Entredeux
Insertion
Entredeux
Fabric
Entredeux

Lace edging

Add this width to the 4" hem allowance and shorten skirt pieces by total

FIGURE 5

8. Sew only one side seam of the dress. Attach the entredeux edge of the fancy band to the dress the same way the fabric strips were attached to the band in step b in this section. Sew the remaining side seam and finish the dress.

XVI. Finishing the Dress

A. Buttonholes and Buttons

Beauty pins may be used in place of buttons and buttonholes.

1. Mark buttonhole placement on the right back bodice.

2. Place stabilizer under the buttonhole marks and work buttonholes.

3. Attach buttons to the back left bodice.

B. Sash Loop

A sash loop is optional, but it will help keep the bow from sagging.

1. Thread a hand needle with a double strand of thread and knot the end. At the center back waist, attach the thread to the inside of the right back bodice with a knot.

2. Bring the needle to the right side of the garment and take a small stitch to create a loop in the thread, but do not pull the loop tight. Holding the needle in the left hand, reach through the loop with the right index finger and pull a loop of the needle thread through the first loop (**fig. 1**).

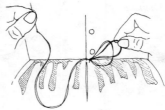

FIGURE 1

3. Pull on the second loop to tighten the first loop down close to the fabric. Use the right hand to pull a new loop through and tighten down the previous loop (**fig. 2**).

FIGURE 2

4. When the chain is long enough to make a loop that the sash will pass through, pull the needle through the last loop and tighten it into a knot (**fig. 3**).

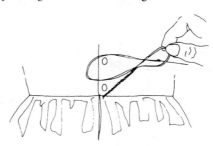

FIGURE 3

5. Insert the needle through the fabric to the wrong side and tie off with a secure knot. ▨

113

Morgan Ross Dress Variations

Kelly Michelle

Kate Irene

Summer
Delight

Misty

Nosegay Lace
Bouquet Collar

Sophisticated
Elegance
Collar

Sweetheart
Collar

Grapevine Heart
Collar

Peek–A–Boo
Bunnies Collar

Daisy Collar

Heartfelt
Inspirations Collar

Heritage Baskets

High Back Yoke
Dress

Dress Back
with Sash

Silk Ribbon Collars

Daisy Collar

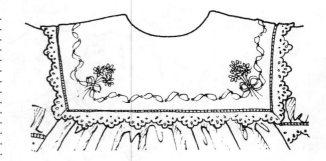

Using pale blue handkerchief linen for the background of this collar, the silk ribbon is truly a breath of spring. White daisies of silk ribbon have yellow French knots for the centers. Yellow silk ribbon has been cascaded all the way around the bottom of the collar, and it is tied in a bow as if to catch the bouquet of daisies in each corner of the front of the collar. An entredeux-edged Swiss trim is mitered on the corners and stitched flat all the around the collar. The stems are green embroidery floss and the leaves are green silk ribbon.

Materials

❧ Silk Ribbon Colors Used:

   4mm: #3 white, #12 yellow

   2mm: #18 green

❧ DMC floss: #563 green

❧ Square Collar Pattern found on pull-out

❧ Color photo - page 31

Silk Ribbon Stitches

Lazy Daisy Stitch - page 167   French Knot - page 164

Stem Stitch - page 173   Straight Stitch - page 173

Bullion Lazy Daisy - page 158

Directions

Refer to "Dress Construction - IX. Dollar Embellishment for Flat Collars - A. Embroidery" before beginning the collar. Collar pattern found on pullout.

1. Trace the collar with the flower design onto a block of fabric.

2. Using 2 strands of #563 green floss for the daisy stems, work a stem stitch.

3. The daisies are worked in 4mm #3 white silk ribbon using bullion-tipped lazy daisy stitches. When working the daisy petals, leave a small circle in the center. The longer petals have 3 wraps each in the bullion stitch and the shorter petals have 2 wraps each. See template for placement.

4. The centers of the daisies are filled with single wrap French knots using 4mm #12 silk ribbon.

5. Using straight stitches in 2mm #18 green silk ribbon, work the leaves along the stems. See template for placement.

6. The bow is worked with two very loose lazy daisy stitches using 4mm #12 yellow silk ribbon. The cascading streamers are made with loose straight stitches around the edge of the collar. You may draw a line as a guide for the streamers or work them in free-form.

7. Using 4mm #12 yellow silk ribbon, work a single wrap French knot where the straight stitches enter and exit the fabric. ▩

Silk Ribbon Template

Grapevine Heart Collar

Create a masterpiece for your heirloom collection by stitching this grapevine heart collar to go on an ecru silk dupioni dress for your child or a blouse for yourself. It is stitched on the V collar pattern from this book. The silk ribbon colors are two shades of purple, two shades of green and brown. The tendrils are worked in Kanagawa silk thread. This heart would be magnificent framed, on a pillow or on any sophisticated piece of embroidered home decorating projects.

Materials

❧ Silk Ribbon Colors Used:

   4mm: #23 purple, #84 purple, #56 green, #143 green, #37 brown

❧ Kanagawa silk thread: #820 green

❧ Pointed Collar Pattern found on pull-out

❧ Color photo - page 27

Embroidery Stitches

Colonial Knot - page 161   Stem Stitch - page 173

Lazy Daisy Stitch - page 167   Whipped Running Stitch - page 176

Couching - page 162

Directions

Refer to "Dress Construction - IX. Dollar Embellishment for Flat Collars - A. Embroidery" before beginning the collar. Collar pattern found on pullout.

1. Using a washout marker, trace the collar shape and heart design onto a block of fabric.

2. The heart is made using 4mm #37 brown silk ribbon. The heart is completed by working a whipped running stitch on the drawn lines - 1 wrap per stitch (see graph on next page.

3. Work the basic center heart shape first. Allow the stitches to hug the straight stitches but do not wrap them tightly. The ribbon should remain flat with each stitch.

4. The second and third which serpentine lines around the heart are worked with a whipped running stitch that is looser than the one worked for the basic heart shape.

5. The grape clusters are worked in colonial knots using #23 and 4mm #84 purple silk ribbon. Stitch several clusters of grapes around the heart following the template for placement.

6. Using 4mm #56 and #143 green silk ribbon, work the grape leaves using a lazy daisy stitch.

7. The tendrils worked in #820 green Kanagawa silk thread. They are randomly couched in place around the heart. See template for placement. ❖

Silk Ribbon Template

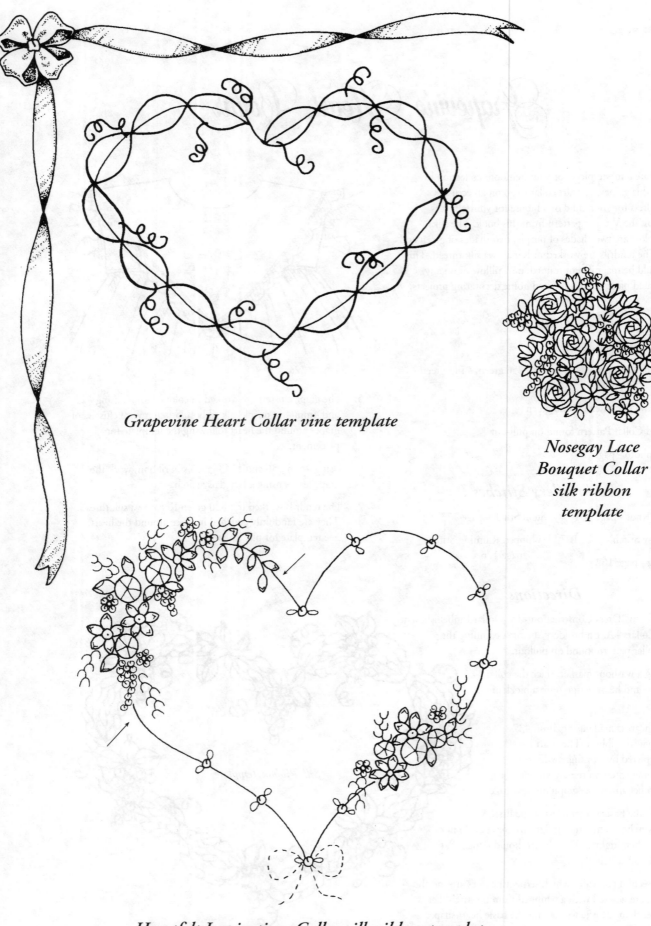

Grapevine Heart Collar vine template

*Nosegay Lace
Bouquet Collar
silk ribbon
template*

Heartfelt Inspirations Collar silk ribbon template

Heartfelt Inspirations Collar

Romantic is the best word for this pastel heart of flowers on this beautiful white round collar of Swiss batiste. Entredeux and white French edging finish the edge of the collar. The silk ribbon heart is a pastel blue with pink roses holding the edges of the heart down. The bottom of the heart features a perky bow and a pink rose. Roses and other flowers are found in the upper right hand corner and the lower left corner. The colors are lavender, pink, blue, yellow, white and green for the stems and leaves. This would be a beautiful design to stitch and frame for a special gift for any lady on your list. It would also be beautiful to stitch in the middle of a ring bearer's pillow for a wedding.

Materials

❀ Silk Ribbon Colors Used:

    4mm: #125 blue, #8 pink, #22 lavender, #1 white, #12 yellow, #31 green

❀ DMC Floss: #504 green, #3078 yellow (Use 2 strands of floss throughout this design).

❀ Silk Ribbon Template - page 118

❀ Round Collar Pattern found on pull-out

❀ Color photo - page 30

Embroidery Stitches

Colonial Knot - page 161	Lazy Daisy Stitch - page 167
Feather Stitch - page 164	Loop Stitch - page 168
French Knot - page 164	Running Stitch - page 171
Japanese Ribbon Stitch - page 167	Spider Web Rose - page 172

Directions

Refer to "Dress Construction - IX. Dollar Embellishment for Flat Collars - A. Embroidery" before beginning the collar. Collar pattern found on pullout.

1. Using a washout marker, trace the collar and heart design onto a block of fabric.

2. Work a loose running stitch around the heart using #125 blue 4mm silk ribbon. The running stitch is worked between the arrows. For a natural appearance, twist the ribbon once for each stitch.

3. Using 4mm #8 pink silk ribbon, work a one wrap colonial knot over each spot where the running stitch enters and exits the fabric. See template for placement.

4. The bow is formed by working two loop stitches with 4mm #125 blue silk ribbon. The tails are loose straight stitches.

5. Using 4mm #8 pink silk ribbon, work a one wrap colonial knot in the center of the bow for a knot.

6. Using #504 green floss, work two lazy daisy leaves on either side of each colonial knot.

7. Using #3504 green floss, work the feather stitches in the design. See template for placement.

8. Using 4mm #8 pink silk ribbon, work three spider web roses. See template for placement.

9. Using the template for placement, work the stem stitches in #504 green floss.

10. The large white flowers are six-petal straight stitch flowers made with 4mm #1 white silk ribbon. The centers of the flowers are worked with small loop stitches using 4mm #12 yellow silk ribbon.

11. Using #3078 yellow floss, work a single-wrap French knot to anchor the loop stitches in the center of the white flower.

12. There are several small blue flowers that are worked using 4mm #125 blue silk ribbon French knots with a single wrap French knot center in 4mm #12 yellow silk ribbon. See template for placement.

13. The Wisteria clusters are French knots worked with 4mm #22 lavender silk ribbon. See template for placement.

14. The green leaves are worked with 4mm #31 green silk ribbon and the Japanese ribbon stitch. See chart for placement. ❈

Peek-A-Boo Bunnies

Two precious little silk ribbon bunnies peek out from this beautiful brown basket. The fabric for this child's collar is sea foam green linen; the edge of the collar is trimmed with entredeux and tatting. The bunnies are white, the carrots are peach, the ribbons are yellow and the carrot tops are green. The bunnies have pale pink ears with deeper pink French knot eyes. Yellow Kanagawa silk twist thread is used for a feather stitch border around this magnificent collar. The adorable basket is woven from two colors of brown silk ribbon.

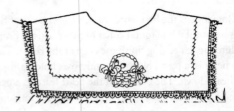

Materials

❧ Silk Ribbon Colors Used:
  4mm: #65 beige, #24 coral, #12 yellow, #5 pink, #139 brown
  2mm: #18 green
  7mm: #1 white

❧ Kanagawa silk twist: #196 yellow

❧ Square Collar Pattern found on pull-out

❧ Color photo - page 26

Embroidery Stitches

Feather Stitch - page 164

French Knot - page 164

Japanese Ribbon Stitch - page 167

Loop Stitch - page 168

Stem/Outline Stitch - page 173

Straight Stitch - page 173

Weaving - page 172

Wrapped Straight Stitch - page 175

Directions

Refer to "Dress Construction - IX. Dollar Embellishment for Flat Collars - A. Embroidery" before beginning the collar. Collar pattern found on pullout.

Basket Guide

1. Using a washout marker, trace collar and the basket shape onto a block of fabric.

2. Using 4mm #139 brown silk ribbon, work the basket spokes with a straight stitch.

3. Using 4mm #65 beige silk ribbon, weave the ribbon over one spoke and under one spoke. It may be necessary to crowd the weaving in order to make nine rows fit in the basket area.

4. The basket handles, rim, and base are worked in 4mm #139 brown silk ribbon using an outline stitch.

5. The carrots are worked in #24 coral 4mm silk ribbon. Work 3 straight stitches close together and wrap each stitch 5 or 6 times completely covering the straight stitch.

6. The bow is worked with 4mm #12 yellow silk ribbon. Work two sets of loop stitches containing three loops each. These sets of stitches are centered above the carrots. The knot for the bow is a straight stitch worked between the two sets of loop stitches. The bow streamers are made by working a loose straight stitch below the knot on each side of the bow.

7. Using 2mm #18 green silk ribbon, work several straight stitches at the top of the carrots for the carrot tops. You may want to give a slight twist to the ribbon to give it a more natural appearance.

8. The bunny heads are worked using 7mm #1 white silk ribbon. Work two straight stitches for the head, side by side. The third stitch is centered between these two previous stitches and will overlap most of the first two. Keep each of the straight stitches as flat as possible and do not allow the ribbon to "bunch up", allowing the full width of the ribbon to be used.

9. Work the ears using #1 white 7mm silk ribbon and #5 pink 4mm silk ribbon. Thread 1 strand of each color of ribbon into a single needle. The ears are worked with a Japanese ribbon stitch, making sure that the pink silk ribbon is centered on top of the white.

10. Work the bunnies eyes with two wrap French knots using a single strand of #196 yellow Kanagawa silk thread.

11. Using a washout marker, lightly draw a line 1¼ inch from the cut edge of the collar. Using #196 yellow Kanagawa silk thread, work a feather stitch on the drawn line.

Silk Ribbon Template

Nosegay Lace Bouquet Collar

Absolutely adorable and beautiful also is this round collar of white linen. The bouquet of silk ribbon flowers is placed within gathered white French lace edging to give the sweetest look. The flowers are peach, pale peach, lavender, yellow and blue; the leaves are green. The silk ribbon bow at the bottom of this bouquet is peach; it is stitched down with a few basting stitches.

Materials

❀ Silk Ribbon:

　　2mm: #101 lavender, #13 yellow, #125 blue, #169 peach

　　4mm: #111 med. rose, #110 lt. rose, #154 green, #6 pink

❀ DMC Floss: #320 green, #963 peach

❀ 8" of lace edging 1" wide

❀ Silk Ribbon Template - page 118

❀ Scalloped Collar II pattern found on pull-out

❀ Color photo - page 28

Directions

Refer to "Dress Construction - IX. Dollar Embellishment for Flat Collars - A. Embroidery" before beginning the collar. Collar pattern found on pullout.

1. Using a washout marker, trace the collar with the circle design onto a block of fabric.

2. Gather the lace edging into a circle. Stitch the edges of the lace circle together by hand or machine.

3. Place the circle of lace edging in the center of the drawn circle. The edge of the lace circle should be 1³/₄" from the cut edge of the collar. Pin the lace circle to the collar.

4. You may baste the lace circle to the collar or attach it with the silk ribbon embroidery.

5. Complete the silk ribbon embroidery following the instructions given below.

6. Using 4mm #169 peach silk ribbon, make a six loop bow with streamers. Carefully slip the bow underneath the lace edging and tack through the center using #963 peach floss.

7. Shape the streamers of the bow and attach to the collar using #963 peach floss.

Embroidery Stitches

Fly Stitch - page 163

Japanese Ribbon Stitch - page 167

Lazy Daisy Stitch - page 167

Loop Stitch - page 168

Spider Web Rose - page 172

Straight Stitch - page 173

1. Work five spider web roses using 4mm #111 med. rose silk ribbon. See template for placement.

2. Work three small loop stitch flowers using 2mm #101 lavender silk ribbon. See template for placement.

3. Using 2mm #13 yellow silk ribbon, work a single-wrap French knot in the center of the lavender loop stitch flowers.

4. Work three straight stitch flowers using 2mm #13 yellow silk ribbon. See template for placement.

5. Using 4mm #6 pink silk ribbon, work the buds using a lazy daisy stitch. See template for placement.

6. Using 4mm #169 peach silk ribbon, work straight stitch flowers. See template for placement.

7. Using #320 green floss, work a fly stitch at the base of each small peach bud.

8. Using 2mm #125 blue silk ribbon, work clusters of one wrap French knots throughout the design. See template for placement.

9. Using 2mm # 154 green silk ribbon, work straight stitch and Japanese stitch leaves around the flowers in the design.

10. Once the design has been completed, look closely at the finished project and determine if there are any empty spaces. If you find these empty spaces, fill them in with a mixture of colors and stitches already used. ❀

Sophisticated Elegance

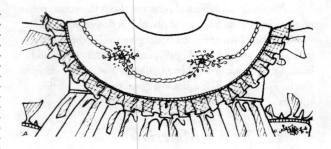

Silk dupioni has been one of my favorite fabrics since I was a little girl. Several years ago on a trip to Australia, I fell in love with the fabric once again since most of the wedding dresses in the windows of the Queen Victoria building in Sydney were of this fabric. This round collar of ecru silk dupioni has navy, burgundy, green, gold, white and rose silk ribbon embroidery. The scalloped design runs around the collar and the bouquets of flowers are spaced at the crest of each scallop of the blue ribbon. This design is simple, easy to stitch, and pretty as a picture. The collar is finished with ecru entredeux and gathered ecru French edging.

Materials

❋ Silk Ribbon Colors Used:

4mm: #184 navy, #129 burgundy, #33 green, #51 gold, #3 white

7mm: #128 rose

❋ DMC Floss: #500 green

❋ Round Collar Pattern found on pull-out

❋ Scallop Template found on pull-out

❋ Color photo - page 29

Embroidery Stitches

French Knot - page 164   Split Stitch - page 173

Japanese Ribbon Stitch -   Stem Stitch - page 173
    page 167
                             Straight Stitch - page 173

Loop Stitch - page 168

Directions

Refer to "Dress Construction - IX. Dollar Embellishment for Flat Collars - A. Embroidery" before beginning the collar. Collar pattern and scallop template found on pullout.

1. Using a washout marker, trace the collar with the scallop and silk ribbon design onto a block fabric.

2. Using 4mm #184 navy silk ribbon, work a split stitch along the scallop line.

3. Using two strands of #500 green floss, work the stems of the silk ribbon design with a stem stitch.

4. Using 4mm #129 burgundy silk ribbon, work the loop stitches on the stems as follows: three loop stitches on the upper short stems and five on the lower stems. Follow silk ribbon template for placement.

5. Using the Japanese ribbon stitch and 4mm #33 green silk ribbon, stitch the leaves, following silk ribbon template for placement.

6. Using the template for placement, work the five petal center flower with a loop stitch using 7mm #128 rose silk ribbon. Leave a small opening in the center of the flower.

7. After completing the five loops, work a straight stitch over each loop using 4mm #129 burgundy silk ribbon. These straight stitches will anchor the loops of the flower to the fabric.

8. Work one wrap French knots in the center of the large flower using 4mm #51 gold silk ribbon.

9. Using 4mm #3 white silk ribbon, work one wrap French knots around the center flower. Follow template for placement. ❋

Silk Ribbon
Template

Sweetheart Collar

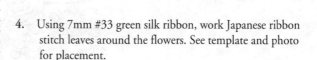

Perhaps you will recognize this collar as the one I use on the introductory portion of our television series, *Martha's Sewing Room.* I love this collar with its scalloped edges and the tatting attached around those scallops. The edge of the collar has been machine wing needle entredeux stitched. Silk ribbon lazy daisies are used to stitch the heart on the bottom of the collar. Japanese ribbon stitches make the green leaves on all of the flowers. Crystal beads are stitched all around in the design as well as in the center of each rose colored flower. This adds some elegant sparkle to the design. Entredeux and tatting finish the top of the collar. This particular silk ribbon heart would be just as beautiful on a pillow as it is on this collar. It would also be beautiful on a smocked dress by using two-step waves all over the smocking design and embroidering this heart on top of the waves. Enjoy!

Materials

❧ Silk Ribbon Colors Used:

   4mm: #129 dark rose, #128 med. rose

   7mm: #33 green

❧ Clear glass beads

❧ Scalloped Collar I Pattern found on pull-out

❧ Color photo - page 25

Embroidery Stitches

Japanese Ribbon Stitch - page 167

Lazy Daisy Stitch - page 167

Directions

Refer to "Dress Construction - IX. Dollar Embellishment for Flat Collars - A. Embroidery" before beginning the collar. Collar pattern and scallop template found on pullout.

1. Using a washout marker, trace the collar with the heart design onto a block of fabric.

2. With 4mm #129 dark rose silk ribbon, work a series of five petal lazy daisy flowers around the heart. See template and photo for placement.

3. Using 4mm #128 med. rose ilk ribbon, repeat the instructions given in step 2, spacing the medium rose flowers between the dark rose flowers. See template for placement.

4. Using 7mm #33 green silk ribbon, work Japanese ribbon stitch leaves around the flowers. See template and photo for placement.

5. Using beading thread or regular sewing thread, stitch a crystal bead in the center of each flower and scatter beads around the heart.

6. Stitch a single lazy daisy flower in the center of each scallop, alternating colors. Stitch a single bead in the center of each flower. ❧

Heart Template

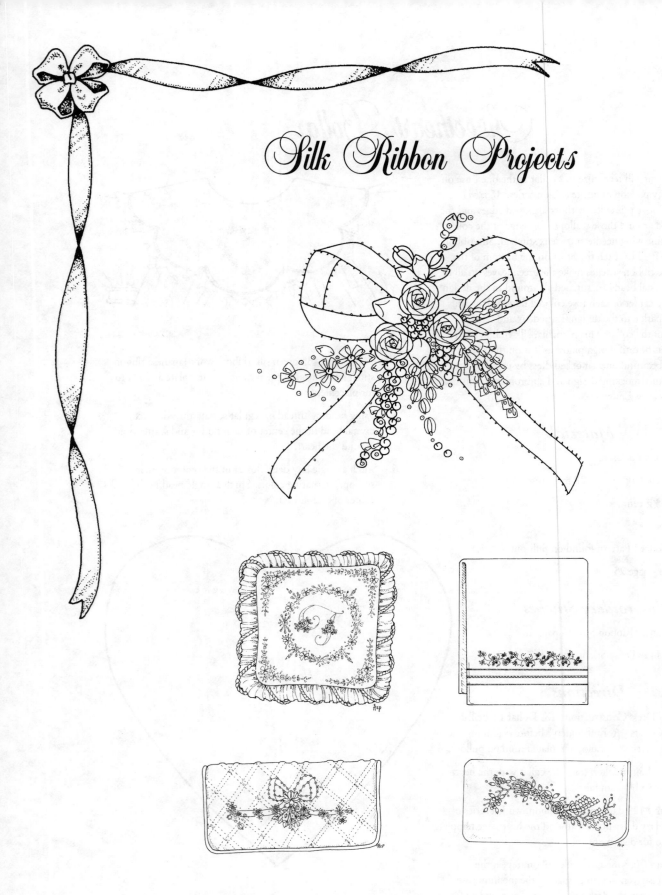

Silk Ribbon Projects

Ring Bearer Pillow

Matching the smocking design plate of the dress made of the same fabric, is this beautiful pillow designed for a ring bearer in the wedding. It would be perfectly adorable for the little flower girl to wear the matching dress of ecru silk dupioni and have the ring bearer carry this pillow. A little Eton suit made of this silk dupioni would be beautiful for him to wear. There is a pink silk ribbon bow in the middle to tie the ring to the pillow. The finished pillow measures 14¹/₂" by 13". The smocking is of ecru Marlitt rayon floss and is stitched with two step waves. The lazy daisy flowers are of pale dusty pink, pale dusty blue/green, yellow and deep dusty rose. Gold beads are stitched at random for a sweet effect. The ruffle around the pillow is trimmed with 1¹/₄" wide ecru French lace. The pillow slips into the pillowcase via a pocket opening in the back.

Materials

❋ Silk Ribbon Colors Used:

    4mm: #160 light mauve, #15 yellow, #155 light green, #163 mauve

❋ Marlitt #1036 rayon floss

❋ Gold Seed Beads

❋ ³/₄ yd. of ecru silk dupioni

❋ Stuffing: pillow form or polyfil

Optional:

❋ 2-9" squares of fabric if making pillow form

❋ #7 or #8 crewel needle for smocking

❋ #26 tapestry needle for silk ribbon embroidery

❋ Color photo - pages 18,19

❋ Smocking graph - page 127

Directions

Seam allowance ¹/₂" unless otherwise specified.

1. Cut a piece of fabric 9" x 45". Tie off to 9".

2. Pleat 24 rows. The top and bottom rows are stabilizer rows and are not numbered on the graph. Smock 22 rows.

3. Using two strands of #1036 Marlitt floss, begin on row 1¹/₂ with a down cable. Work a 2-step ¹/₂ space wave up to row 1, up cable, 2-step ¹/₂ space wave down to row 1¹/₂. Repeat across the row.

4. Begin on row 1¹/₂ with an up cable. Work a 2-step ¹/₂ space wave down to row 2, down cable, 2-step ¹/₂ space wave up to row 1¹/₂. Repeat across the row.

5. Repeat instructions given in steps 2 and 3 until you have smocked 22 rows.

Embroidery Stitches

French Knot - page 164   Pullen Knot - page 168

Lazy Daisy Stitch - page 167   Straight Stitch - page 173

1. Following the graph for placement, work five petal lazy daisy flowers using 4mm #160 light mauve silk ribbon.

2. Work 4mm #15 yellow silk ribbon French knots for the center of the flowers.

3. Using 4mm #155 light green silk ribbon, work three or four straight stitch leaves around each flower.

4. Scatter Pullen knot buds using 4mm #163 mauve silk ribbon.

5. Once the design is completed, fill in with gold beads where desired.

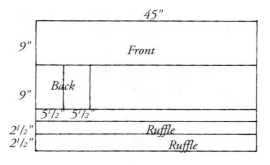

Construction

1. Block the smocked pillow into a 9" square.

2. Cut two pieces of fabric 9" x 5½" for the pillow back. Cut two strips of fabric 45" long and 2½" wide. Seam together with a rolled hem or French seam.

3. Attach the lace edging to one cut edge of the pillow with a serged rolled hem or by using the technique flat lace to flat fabric. Press.

4. Run two gathering threads ¼" and ½" from the raw edge of the ruffle.

5. Fold the ruffle in quarters and mark. Pin the marks at each corner of the pillow, right sides together (**fig. 1**).

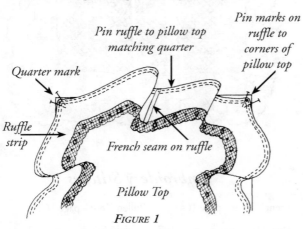

Pin ruffle to pillow top matching quarter

Pin marks on ruffle to corners of pillow top

Quarter mark

Ruffle strip

French seam on ruffle

Pillow Top

FIGURE 1

6. Gently pull the gathering threads until each segment of the ruffle fits the pillow top.

7. Working with one of the 9" x 5½" pieces of fabric for the pillow back, working on the 9" length, turn under ⅛" and ⅛" again and stitch by machine or hand. This will hem the cut edge (**fig. 2**). Repeat on other piece of fabric.

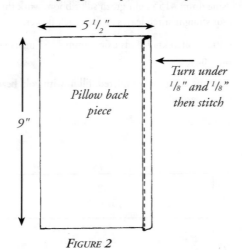

← 5½" →

Turn under ⅛" and ⅛" then stitch

Pillow back piece

9"

FIGURE 2

8. Overlap the hemmed edges until the block measures 9" x 9" square. Pin to hold in place (**fig 3**).

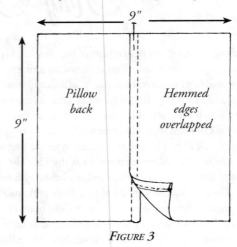

9"

Pillow back

Hemmed edges overlapped

9"

FIGURE 3

9. Place the right side of the back over the pillow top and ruffle, right sides together. Pin in place.

10. Stitch the pillow back, ruffle, and top together using a ½" seam allowance. Turn the pillow to the right side through the back opening.

11. Stuff the pillow with a pillow form or follow optional construction steps below.

Optional Construction

1. If you do not want to make a separate pillow form, you may cut a 9" square of fabric, place the right side of the pillow back on top of the ruffle, stitch in place leaving a 6" opening to turn the pillow.

2. Fill the pillow with fiberfill and stitch the 6" opening closed by machine or hand.

Optional Pillow Form

1. If you cannot purchase a 9" square pillow form, it will be necessary to make one.

2. Stitch the two 9" squares of fabric for the pillow form together, leaving a 6" opening to turn the squares.

3. Stuff the form with polyfil and slipstitch the 6" opening closed.

4. Slip the pillow form inside the pillow. ▧

Ring
Bearer
Pillow
Smocking
Graph

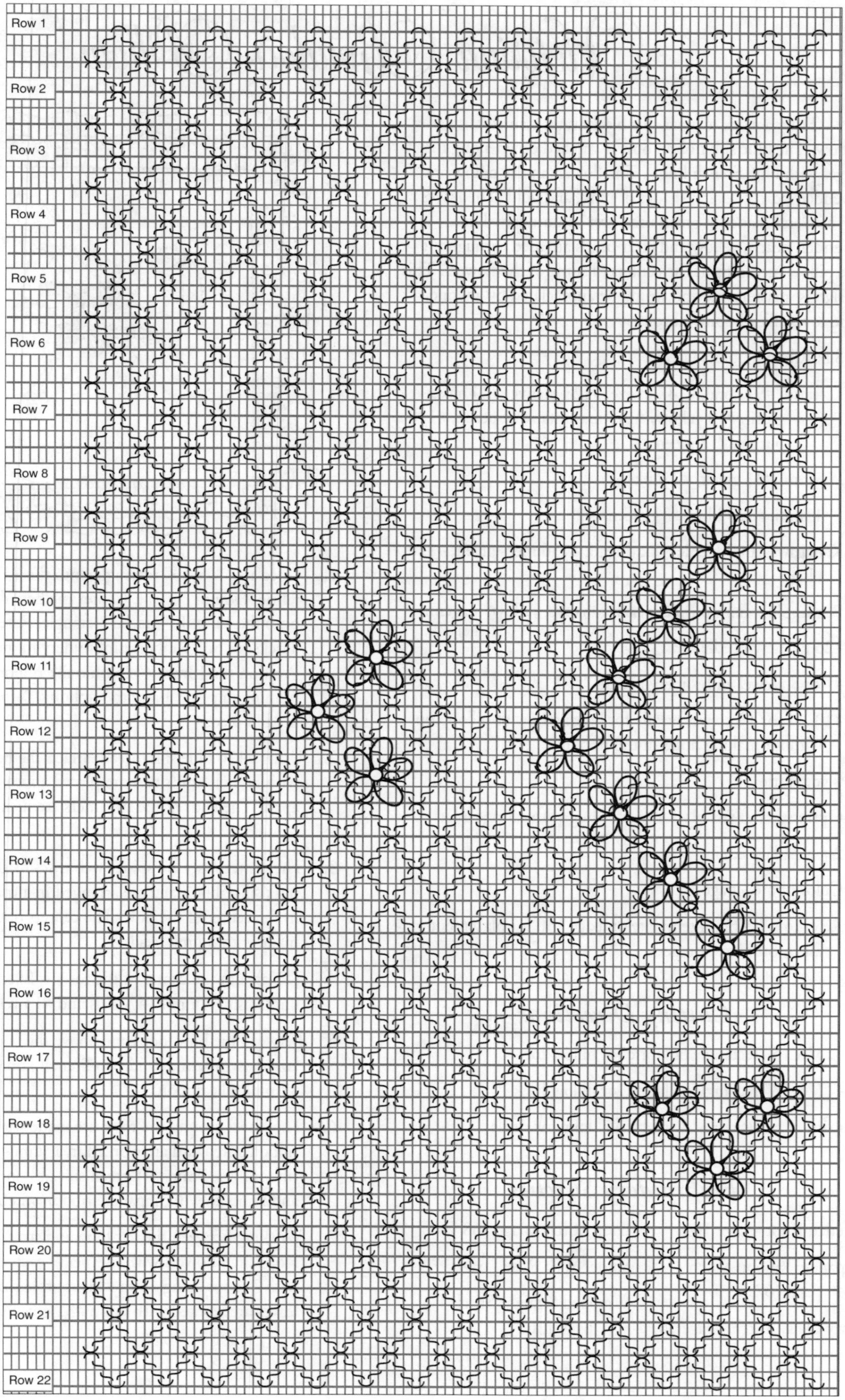

Row 1
Row 2
Row 3
Row 4
Row 5
Row 6
Row 7
Row 8
Row 9
Row 10
Row 11
Row 12
Row 13
Row 14
Row 15
Row 16
Row 17
Row 18
Row 19
Row 20
Row 21
Row 22

Victorian Boudoir Pillow

Truly a work of art is this black water stained taffeta pillow. The blue silk ribbon bow is stitched down along the edges with blue French knots. The flowers in the pillow are lavender, peach, several shades of pink, and gold. The leaves have several shades of green used ever so uniquely. Pink, lavender, peach, yellow and clear beads are used throughout the pillow including as the centers of some of the flowers. This design is masterpiece and would be appreciated by anyone who loves silk ribbon embroidery.

❋ Silk Ribbon Colors Used:

> 4mm: #91 coral, #147 maize, #128 mauve, #20 moss green, #13 yellow, #145 magenta, #42 peach, #118 purple, #18 green
>
> 7mm: #31 green, #7 pink
>
> 13mm: #125 blue, #31 green

❋ Kanagawa 1000 Denier silk thread: #156 moss green, #120 blue

❋ Beads: pink, dark purple, peach , mauve, yellow, magenta

❋ #26 tapestry needle

❋ #7 or 8 crewel embroidery needle

❋ #10, 11, or 12 crewel needle for basting bow to pillow top without making holes in the ribbon

❋ 1 yd. fabric

❋ Optional: 1½ yds black rope cording with selvage edge

❋ 2½ yds. lace edging

❋ Color photo - page 18

❋ Refer to silk ribbon template on page 130 for placement of all embroidery stitches.

Cutting Directions

1 - 13" x 15" rectangle of fabric for pillow top

1 - 11" x 13" rectangle of fabric for pillow back

2 strips of fabric cut 8" wide by 45" long for ruffle

Embroidery Stitches

French Knot - page 164

Japanese Ribbon Stitch - page 167

Lazy Daisy Stitch - page 167

Loop Stitch - page 168

Spider Web Rose - page 172

Wrapped Straight Stitch - page 176

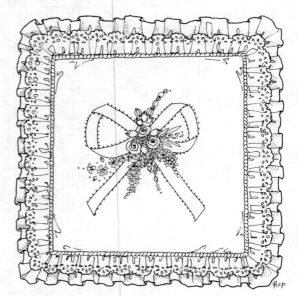

1. Trace an 11" x 13" rectangle onto the 13" x 15" piece of fabric. Do not cut out. Center the bow design and trace onto the 11" x 13" traced rectangle. Refer to Tips and Tricks for Silk Ribbon Embroidery found on page 152. Position the 13mm #125 blue silk ribbon along the guide pinning in place. Baste the ribbon ⅛" from the edge to hold in place.

2. Using #120 blue silk thread, attach the bow to the fabric with French knots that are placed approximately ¼" apart. The ends of the streamers are tucked under and secured.

3. The center roses are spider web roses made of 7mm #7 pink silk ribbon and are arranged in a triangular pattern in the center of the bow. The centers of the roses are made with 3 pink beads.

4. The area in the center of the roses is filled in with French knots using 4mm #147 mais and #13 yellow silk ribbon.

5. Between the bow loops and above the bow loops are two lazy daisy rosebuds and two French knots worked in 7mm #7 pink silk ribbon.

6. The leaves around the roses are made with the Japanese ribbon stitch and are worked in 13mm #31 green silk ribbon. Use 7mm #31 green silk ribbon around the buds and knots to work Japanese ribbon stitch leaves.

7. Working between the left loop and streamer, work two loop stitch flowers with five petals each and one flower with 3 loops using 4mm #118 purple silk ribbon. The leaves are worked with 7mm #31 green silk ribbon using

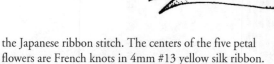

the Japanese ribbon stitch. The centers of the five petal flowers are French knots in 4mm #13 yellow silk ribbon. Dark purple beads are scattered around the flowers.

8. Trailing beneath the lower left rose is a spray of French knots. Some of the knots are worked in 4mm #42 peach and some are worked in 4mm #91 coral silk ribbon. The leaves are worked in Japanese ribbon stitch and loop stitch with 4mm #20 moss green silk ribbon. Peach beads are used to embellish this spray.

9. Next to the coral and peach spray is a spray of lazy daisy stitches worked with 4mm #128 mauve silk ribbon and embellished with mauve beads.

10. Moving counterclockwise, the next motif is a spray of wisteria worked with 4mm #118 purple silk ribbon using French knots and purple beads.

11. Between the right streamer and loop is a spray of gladiola consisting of ribbon loop stitches in alternating rows of 4mm #20 moss green, #13 yellow, and #147 maize silk ribbon. Embellish this spray with yellow beads.

12. The final spray of flowers is a row of short wrapped straight stitches worked with 4mm #145 magenta silk ribbon and arranged in an interlocking manner. The leaves are elongated Japanese ribbon stitches worked with 4mm #18 green silk ribbon. This spray is embellished with magenta beads.

Pillow Construction

1. Cut the top and back of the pillow to 11" x 13" which allows a $^1/_2$" seam allowance on each side.

2. Cut two fabric ruffles 8" wide x 45" long. Stitch the two pieces together to make a circle. The length of the ruffle should be twice the perimeter of the pillow. Fold the ruffle in half lengthwise and run two rose of gathering threads in the ruffle, $^1/_2$" and $^1/_8$" from the cut edge of the ruffle (**fig. 1**).

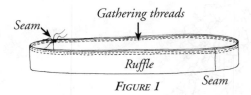

Gathering threads
Seam
Ruffle
Seam
FIGURE 1

3. Place cording on top of the pillow top. Clip the cording tape to turn corners. Let the ends overlap and extend into the seam allowance where they meet (**fig. 2**)

Overlap and extend into seam allowance

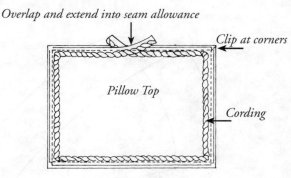

Clip at corners

Pillow Top

Cording

FIGURE 2

4. Sew the lace into a circle and gather to fit the pillow top. Place gathered lace over the cording and pin in place.

5. Place gathered ruffle on top of the lace, adjust to fit the pillow top, and stitch through all layers, attaching them to the pillow top (**fig. 3**).

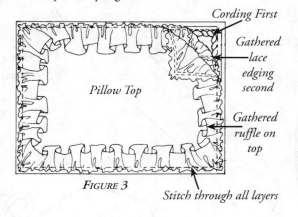

Cording First

Gathered lace edging second

Pillow Top

Gathered ruffle on top

FIGURE 3

Stitch through all layers

6. Place the pillow back over the pillow top, right sides together, and stitch in place leaving a 6" opening to turn. Clip corners where necessary (**fig. 4**).

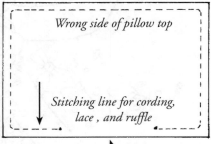

Wrong side of pillow top

Stitching line for cording, lace , and ruffle

FIGURE 4 *Stitch and leave open to turn*

7. Turn pillow to the right side, stuff and slip stitch opening closed. ▨

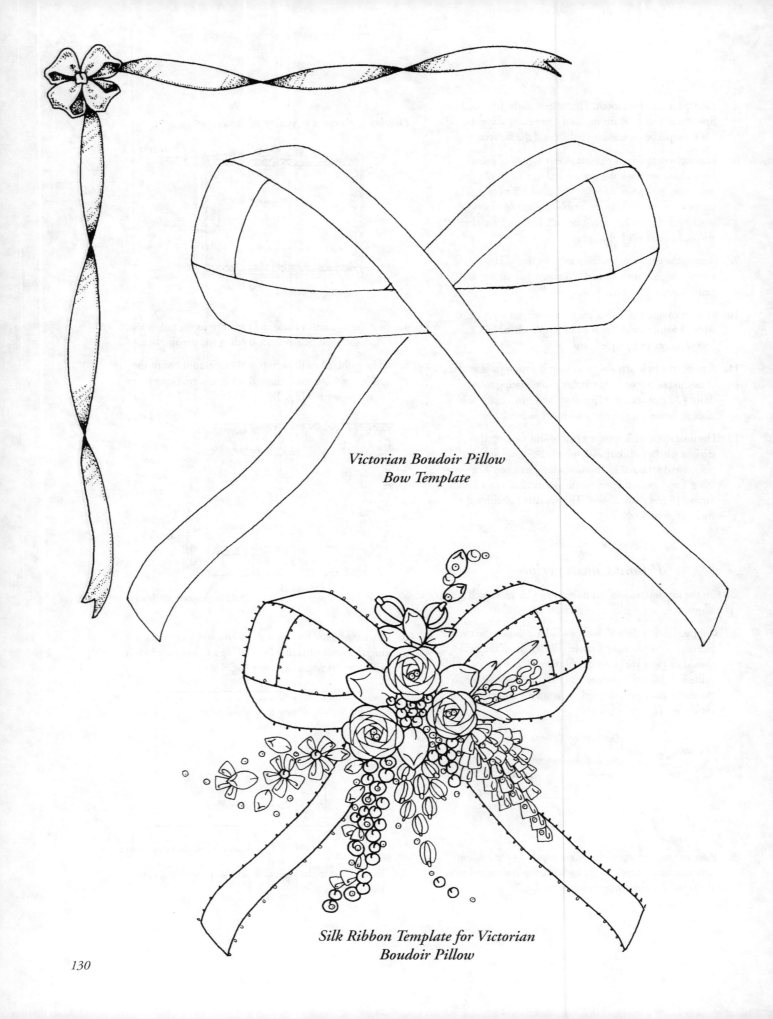

Victorian Boudoir Pillow
Bow Template

Silk Ribbon Template for Victorian
Boudoir Pillow

Emerald Elegance

Using a built in monogram from a sewing machine with embroidery capabilities, this gorgeous pillow is made of forest green silk dupioni. The square pillow measures 14" by 14" which includes the puffed edges wrapped with off white silk cording. The design in the center has the machine embroidered letter trimmed with pink, ecru and pale green silk ribbon. In the circle of gorgeous flowers are the colors peach, grass green, pale green, palest green, orange, dark purple, white, off white, and dusty pink. Beautiful beads in white, gold, copper, and clear are placed in the centers of the flowers and scattered around the design. The four points of the pillow have flowers, beads and leaves using the same colors of silk ribbon. The puffed band around the pillow is gorgeous and it is wrapped with off white silk cording.

Materials

❧ Silk Ribbon Colors Used:

  7mm : #8 pink, #154 green, #162 mauve, #156 maize

  4mm : #154 green, #87 peach, #3 white, #20 green, #12 lt. maize, #8 pink, #145 hot pink, #55 gold, #57 tan, #185 navy

❧ Bugle beads, pearl beads, gold beads

❧ Monofilament thread

❧ 3^1/$_2$ yds. of satin drapery rope trim

❧ 1^1/$_8$ yds. of fabric for pillow

❧ Quilt batting

❧ Polyfill or pillow form

❧ Color photo on page 18

Cutting Directions

Refer to the cutting diagram on page 133

1 - 16^1/$_2$" x 16^1/$_2$" square of emerald green silk dupioni for pillow top

1 - 12^1/$_2$" x 12^1/$_2$" square of emerald green silk dupioni for pillow back

4 strips of fabric 5^1/$_2$" wide x 45" long for ruffle

A strip of quilt batting 5" wide by 46" long

Center Circle

Embroidery Stitches

Bradford Rose - page 156

Elongated Fly Stitch - page 163

French Knot - page 164

Japanese Ribbon Stitch - page 167

Lazy Daisy Stitch - page 167

Loop Stitch - page 168

Pullen Knot - page 168

Spider Web Rose - page 172

Twisted Chain Stitch - page177

Wrapped Stitch - page 175

1. Following the instructions for design transfer given on page152, trace the silk ribbon design onto the 16^1/$_2$" square of fabric, making sure that the design is centered. The square of fabric should be 2 inches larger than the overall design and I suggest that you serge or edge finish the fabric before beginning the project to prevent raveling. See cutting diagram on page 133.

2. The initial in the center was worked by machine. This particular initial was worked on the Viking #1 Plus. The embroidered flowers were omitted and replaced with silk ribbon flowers. You may also use the initials provided on pages 145 to 151 to monogram the center of your design.

3. Using 7mm #8 pink silk ribbon and 7mm #156 maize silk ribbon, work a spider web rose as indicated on template.

4. Using 7mm #154 green silk ribbon, work twisted chain stitch leaves around the spider web roses as indicated on template.

5. Work Bradford roses around the outer circle using 7mm #156 maize silk ribbon. See template for placement.

6. Using 4mm #87 peach silk ribbon and 4mm #3 white silk ribbon, work loop stitch flowers around the center circle, alternating the two colors for the center and outer rows of petals. See the template for placement.

7. Attach pearl beads and gold beads for the centers of the loop stitch flowers with monafilment thread.

8. Using 4mm #12 lt. maize silk ribbon, #145 hot pink silk ribbon, #8 pink silk ribbon, #87 peach silk ribbon, #185 navy silk ribbon, #3 white silk ribbon, #57 tan silk ribbon, work Japanese ribbon stitch buds around the center circle. See template for placement.

9. Using 4mm #154 green, work elongated fly stitches at the base of each bud. You may also work the twisted chain stitch leaves at the top of the Bradford rose. See template for placement.

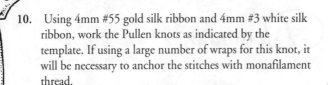

10. Using 4mm #55 gold silk ribbon and 4mm #3 white silk ribbon, work the Pullen knots as indicated by the template. If using a large number of wraps for this knot, it will be necessary to anchor the stitches with monafilament thread.

11. I replaced the French knots located at each corner of the center circle with glass bugle beads.

Corners

It will be impossible to work the corner designs with a hoop because of crushing the center circle. Just remember to keep the thread tension loose to prevent distorting the stitches.

1. Using 4mm #55 gold silk ribbon, work a Bradford rose in the corner.

2. Using 4mm #20 green silk ribbon, work lazy daisy leaves around rose. See template for placement.

3. Using 4mm #12 lt. maize, work Japanese ribbon stitch flowers, with 4mm #154 green silk ribbon elongated fly stitches worked at the base of each flower group for the leaves and stem.

4. Using 7mm #162 mauve silk ribbon and 7mm #156 maize silk ribbon, work French knot loop stitch flowers. The center of the mauve flower is worked with 4mm #12 lt. maize and the lt. maize flower center is filled with pearl beads.

5. Using 4mm #12 lt. maize and 4mm #8 pink silk ribbon, work Bradford stitch roses. See template for placement.

6. Using 4mm #145 hot pink silk ribbon, work Japanese ribbon stitch buds with 4mm #154 green silk ribbon elongated fly stitches at the base of each bud for leaves and stem.

7. The vines are worked using 7mm #154 green silk ribbon wrapped stitch stems and Japanese ribbon stitch leaves.

Construction

Seam allowances: ¹/₂" unless otherwise specified.

1. Trim the embroidered block of fabric to a 12¹/₂" square.

2. Cut 4 strips of fabric 5¹/₂" wide x 45" long. Seam the 4 strips together making a strip 180" long. Run a gathering thread ¹/₄" and ¹/₂" from both cut edges of the strip of fabric. Pull the gathering threads until the strip of gathered fabric is long enough to go around the top of the pillow top and has 2" on each end for an overlap (**fig. 1**).

Ruffle — allow 2" on each end for overlapping

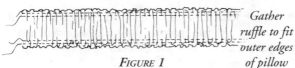

Gather ruffle to fit outer edges of pillow

FIGURE 1

3. Cut a strip of quilt batting 5" wide x 46" long and roll the batting into a tight tube. Fold the strip of gathered fabric over the rolled batting, leave a 2" overlap at each end of the gathered ruffle. Pin the strip of fabric together encasing the rolled batting (**fig. 2**).

4. Stitch the strip of gathered fabric and batting together using a ³/₈" seam allowance. Do not stitch the overlaps together (**fig. 2**).

Fold gathered ruffle over rolled batting and pin gathered edges together

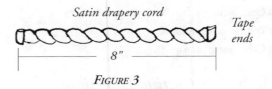

Stitch with ³/₈" seam

Do not stitch together the 2" at each end, to be overlapped

Quilt batting rolled in tight tube, encased in gathered ruffle

FIGURE 2

5. Cut the satin drapery cord into 8" lengths. It will be necessary to place a small piece of tape on the cut edges of the trim to prevent it from unraveling (**fig. 3**). Pin to the right side of the embroidered piece of fabric at equal intervals around the pillow (**fig. 4**).

Satin drapery cord

Tape ends

|———— 8" ————|

FIGURE 3

Embroidered Pillow Top

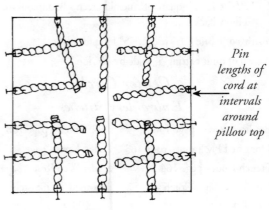

Pin lengths of cord at intervals around pillow top

FIGURE 4

6. Pin the ruffle to the right side of the pillow, leaving one end of each satin cording free. Tuck the ruffle overlaps in 1" and fold one end over the opposite end, covering it 1". The ends of the rolled batting should butt together inside the ruffle. Stitch to pillow front using a $^1/_2$" seam allowance (**fig. 5**).

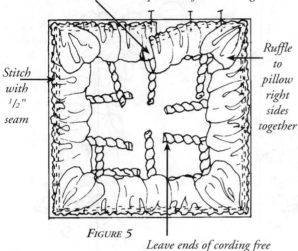

Tuck in ends 1", overlap ends before stitching

Stitch with $^1/_2$" seam

Ruffle to pillow right sides together

Leave ends of cording free

FIGURE 5

7. Pull the satin cording over the ruffle to the edge of the pillow. The satin cording is cut in lengths that allow you to pull it at an angle to give it the appearance of wrapping the ruffle (**fig. 6**). Pin in place.

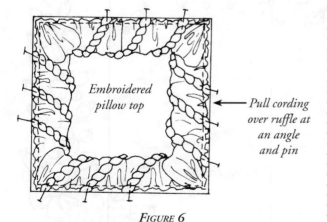

Embroidered pillow top

Pull cording over ruffle at an angle and pin

FIGURE 6

8. Place the pillow back on top of the pillow front, right sides together, sandwiching the ruffle and satin drapery cord between the top and back (**fig. 7**). Stitch the back to the front using a $^1/_2$" seam allowance. Leave a 6" opening to turn the pillow.

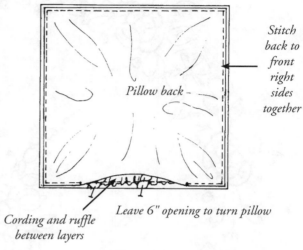

Pillow back

Stitch back to front right sides together

Cording and ruffle between layers

Leave 6" opening to turn pillow

FIGURE 7

9. Clip the corners and turn. You may stuff the pillow with polyfill or use a pillow form. Slipstitch the opening closed and fluff the ruffle. �֍

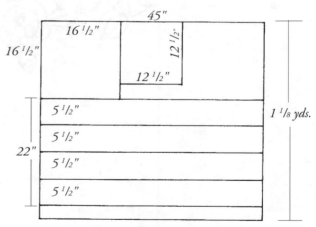

45"

16 $^1/_2$"

16 $^1/_2$"

12 $^1/_2$"

12 $^1/_2$"

22"

5 $^1/_2$"

5 $^1/_2$"

5 $^1/_2$"

5 $^1/_2$"

1 $^1/_8$ yds.

CUTTING DIAGRAM

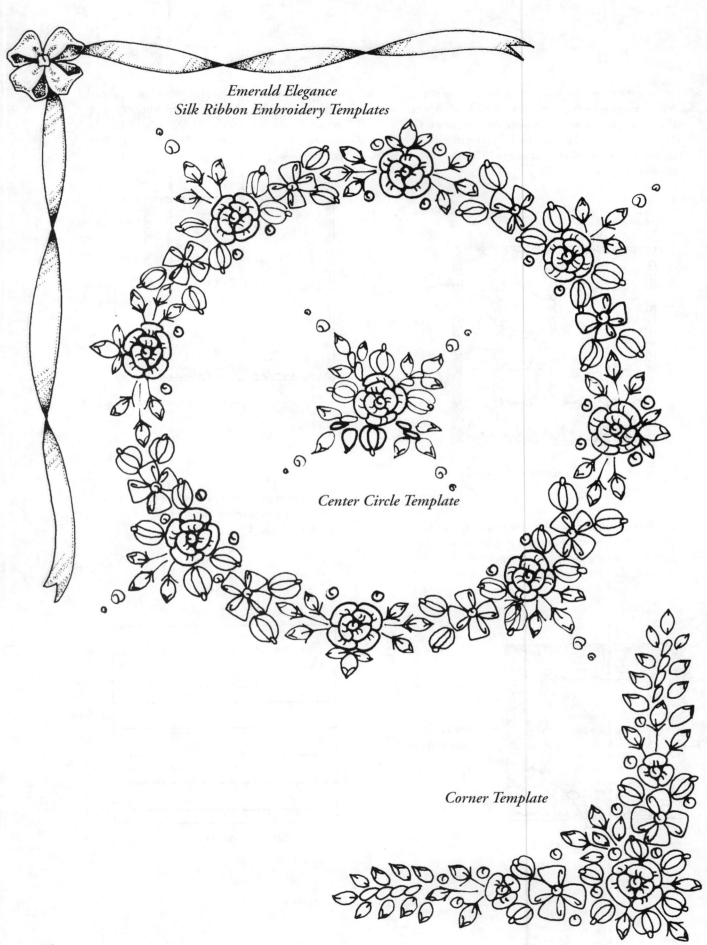

Emerald Elegance
Silk Ribbon Embroidery Templates

Center Circle Template

Corner Template

Initial Pillow

P stands for Pullen and you can choose your initial when you make this easy to sew pillow with our beautiful silk ribbon alphabet. The outline is in navy blue floss and all the rest of the embroidery is completed with silk ribbon stitches which are so fast and easy to make. Actually all of the flowers are simple lazy daisies. The pillow measures 19 inches by 19 inches from tip of the ruffle to tip of the ruffle. The double ruffle is topped with a beautiful ecru French lace gathered in with the ruffle..

Materials

* 1 yard of fabric
* 3³/₄ yds. of 2¹/₂" wide lace edging
* 2 yds. of ³/₈" cord for piping
* Thread to match fabric
* Polyfil
* Color photo - page 19

Cutting Directions

2 squares of fabric 15" x 15" for pillow top and pillow back

l square of 15" x 15" to be cut into 2" bias strips for piping

3 strips of fabric cut 7" x 45" for ruffle

Seam allowance ¹/₂"

Directions

1.   Cut the fabric into the dimensions given above (**fig. 1**).

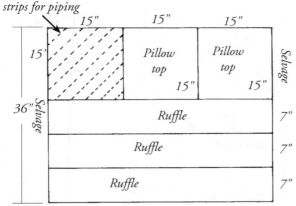

FIGURE 1

2.   Stitch the 3 strips of fabric for the ruffle together. Press the seams open.

3.   Fold the ruffle strip in half along the length and press (**fig. 2**).

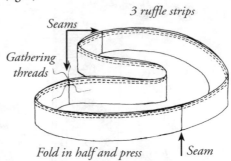

FIGURE 2

4.   Following the instructions given in the design transfer section, page 152, trace the silk ribbon design onto the pillow top. Complete the silk ribbon embroidery.

5.   Using the third 15" square of fabric, cut it into bias strips 2" wide. Seam these strips together forming a single strip 64" long (**fig. 3**). Using the baby piping instructions

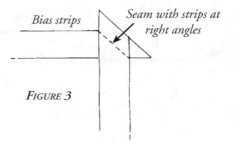

FIGURE 3

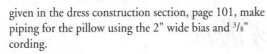

given in the dress construction section, page 101, make piping for the pillow using the 2" wide bias and ³/₈" cording.

6. Place piping on top pillow. Clip the seam allowance of the piping at the corners, letting the ends of the piping overlap and extend into the seam allowance as they meet or turn to the ouside at one corner (**fig.** 4).

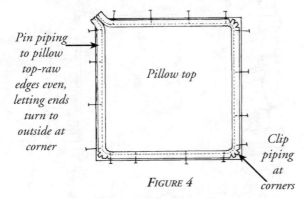

Pin piping to pillow top-raw edges even, letting ends turn to outside at corner

Pillow top

Clip piping at corners

FIGURE 4

7. Place gathered lace edging on top of piping. Turn the ends of the lace to the wrong side and overlap the ends of the lace as they meet (**fig.** 5).

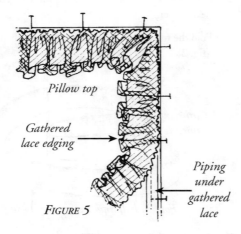

Pillow top

Gathered lace edging

Piping under gathered lace

FIGURE 5

8. Run a gathering thread ¹/₄" and ¹/₂" from the cut edge of the ruffle strip. Fold the ruffle strip in quarters and mark. Pin each quarter mark to a corner of the pillow top (**fig.** 6).

Pin ruffle over gathered lace edging matching quarter marks at corners of pillow

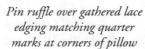
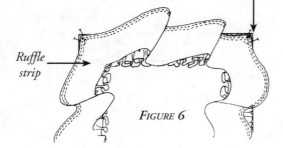

Ruffle strip

FIGURE 6

9. Pull the gathering threads until the ruffle fits the pillow top. Remember, it will be necessary to have a few more gathers in each corner to keep the ruffle from flipping inward.

10. Place the gathered ruffle on top of the lace and cording, stitch through all layers using a ¹/₂" seam allowance (**fig.** 7).

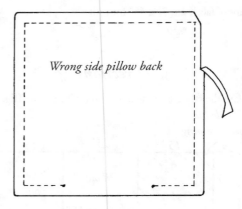

Stitch with ¹/₂" seam

Pillow top

Ruffle is stitched over piping and gathered lace edging

FIGURE 7

11. Place the pillow back on pillow top, right sides together and stitch in place leaving a 6" opening to turn. Clip corners where necessary (**fig.** 8).

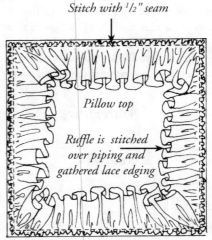

Wrong side pillow back

FIGURE 8

12. Turn pillow to the right side, stuff and slip stitch opening closed. ▨

Linen Guest Towel

Stitched on a crisp white linen hemstitched tea towel is this design of pure opulence. Pale green silk thread creates the leaves and the stems. Magnificent flowers of pink, peach, yellow and darker pink are scattered throughout the design. Flowers of lavender beads add enchantment to the floral design. Clear bugle beads are placed at several locations on the outside edges of the larger flowers. Sure to please anyone on your gift list, the stitching is fun and easy.

Materials

✻ Silk Ribbon Used:

    2mm: #156 maize

    4mm Silk Ribbon: #31 green, #14 yellow, #5 light pink, #127 rose, #1 white, #87 peach

✻ Kanagawa 1000 denier silk thread #730 pale green

✻ Clear bugle beads

✻ Iridescent purple glass beads

✻ Monofilament thread

✻ 1 purchased linen guest towel

✻ Color photograph - page 20

Directions
Embroidery Stitches

French Knot - page 164   Stem Stitch - page 173

Fly Stitch - page163

Japanese Ribbon Stitch - page 167   Straight Stitch - page 173

1. Using a washout marker or quilter's pencil, trace the design on the tea towel. The template given may be repeated as many times as desired.

2. Using Kanagawa silk thread #730 pale green, work stem stitch vines.

3. Using the Japanese ribbon stitch and a color combination of your choice, work the outer petals of the flowers and fill the flower centers with French knots using a contrasting color of silk ribbon. The larger flowers use 2mm silk ribbon for the centers.

4. Using 4mm #31 green silk ribbon, work fly stitch clusters forming fern fronds at the places indicated on the design.

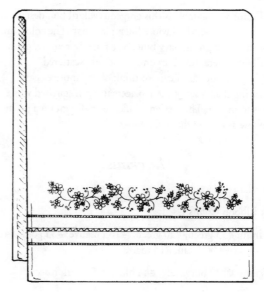

5. The single leaves are worked using a straight stitch in 4mm #31 green silk ribbon.

6. You may add as many or as few French knot clusters at the end of the vines as desired. The French knot clusters are worked using 4mm #87 peach silk ribbon. See the silk ribbon template on page 137 for placement.

7. Using Kanagawa silk thread #730 pale green, work clusters of three French knots at the places indicated on the graph.

8. Using monafilament thread, stitch the iridescent purple glass beads in a cluster for the remaining flowers. I substituted the glass beads for French knots.

9. Using 4mm #31 green silk ribbon, work straight stitch leaves in and around the clusters of iridescent beads.

10. I added the bugle beads around the large flowers to replace the French knots. ▓

Linen Hand Towel Embroidery Template

Placemat

Fit for a royal table is this gorgeous silk ribbon design on a purchased, hemstitched white linen placemat. The colors are several shades of green, navy blue, pale blue, burgundy, gold, and yellow. Several tiny burgundy beads are scattered throughout the design. I cannot think of any more elegant table setting than a set of these placemats with starched white napkins to match. This design would be as elegant on a collar or a pillow as it is on these placemats.

Materials

❋ 1 purchased placemat

❋ Silk Ribbon Colors Used:

4mm: #33 green, #20 green, #163 mauve, #55 gold, #47 navy, #35 tan, #13 maize

7mm: #129 burgundy, #44 blue, #159 dark rose,

❋ Burgundy glass beads

❋ Color photo - page 21

❋ Silk Ribbon Template - page 139

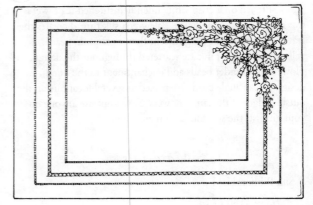

Directions

Embroidery Stitches

Chain Stitch - page 161

Elongated Fly Stitch - page 163

French Knot - page 164

Loop Stitch French Knot - page 168

Spider Web Rose - page 172

Wrapped Stitch - page 175

1. Using a washout marker, draw the design on the placemat.

2. If you want to work with an embroidery hoop, it will be necessary to baste fabric to the edge of the placemat to have enough fabric to fit in a hoop large enough for the design. This design was worked without a hoop. If you decide to work without a hoop, be very careful with your tension and do not pull the ribbon too tightly.

3. Work a large spider web rose in the center of the design using 7mm #44 blue silk ribbon.

4. Using 4mm #33 green silk ribbon, work a wrapped stem stitch for the vines. Add straight and Japanese ribbon stitch leaves along the vine where desired.

5. Using 7mm #129 burgundy silk ribbon, work a spider web rose on each vine.

6. Using 4mm #47 navy silk ribbon, work a spider web rose to the left of the large spider web rose at the center of the design.

7. Using 4mm #163 mauve silk ribbon, work another spider web rose on the right side of the large spider web rose at the center of the design.

8. Using 7mm #129 burgundy silk ribbon, work three French knot loop stitch flowers around the spider web roses in the center of the design.

9. Using 4mm #55 gold silk ribbon, stitch two clusters of French knots above the center French knot loop stitch flower.

10. Using 4mm #163 mauve silk ribbon, work twisted chain stitch buds around the large spider web rose in the center of the design.

11. Work an elongated fly stitch at the base of each bud using 4mm #20 green silk ribbon. This elongated fly stitch will cup the base of the bud and form the stem.

12. Using 4mm #13 maize silk ribbon, scatter clusters of French knots around the group of flowers. Follow template on page 139 for placement.

13. Using 4mm #20 green silk ribbon, scatter chain stitch leaves around the design mixed with French knot loop stitch stems, and Japanese ribbon stitch leaves. See template on page 139 for placement.

14. Scatter the burgundy beads throughout the design. ❋

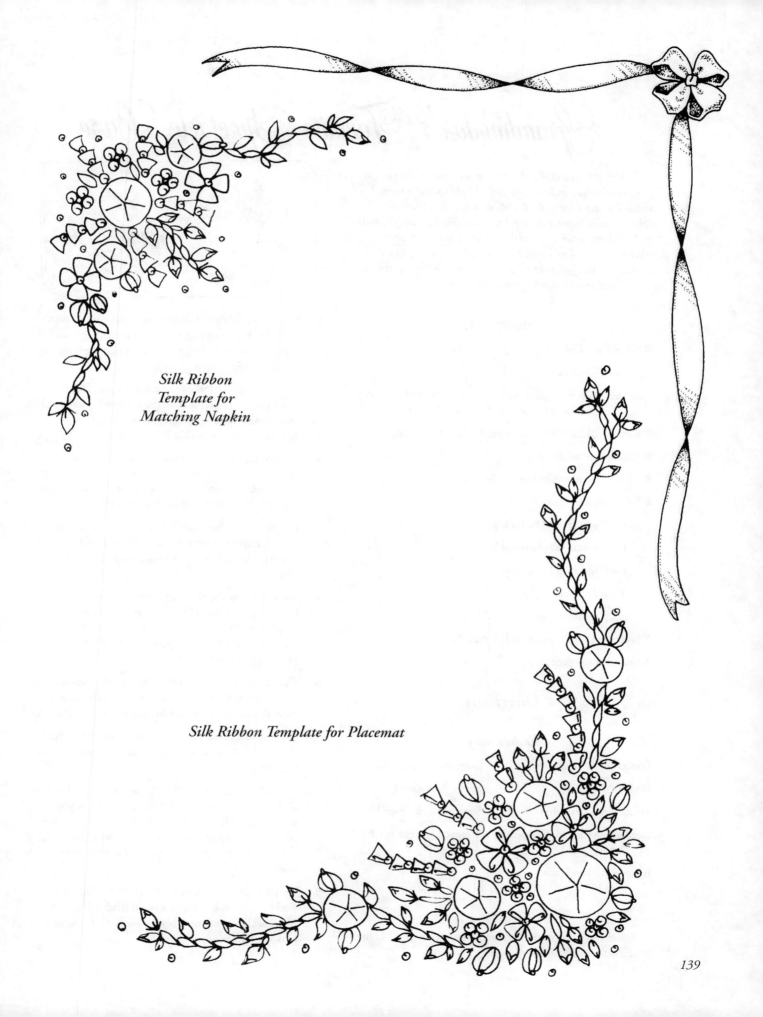

Silk Ribbon
Template for
Matching Napkin

Silk Ribbon Template for Placemat

139

Grandmother's Favorite Spectacle Case

This very practical and very beautiful eyeglass case might be something you make for yourself. The black water stained taffeta features a spray of silk ribbon embroidery featuring colors of pink, green, peach, gold, red, white, deep purple, and pink. Delicate little sprays of flowers using many different stitches make this a treasure for many years to come. The opening of the eyeglass case has black taffeta piping and the case is lined in a contrasting black fabric.

Materials

✿ Silk Ribbon Colors Used:

    2mm: #3 white

    4mm: #20 moss green, #26 pale pink, #147 mais, #26 pink, #118 purple, #91 pink, #93 red

✿ Kanagawa 1000 Denier silk thread: #156 moss green

✿ #26 tapestry needle

✿ #7 or 8 crewel embroidery needle

✿ Fabric requirements:

    1 - 9" square of fabric for top

    1 - 9" square of lightweight batting

    1 - 9" square of lining fabric

    1/2 yard of piping

    black sewing thread

✿ Spectacle Case Pattern found on page 142

✿ Color Photo - page 21

Directions

Embroidery

Feather Stitch - page 164	Loop Stitch - page 168
Fly Stitch - page 163	Spider Web Rose 172
French Knot - page 164	Straight Stitch - page 173
Interlocking Curved Whipped Stitch - page 175	Wrapped Straight Stitch - page 175
Japanese Ribbon Stitch - page 167	

Refer to silk ribbon embroidery template on page 141 for placement of all embroidery stitches.

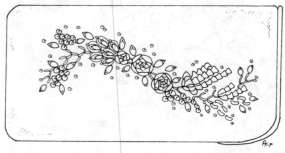

1. Fold the top fabric in half and trace spectacle case pattern on folded fabric, making sure that you mark the notches. Using the vine template, mark the vine on the front side of the case (**fig. 1 on page 142**).

2. Using Kanagawa #156 moss green silk thread, feather stitch the vine, working from the top to the middle and then turning to complete the vine, working from the opposite end to the middle Refer to fig. 1.

3. Using 4mm #93 red silk ribbon, work a large spider web rose at the center of the vine and then work two smaller spider web roses on either side of the large one. The size is determined by the size of the base fly stitch.

4. The pink and yellow buds below the roses are lazy daisy stitches worked in 4mm #91 pink silk ribbon. Fill in the center of the buds using a straight stitch in 4mm #147 maize.

5. Working below the pink and yellow buds, work the wisteria spray in small French knots using 4mm #118 purple silk ribbon. The number and placement of the French knots is at your discretion, think of a bunch of grapes as you stitch.

6. Work a similar spray of French knots on the opposite side of the vine, using a needle threaded with two pieces of 4mm silk ribbon in colors #26 pink and #20 moss green.

7. Working toward the top of the vine, follow the instructions in step 5 and work a second spray of wisteria above the center roses.

8. The gladiolas are worked in a ribbon loop stitch. The large glad is a center row of 4mm #147 maize ribbon with a row of 4mm #20 moss green silk ribbon used on either side. The small glad is one row of 4mm #147 maize and one row of 4mm #20 moss green and it contains fewer loops.

9. The pink sprays on the opposite side of the vine are worked with small wrapped straight stitches placed in an "interlocking" position. They are worked using 4mm #26 pink silk ribbon.

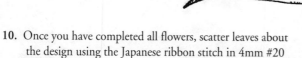

10. Once you have completed all flowers, scatter leaves about the design using the Japanese ribbon stitch in 4mm #20 moss green silk ribbon.

11. Work French knot baby's breath throughout the design using 2mm #3 white silk ribbon.

Construction

1. Cut out case, batting, and lining.

2. Stitch the piping to the top edge of case, matching raw edges and stitching from notch to notch (**fig. 2**).

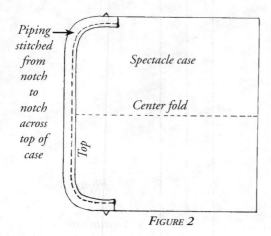

Piping stitched from notch to notch across top of case

Spectacle case

Center fold

Top

FIGURE 2

3. Place batting on the wrong side of case, and place the lining, right side facing down on top of the case. Stitch from notch to notch (**fig. 3**).

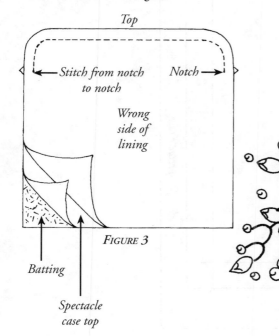

Top

Stitch from notch to notch

Notch

Wrong side of lining

Batting

Spectacle case top

FIGURE 3

4. Pull lining away from the batting and case and fold lengthwise with right sides together. Stitch from the end of the lining to the notch. Clip to the notch. Stitch from the end of the case and batting to the notch. Backstitch a couple of stitches to reinforce at the notches (**fig. 4**).

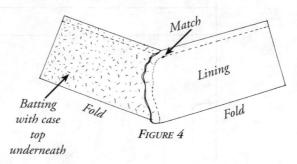

Match

Batting with case top underneath

Fold

Lining

Fold

FIGURE 4

5. Turn the lining to the outside over the case and batting. Serge across the bottom (**fig. 5**). Turn right side out

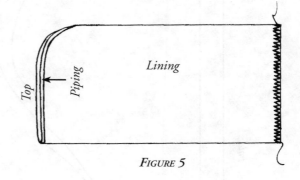

Top

Piping

Lining

FIGURE 5

Silk Ribbon Template

141

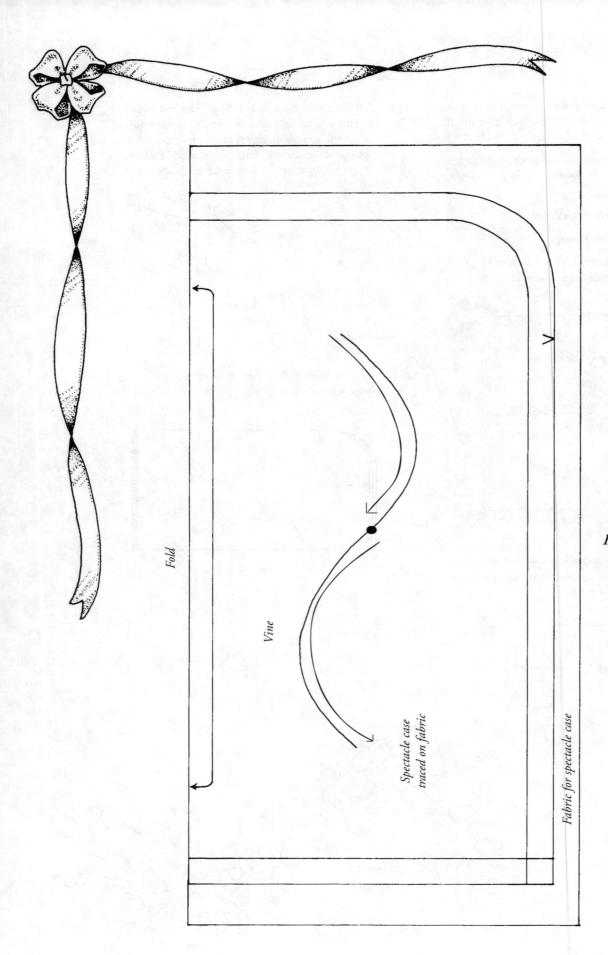

Fold

Vine

Spectacle case
traced on fabric

Fabric for spectacle case

Figure 1

*Grandmother's
Favorite Spectacle
Case*

Victorian Needle Case

Straight from the pages of a Godey's book a la 1900 is this fabulous needle case. Measuring 9 inches by 4½ inches, folded, this is a stitchers delight. The outside covering of the case is navy blue velveteen with corded double needle pintucks. Using navy thread; these pintucks are crossed making a waffle effect. Burgundy piping travels around the outside of the case. The inside is a beautiful upholstery print damask in shades of burgundy, green, blue, and beige. There are places for eight packages of needles inside the case. It closes with a large snap.

Exquisite is what I would call the silk ribbon design on the outside of this case. The large burgundy bow is stitched down with colonial knots. The streamers are secured with grape like bouquets of colonial knots in pale rose, green and blue. Several little yellow colonial knots are scattered throughout these clusters also. Stems and roses of green, dark rose, and pale blue are found in the lower center of the bow and lazy daisies in pale pink and green complete the center of the bow. Beads of white and burgundy are stitched throughout the design making it absolutely sparkle with creativity.

Materials

✳ Silk Ribbon Colors Used:

    7mm: #129 burgundy, #163 mauve, #125 blue, #33 green

    4mm: #33 green, #34 ecru, #128 dark mauve, #9 light blue, #144 pink, #159 mauve, #163 mauve, #129 burgundy

✳ Kanagawa Silk Thread: 80 denier #113 green

✳ White and burgundy glass beads

✳ 2½ yds. cord for corded pintucks

✳ 1⅛ yds. piping

✳ ⅓ yd. fabric for lining

✳ 15" x 15" square of fabric for top

✳ 12" x 12" square of lightweight batting for padding

✳ Color photo - page 20

✳ Silk Ribbon Template - page 145

Directions

Embroidery

Colonial Knot - page 161	Loop Stitch - page 168
Curved Whip Stitch - page 175	Pullen Knot - page 168
Fly Stitch - page 163	Stem Stitch - page 173
Japanese Ribbon Stitch - page 167	Twisted Chain - page 177
Lazy Daisy Stitch - page 167	

Refer to the silk ribbon template on page 145 for placement of all embroidery stitches.

1. Using the corded pintuck directions given in the technique section, page 204, pintuck the top piece of fabric.

2. Trace a 9½" square onto the pintucked fabric. Stitch on the drawn line. DO NOT CUT OUT (**fig. 1**).

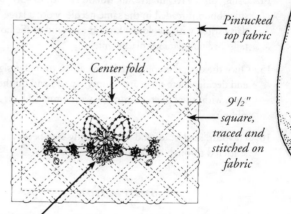

Pintucked top fabric

Center fold

9½" square, traced and stitched on fabric

Embroidery design placement — centered

FIGURE 1

3. Fold the fabric in half and center the embroidery design on one of the folded sides. Refer to the tips section for transferring design to fabric.

4. Shape the bow using 7mm #129 burgundy silk ribbon and pin or baste in place along the selvage edge of the ribbon.

5. Using 4mm #129 burgundy silk ribbon, work colonial knots every ⅛" to ¼" along the finished edge of the ribbon bow loops.

6. Using Kanagawa #113 green silk thread, work a stem stitch for the vines underneath the center flower.

7. Using 7mm #163 mauve silk ribbon, work a series of Japanese ribbon stitches radiating out from a center point to form the center flower.

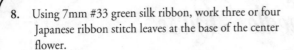

8. Using 7mm #33 green silk ribbon, work three or four Japanese ribbon stitch leaves at the base of the center flower.

9. Work twisted chain stitches using 7mm #125 blue silk ribbon at the end of each stem. Varying the size of the stitch will give different size buds.

10. Using 7mm #33 green silk ribbon, work a fly stitch immediately underneath each blue bud. This fly stitch forms the leaves for the bud.

11. Scatter curved whip stitches between the buds using 4mm #159 mauve silk ribbon.

12. Thread 4mm #163 mauve silk ribbon and 4mm #33 green silk ribbon in the same needle and work clusters of colonial knots. See template for placement. When working these colonial knots, use different tensions when creating each knot for a more natural appearance.

13. The loop stitch flowers are worked in 4mm #34 ecru silk ribbon with French knot centers worked in 4mm #144 pink silk ribbon.

14. Using 4mm #163 mauve silk ribbon and 4mm #33 green silk ribbon threaded in the same needle, work a large lazy daisy stitch with a colonial knot at each end of the bow tails. See template for placement.

15. Once the design is completed, look at the overall design and decide where there are "empty" spaces and fill these areas with the Pullen knot made with 4mm #9 light silk ribbon.

16. The pearl seed beads and the burgundy seed beads are scattered throughout the design.

Construction

1. Cut out the fabric for the top, cutting outside the stitched line and cut the lining the same size as the top.

2. Cut two strips of lining fabric 9½" long and 3¼" wide. Fold in half along the length and press. These strips are used for the needle pockets (**fig. 2**).

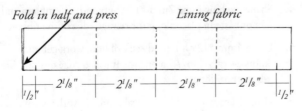

Mark lines at these intervals to create pockets

FIGURE 2

3. Starting ½" from one end, measure across the folded fabric 2⅛" and mark. Repeat until you have three lines drawn that will create four needle pockets. Repeat for second strip of fabric (**fig. 3**).

4. On the right side of the lining, place the cut edge of the folded fabric along the cut edge of the lining, placing the folded edge of the strip of fabric toward the center of the lining strip. Carefully line up the drawn lines on each strip of fabric. Draw a line across the lining fabric connecting the needle pockets. Pin in place (**fig. 3**).

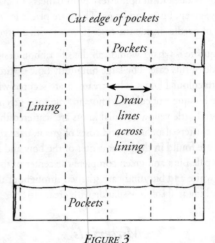

FIGURE 3

5. Place the batting to the wrong side of the lining and pin in place.

6. Stitch on the drawn lines by hand or machine, stitching from cut edge to cut edge. This creates the pockets to hold the needle packs and anchors the batting to the back of the lining.

7. Attach the piping to the lining fabric by placing the piping along the cut edge, right sides together. Let the ends overlap and extend into the seam allowance. Pin in place. It will be necessary to clip the piping on the corners to get a smooth turn (**fig. 4**).

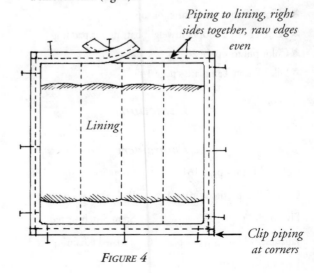

Piping to lining, right sides together, raw edges even

Clip piping at corners

FIGURE 4

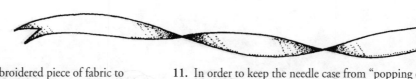

8. Place the right side of the embroidered piece of fabric to the right side of the lining. Stitch through the batting, lining, piping, and top. Clip corners where necessary.

9. Leave a six inch opening to turn the needle case. Turn the needle case and press the seam allowance.

10. Slip stitch the opening closed.

11. In order to keep the needle case from "popping open" in the center, stitch across the needle case on the center fold mark (**fig. 5**).

12. Stitch a large snap to the inside of the needle case to keep it closed. ▦

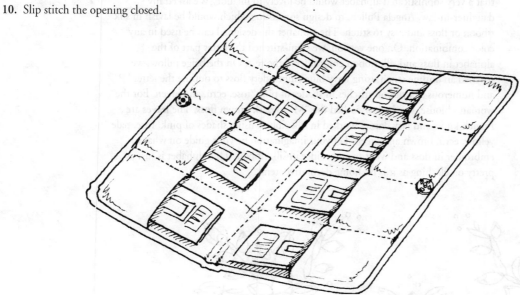

Figure 5

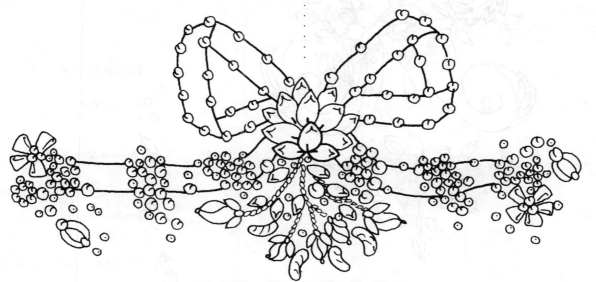

Silk Ribbon Template for Needle Case

Angela's Silk Ribbon Alphabet

Upon finalizing the last designs to include in this beautiful book, we decided that a very sophisticated alphabet would be lovely to include. We asked my daughter-in-law, Angela Pullen, to design something which would be lavish in silk ribbon or floss and easy to stitch. The alphabet she designed can be used in any color combination. On one version, we stem-stitched the letter part of the alphabet in floss and silk ribbon embroidered the rest. On the beige pillow, we stitched an outline stitch using navy blue embroidery floss to outline the letter "P" and numerous silk ribbon stitches in shades of pink, rose, ecru, and green. For the woman's blouse, we shadowworked the "M" in dark brown floss. The leaves are French knots and lazy daisies worked in silk ribbon using shades of pink, rose, pale yellow, ecru, brown and green. Let your imagination be your guide on what to embroider in floss and what to embroider in silk ribbon. This alphabet is just as pretty on clothing as it is on home decorative items.

A

STITCH GUIDE

French Knots

Ribbon Stem Stitch

Floss Stem Stitch

Lazy Daisy with French Knot

Japanese Ribbon Stitch

Straight Stitches with Ribbon

B

C

D

E

F

G

H

I

J

K

L

M

N

O

P

Q

R

S

T

U

V

W

X

Y

Z

White Linen Blouse

Since this blouse is for me, the letter is an *M*. The letter is shadow embroidered in dark brown with the rest of the embroidery's being done in silk ribbon stitches in various shades of pink, green, ecru, brown, pale yellow and green. The blouse pattern is from my book, *Heirloom Sewing For Women*, and the silk ribbon embroidery is the perfect embellishment for this very tailored blouse. The sleeves are hemmed by using a pin stitch and a wing needle.

Initial Pillow

You can choose your initial when you make this easy to sew pillow with our beautiful silk ribbon alphabet. The outline is stitched in navy blue floss and the remainder of the embroidery is completed with silk ribbon stitches which are so fast and easy. The pillow measures 19 inches by 19 inches from tip of the ruffle to tip of the ruffle. The double ruffle is topped with a beautiful ecru French lace gathered in with the ruffle.

Instructions for making this pillow begin on page 135.

Tips and Tricks
For Silk Ribbon Embroidery

by Margaret Taylor

Silk ribbon embroidery is easy, quick and fun to do. Silk ribbon comes in five sizes; 2mm ($^1/_{16}$ inch), 4mm ($^1/_8$ inch), 7mm ($^1/_4$ inch), 13mm ($^1/_2$ inch), or 32mm ($1^1/_4$ inch). The size ribbon you choose will be determined by the desired texture, the design, and size of your project.

Embroidering with silk ribbon is different from using embroidery floss. You must keep the ribbon under control to make the stitches appear natural and untwisted. There are, however, specific stitches that require the ribbon to be twisted. Some people use a laying tool to smooth out the wrinkles in the silk ribbon or to fluff the ribbon to finish the stitch. A laying tool can be a large needle, a shish kabob wooden skewer, a corsage pin, or a trolley needle. You may even use your finger to straighten the ribbon.

Needles

For many types of embroidery, one uses a very small needle. Because of the size of silk ribbon, it is necessary to use a much larger needle. The width of the ribbon chosen for your project must slip easily through the needle eye. The size of the needle shaft will correspond with the size of the eye; the larger shafts will make a larger hole in your fabric to allow the ribbon to pass through easily. If the needle shaft isn't large enough to make an ample hole, the ribbon will fray as it is pulled through the fabric.

In order to get the wider ribbons through the eye of the needle, it may be necessary to fold the ribbon in half. In some cases, when wide ribbon is used, it is difficult to pull the ribbon through the fabric. If this happens, use a stiletto to pierce the fabric; this should allow the ribbon to pull through with ease.

As in all cases, there are exceptions to the rule. It is important that the needle size not only correspond to the ribbon size but also to the fabric being used. If the fabric is tightly woven or has a pile such as velvet, it will be necessary to use a larger needle even with smaller ribbon. A needle that is too small, will cause the ribbon to distort and change the look of the stitches. It is suggested that you always do a small test on a scrap piece of fabric to determine the proper needle size for the project you are beginning. Read in the "Beginning to Stitch" section for specific types of needles.

Fabrics and Linings

The fabric you choose for your project should enhance the embroidery and not overpower it. Always allow at least four inches on all sides of your design. This allowance makes it easier to handle and finish the project.

You may use any type of fabric, but it will quickly become clear that not all stitches work well on all fabrics. If a fabric is plush, such as wool or velvet, it will be necessary to use stitches that sit on top of the fabric in order to keep them from getting lost in the texture. If the fabric is sheer, such as lightweight silk, organza, and some batiste, it should be backed with a second layer of fabric to prevent the ends of the ribbons from showing through when finished. To be more specific, if a second layer of fabric is needed, the first choice would be to use the same fabric as the top layer. For example, Swiss batiste would be lined with Swiss batiste and organza would be lined with organza. If two layers of fabric are still too sheer, the second layer can be Swiss batiste or another slightly heavier fabric. Keep in mind when choosing your lining fabric that both fabrics should receive the same care in laundering.

After choosing your lining fabric, baste the two layers together around the edges by hand or machine. Work your silk ribbon embroidery leaving tails, not tying knots on the back. Work the tails into the next stitch to secure them to the back and cut them as short as possible after this process is completed. Remember, you do not want the back of the embroidery to show through the fabric.

There are two options for lining after the work is finished. First, leave the second layer intact and have a fully lined piece. Second, cut away the second layer on the back side, cutting very carefully and very close to the stitching. You do not have to finish these cut edges because if you do, they will show through on the right side.

It is my suggestion that you check all fabrics and ribbons for color fastness before beginning your project. To do this, either wash the fabric before beginning your project or test a piece of fabric or ribbon in the following manner. Wet a scrap of the fabric or ribbon; rub it with a white paper towel to see if any color comes off on the paper towel. You might say, "What if I am not going to wash the pillow or jewel case?" Test it anyway, because it might get wet in some way. For instance, when you work silk ribbon embroidery on a dark green silk dupioni, it is necessary to transfer your design onto a water soluble stabilizer. Then, you work the embroidery through the stabilizer and the silk dupioni. It is necessary to wet the water soluble stabilizer to remove it from behind the silk ribbon embroidery and from the rest of the pillow. Do you see why you need to test the fabric?

Threads

Silk ribbon embroidery takes on a different dimension when combined witsêother threads. When adding other threads to your design, keep in mind your choice of fabric and the intended use of the design. You may use perle cotton, crewel yarn, floche, rayon embroidery thread, metallic thread, silk buttonhole twist, silk floss, or any other thread you find available in your area. These threads add texture and dimension to a design and may be used with the ribbon to work flowers, leaves, stems, French knots, or any other part of the design.

Hoops

"Should I work with or without a hoop?" If this question were asked to a group of women, their answers would be split 50/50. The size of the hoop is determined by the size of your hand. Your thumb and fingers should reach comfortably to the center of the hoop to work your stitches. Usually, a size 6" or 7" works best. The size of the hoop must be larger than the design area being worked to keep from distorting finished stitches.

Hoops are made of plastic, metal, or wood. The choice is up to the user. I find that a wooden hoop with a screw for tightening will hold the fabric better than any others I have worked with. I also wrap the center circle of the hoop with a stretchy gauze used for bandages. This holds the fabric taut and helps prevent the inner ring from causing damage to the fabric. Always remove the hoop from the fabric when putting your work away. This will prevent the hoop from making "rings" on your design.

To load the hoop, lay the design over the inner ring, keeping the grain of the fabric straight. If you are using a backing or lining for your fabric, place this on the inner ring first, add the base fabric, and then the top circle. Tighten the screw and gently pull the fabric taut, removing all wrinkles.

Transferring Designs to Fabric

Designs for silk ribbon embroidery can be found in many places. Designs originally meant for floss can be used by simply changing from floss to ribbon and eliminating some of the stitches because of the coverage of silk ribbon. You may use a washout marker, fade away pen, white pencil, or #2 pencil to transfer a design to fabric. If using a fade away pen, make sure that you will be able to finish in one day because the pen fades

overnight. A light box makes it easy to transfer a design or you may tape the design to a window and trace. Always anchor the fabric to the design to keep them from shifting during tracing and use a light hand when transferring any design to fabric.

When the base fabric is dark, it becomes necessary to use other transfer mediums. You may use dressmakers carbon paper for your smoother fabrics or a white pencil. One thing that I found invaluable was Solvy™ or water soluble stabilizer. When working with Solvy™, keep in mind this stabilizer will disintegrate with moisture. You may trace your design directly on the Solvy™ by using a fine point black Sharpie marker. This marker will not dissolve the stabilizer but will wash away when the project is finished and placed in water to rinse away the Solvy™. Please remember that the Sharpie marker is a permanent pen and should never be used to trace a design on the fabric.

Embellishments

It is surprising how beads, buttons, or charms will add pizzazz to your design. Small seed or glass beads can be used to fill in the centers of flowers or to add sparkle to any area. Because of the size of the beads used, you must have a beading needle. Attach the beads with beading thread to prevent deterioration with time or cleaning.

Buttons of all types and varieties may be added to your design. For pastel colors, I recommend mother-of-pearl or small antique buttons. If the fabric is plush, keep in mind that the smaller buttons may become lost in the design and pile of the fabric.

The selection of charms in both brass and silver allows you to add a variety of shapes and designs to your projects. This will greatly enhance the overall look of the finished project.

Keep in mind that sometimes "less is best. " It is wise to be selective in your embellishments and not allow them to become the focus of the design. The silk ribbon embroidery should be the focus of the project and not the "highlights."

Ribbon Tension

As with any new technique, it takes practice. When beginning to work with silk ribbon, you will find that the ribbon does not work as well and the stitches do not look as pretty if your tension is tight. Many first time silk ribbon embroiders have a tendency to "jerk" the ribbon as if it were floss. Even though the ribbon is strong, pull it through the fabric as though it were a thin strand of glass. If you make this a practice, you will find that your ribbon stitches look much better because you are allowing the ribbon to do the work for you. Remember, always allow the ribbon to "sit" on top of the fabric, which means using tension that is not too loose and not too tight. ▓

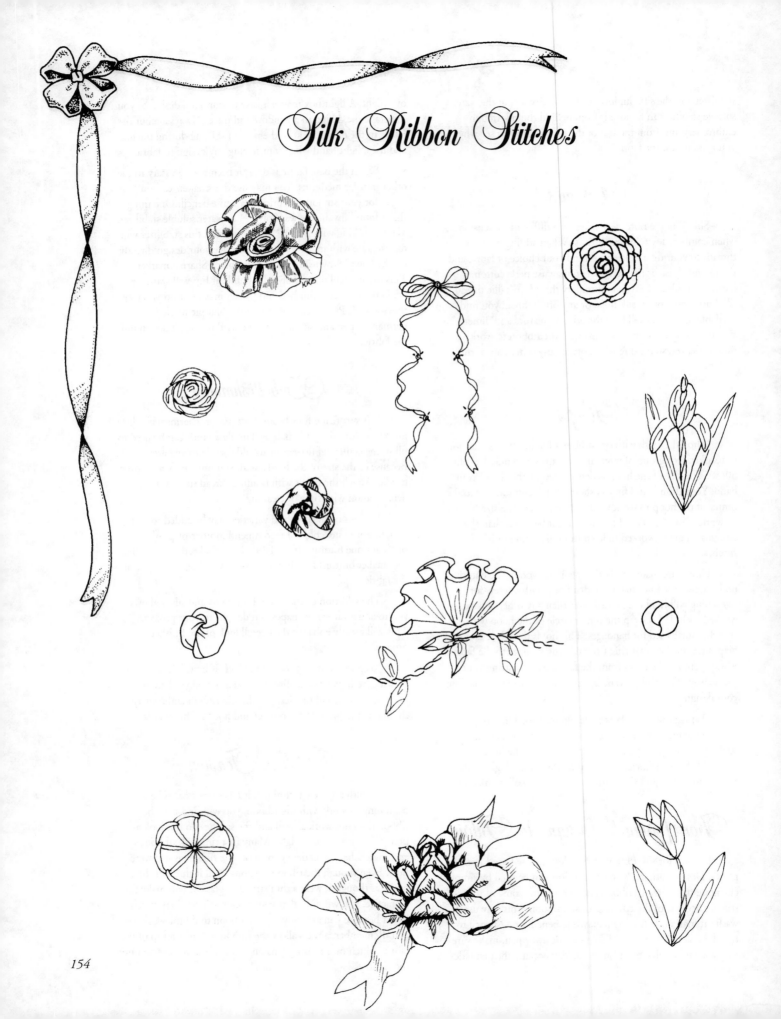

Silk Ribbon Stitches

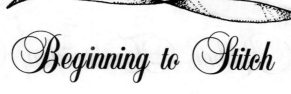

Beginning to Stitch

As you begin to embellish your special projects with silk ribbon you will find that it is actually much easier than it looks and it takes far less time than floss embroidery to complete a design. The craft of silk embroidery is little more than mastering a few basic stitches and using those stitches in combinations with each other. With a change in color and ribbon width, a basic leaf becomes a rose or a tulip. A French knot is babies' breath in one design and a rose or a hyacinth in another design simply by a change in the ribbon or number of twists on the needle. As you fill in your design you will find that silk ribbon is very forgiving and mistakes are easily corrected. You will become familiar with what works best for you as you play with different needles, ribbons, and fabrics. We use YLI Silk Ribbons. They're gorgeous!

Fabrics

Many fabrics are suitable for silk ribbon embroidery; of course, some are easier to work with than others. All of the natural fiber fabrics are beautiful and very suitable. Some are cotton, linen, cotton velveteen, silk taffeta, raw silk, silk dupioni, natural silk, and batiste. The following synthetic fabrics are also useful; moire taffeta, tapestry, lightweight polyester taffeta, organdy, and satin. Experiment with several.

Needles

There are a variety of needles used for silk ribbon work, as you experiment, you will find what works best with which fabrics and stitches. Remember, the higher the size number the smaller the needle.

Chenille Needle - A large, sharp pointed needle with a long eye. Sizes range from 18 to 24. Good for wide ribbon and tightly woven fabrics because it punctures a hole that will accommodate a wide ribbon.

Crewel Needle - This needle has a long eye and a sharp point. Sizes range from 1 to 10, however, sizes 3 to 9 are all you will ever need.

Tapestry Needle - A large eyed needle with a blunt end. It prevents snagging, and is great for passing through other ribbon; good for loosely woven fabrics. Sizes range from 13 to 26, with 18 to 26 being the most useful.

Straw Needle - This needle is a long, narrow needle, also called a milliner's needle, which stays the same thickness from top to bottom. Which means the needle does not get fatter at the eye. This aspect makes it a great needle for French and colonial knots.

Darner - A very large eyed, long needle used for wide ribbons and heavy thick threads. Sizes range from 14 to 18.

Beading Needle - This needle is used for assembling roses, gathering stitches, and tacking beads. It is a thin, long needle with a small eye.

Threading

For best results, work with ribbon no longer than ten inches at a time. The ribbon becomes frayed and hard to work with quickly, so if the ribbon is longer than ten inches it will probably be wasted before it can be used.

To keep the needle threaded, insert the needle into the tail of the ribbon after it has been threaded through the eye of the needle (**fig. 1**). Then, pull the tail back over the main ribbon so that it forms a loop (**fig. 2**). Next, pull the main ribbon until the loop is closed (**fig. 3**). (This passes easily through the fabric and keeps the ribbon from coming unthreaded). ✳

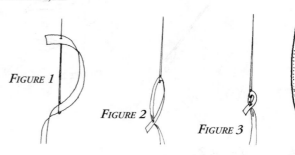

FIGURE 1

FIGURE 2

FIGURE 3

Tying Off

There are two ways to tie on and to tie off the ribbon. One way is to simply tie knots. Knots are best for small projects. The second way is to leave about $1/2$ inch of extra ribbon underneath the fabric, and when the needle is inserted back through to complete a stitch, insert the needle through the extra ribbon to secure it. When cutting the ribbon, leave an extra $1/2$ inch and insert the needle through it when making another stitch. This method helps keep the back side free of so many knots, which can eventually get in the way when working a complicated design. ✳

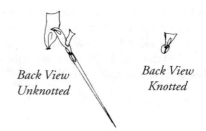

Back View
Unknotted

Back View
Knotted

Silk Ribbon Embroidery Stitches

Bearded Iris

1. With a 2mm, 4mm, or 7 mm ribbon, stitch a lazy daisy (**fig. 1**). Refer to the lazy daisy stitch in this section.

FIGURE 1

2. To create the beards, bring the needle up from under the fabric, below and slightly to the right side of the lazy daisy (**fig. 2**). Insert the needle behind the lazy daisy so that it does not catch the ribbon or the fabric and glides freely between them (**fig 3**).

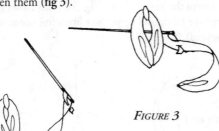

FIGURE 3

FIGURE 2

3. Pull the ribbon through and insert the needle into the fabric on the other side, below and to the side of the lazy daisy (**fig. 4**).

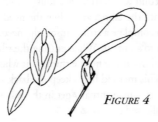

FIGURE 4

4. To complete this flower, add a twisted straight stitch for the stalk and a couple of long straight stitches for the leaves. Note: for added dimension, stitch the stalk and leaves first, and then add the iris to the top of the stalk and allow the beards to lie on top of the leaves. ▓

Bradford Rose

This rose is versatile. For variety, use a dark color for the center knot, a medium shade for the first round of wrapped stitches, and a lighter shade for the outer row.

1. To begin this rose, make a colonial or French knot in the center (**fig. 1**).

FIGURE 1

2. Following the directions for a curved whip stitch on page 175, begin working clockwise around the center knot. Work three wrapped stitches for the first round (**fig. 2**).

FIGURE 2

3. Work four or five curved whipped stitches around the first round (**figs. 3 & 4**). ▓

FIGURE 3

FIGURE 4

You may break, you may shatter the vase, if you will,
But the scent of the roses will hang around it still.

Thomas Moore

Bullion Rose

This ever popular rose embellishes the most elegant embroidery projects. It takes practice, but once the basic bullion stitch is mastered, all of the different bullion roses and flowers will be a cinch.

1. Bring the needle up from under the fabric at A and take a stitch down at B about ³/₈" to ¹/₄" away from A, then come back up through A beside (not through) the ribbon. Do not pull the needle all the way through (**fig. 1**).

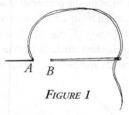

Figure 1

2. Now, hold the end of the needle down with your thumb. This will pop the point of the needle up away from the fabric. Wrap the ribbon coming from A around the needle 5 to 6 times, keeping the ribbon flat (**fig. 2**).

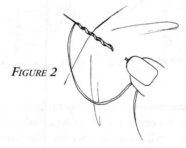

Figure 2

3. With your finger, push the wraps of ribbon to the bottom of the needle next to the fabric so that they are all lined up tightly (**fig. 3**). With your other hand, place your finger under the fabric and your thumb on top of the bullion and gently pull the needle and ribbon through the wraps (**fig. 4**).

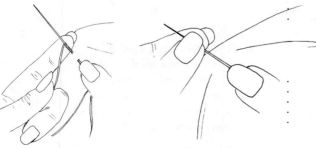

Figure 3   *Figure 4*

4. You almost have a bullion, but first you must lay the coils over to the opposite side and take up the slack ribbon(**fig. 5**). To do this, lay the bullion over and place you finger under the fabric and your thumb on top of the bullion, and gently pull the ribbon until the slack is out (**fig. 6**). Insert the needle into the fabric at the end of the bullion (**fig. 7**) and go on the next stitch, repeating the steps above. Refer to the template for stitch placement.

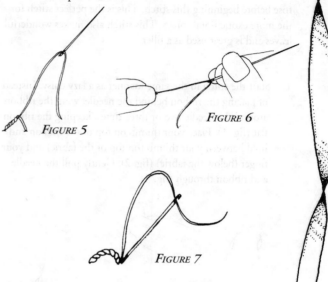

Figure 5   *Figure 6*

Figure 7

Note: The distance from point A to point B will determine the length of your bullion, and the number of ribbon wraps will determine the amount of curve. So, be sure you always have enough wraps to cover the distance. ▓

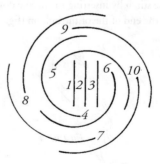

Bullion Rose Template

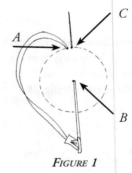

Bullion Lazy Daisy

Flowers and leaves take on a new dimension with this impressive looking silk ribbon stitch. This is a variation of the basic lazy daisy and bullion stitches. Review the lazy daisy instructions and the bullion instructions given for the bullion rose before beginning this stitch. This is the perfect stitch for the more exotic floral sprays. This stitch also makes wonderful leaves and is great used as a filler.

1. Start the stitch in the same manner as a lazy daisy. Instead of placing the ribbon behind the needle, wrap the ribbon around the needle two or three times, keeping the ribbon flat (**fig. 1**). Place your thumb on top of the bullion and hold between your thumb (on top of the fabric) and your finger (below the fabric) (**fig. 2**). Gently pull the needle and ribbon through (**fig. 3**).

| FIGURE 1 | FIGURE 2 | FIGURE 3 |

2. Secure the stitch by inserting the needle down into the fabric at the end of the of the bullion (**fig. 4**).

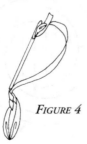

FIGURE 4

3. For added effect, change ribbon color and stitch a straight stitch or a Japanese ribbon stitch on top of each bullion lazy daisy (**fig. 5**). ▨

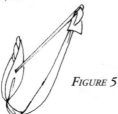

FIGURE 5

Buttonhole Stitch Flower

This wonderful stitch makes unusual flowers that have the appearance of hollyhocks. It is a good filler stitch when you need just something special to fill an area of a design. The buttonhole stitch flower is so easy and quick to do. I know you are going to love this stitch and the flowers you will be able to create with it.

1. The first stitch is a little different from the rest. I call this a starter stitch. Start on the perimeter of an imaginary circle at A. Take a stitch by inserting the needle into the center at B and out through C (**fig. 1**). Notice that C is just next to A for this first stitch. Wrap the ribbon over and around the needle and pull the ribbon through (**fig. 2**).

| FIGURE 1 | FIGURE 2 |

2. Now, to continue with the blanket stitch, insert the needle down into the center at B and make a stitch to the outer edge of the circle a short distance from the first stitch. Wrap the ribbon behind the needle (**fig. 3**) and pull through at D.

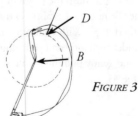

FIGURE 3

3. Repeat these steps, working from the center out all the way around. To end the circle, simply insert the needle down through the fabric at the top of the first stitch (**fig. 4**). ▨

FIGURE 4

Buttonhole Stitch

This stitch is a beautiful way to outline the edge of an appliqué shape. It makes a great fence when used on an embroidered picture. When stitched in a circle, this stitch becomes a hollyhock or a pansy.

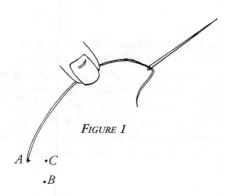

FIGURE 1

A   •C
        •B

1. Bring the needle up through the fabric at A. Pull the ribbon above and to the right of A and hold it in place with your thumb (**fig. 1**).

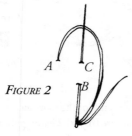

FIGURE 2

2. Insert the needle in B and up through C in one stitch, keeping the ribbon under the needle (**fig. 2**). Pull through.

3. C now becomes A and the sequence repeats. You may see the sequence as A-B, A-B, and on and on (**fig. 3**). Notice that the stitch looks like a series of upside down "L's". ▨

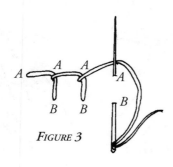

FIGURE 3

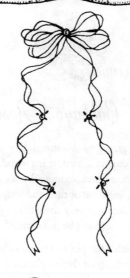

Cascading

This is a beautiful embellishment to add elegance and color when woven loosely through a floral design. It also secures and shapes the tails of a bow.

Bring the needle up through the fabric from underneath a bow or flower, or from wherever your streamers will be attached (**fig. 1**). Next, take a small stitch in the fabric about 1 inch or more away from where you came up and twist the ribbon so that it rolls and loops (**fig. 2**). Pull the ribbon very loosely and let it lie naturally. The loops may be tacked in place with French knots or seed beads. ▨

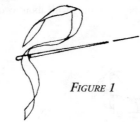

FIGURE 1

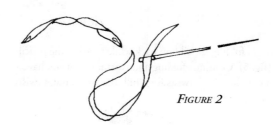

FIGURE 2

Cabbage Rose

Any project graced by this luxurious rose is instantly touched with a Victorian appeal. It is a wonderful ornament for hats, boxes, pillows, and wedding dresses and veils. Technically, it is a variation of the hand wrapped rose. It is made exactly the same way only there is a twist at the end. It takes a little practice so don't be discouraged the first time.

1. Beginning with a flat piece of ribbon about 15 inches long, fold down about three inches at a right angle (**fig. 1**). Fold again, this time folding the ribbon back on itself. This will create a triangle in the corner (**fig. 2**)

FIGURE 1   **FIGURE 2**

2. Place a pointed object such as the sharp tip of a chalk pencil or light colored pencil up through the "triangle" (**fig. 3**) and begin twisting with about two twists (**fig. 4**).

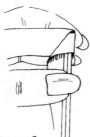   

FIGURE 3   **FIGURE 4**

3. Begin folding the ribbon back while twisting the pencil (**fig. 5**). Continue folding and twisting until you have about 5 to 7 full twists for a full rose and about 4 twists for a small rosette.

FIGURE 5

4. Remove the rose from the pencil and hold it between your thumb and finger. Tack the bottom securely with a needle and thread, leaving the tails dangling (**fig. 6**).

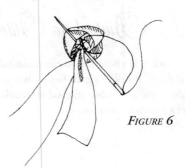

FIGURE 6

5. Now, here's the tricky part. After you have tacked the rose to keep it from falling apart as you finish, take the tail of the ribbon and create loops as you would when making a Christmas bow (**fig. 7**). The point of the loop will be on bottom . Tack stitch each loop as it is formed to the bottom of the rose to secure it. Make four loops, one on each side of the rose. After the last loop, fold the raw edge under and stitch it securely (**fig. 8**).

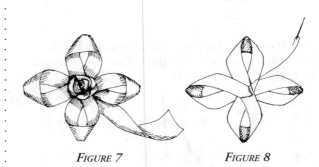

FIGURE 7   **FIGURE 8**

6. Pinch together the ends of the loop and take a couple of tiny stitches to secure (**fig. 9**). Gently pull the tacked ends to the bottom center and take loose stitches to hold it in place. Tie a knot, then go to the next petal and repeat until all of the loops are tacked to the bottom. As you will notice, the tacked loops create puffy petals on the bottom of the rose and give the wrapped rose more volume (**fig. 10**). ❈

Pinch the ends together and tack

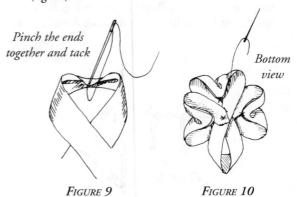

Bottom view

FIGURE 9   **FIGURE 10**

Chain Stitch

This is a glorified lazy daisy stitch that works beautifully on smocking and adds dimension to silk ribbon embroidery. It is a great outline stitch for stems and vines when done with one or two strands of floss.

1. Bring the needle up through the fabric at A. Swing the floss or ribbon around in a loop and hold the loop with your thumb (**fig.** 1).

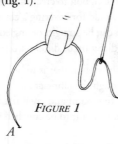

FIGURE 1

2. While holding the loop, insert the needle in at B and out through C in one stitch. Keep the needle and floss or ribbon going over the loop (**fig.** 2).

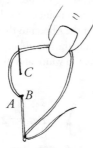

FIGURE 2

3. Instead of inserting the needle to the other side like a lazy daisy, you will make another loop and insert the needle down, right beside C were you last came up, this will become a new A. In the same stitch bring the needle through B and pull (**fig.** 3). Keep the needle over the loop.

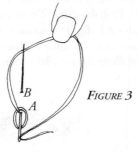

FIGURE 3

4. Continue looping and stitching in an "A, B" - "A, B" sequence. ▧

Colonial Knot

Basic knot stitches are used in a variety of ways. They can be the centers of daisies or the blossoms of hyacinths. Colonial knots make beautiful grape clusters on a vine or tiny rosettes in a bouquet. The colonial knot differs from the French knot in the method of wrapping the floss or ribbon around the needle. It will also make a larger knot than the French knot. If you want the colonial knot to be "fluffy", do not pull the ribbon tight. The knot will "sit tall" on top of the fabric.

1. Come up from beneath the fabric and wrap the needle under the ribbon once (**fig.** 1).

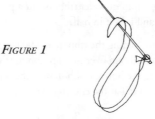

FIGURE 1

2. Next, wrap the ribbon over the needle once (**fig.** 2) and back under once (**fig.** 3). This makes a figure eight.

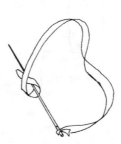

FIGURE 2

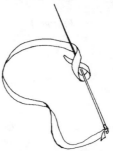

FIGURE 3

3. Insert the needle beside the original hole (**fig.** 4). While holding the needle vertically, pull the slack out of the ribbon so that the knot tightens around the needle (**fig.** 5). Continue holding the ribbon taut until the needle and ribbon have been pulled all the way through. ▧

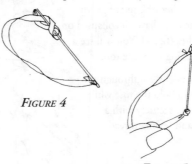

FIGURE 4

FIGURE 5

Concertina Rose

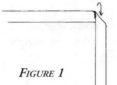

In my experience teaching silk ribbon, I have learned that not everyone can make a hand wrapped rose. The Concertina rose doesn't take quite so many fingers and toes to make, and it can stand in the place of a wrapped rose just as nicely on any project.

Once you try one of these roses, you will probably be reminded of decorating for the prom in high school – remember folding all that tissue. Well, this rose is done the exact same way. And if you've never folded tissue, try this technique the next time you have to decorate for a party!

1. Using 7 mm or wider ribbon, cut a piece 12 to 14 inches long and fold it in half.

2. Start by folding the ribbon at a 90º angle (**fig. 1**). Fold the bottom ribbon over the top ribbon (**fig. 2**). Continue folding the bottom ribbon over the top until it has at least a 1-inch tail at the end (**fig. 3**).

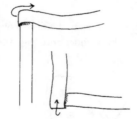

FIGURE 1

FIGURE 2

FIGURE 3

3. Hold the last folded edge of ribbon between your thumb and finger while your other thumb and finger pull the other ribbon tail gently until the folds have all collapsed on each other (**fig. 4**). You will see a rose forming from the top.

4. Stick a straight pin through the bottom to hold the rose while you tack it securely with a needle and sewing thread.

FIGURE 4

Couching

Couching is simply the attachment of ribbon or trim to fabric with tacking stitches. Couching is most often used as an edging method or to outline a shape. It is also very appropriate for silk ribbon smocking. Ribbon can be couched with other ribbon, silk thread, embroidery floss, pearls, or beads. There are many variations of this concept. The ribbon can remain flat or it may curl or loop. Below are the general instructions for couching, along with the technique of couching with pearls.

1. The general technique is to make tack stitches over flat ribbon. Shape the ribbon to create a design or keep it straight as you would for covering a crazy patch seam. This tack stitch can be straight or angled. The angles can be in the same direction or different directions.

2. To start, bring the ribbon that is to be couched up through the fabric at an appropriate starting point and lay it flat in the direction you want it to be couched (**fig. 1**).

FIGURE 1

3. Thread a needle with ribbon or floss in a matching or contrasting color. Bring the needle up just beside the ribbon at the starting point of the flat ribbon in figure 1. Take a stitch over the ribbon to the other side (**fig. 2**). Continue wrapping the flat ribbon with the tack stitches, keeping them even in width and distance (**fig. 3**).

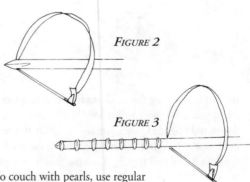

FIGURE 2

FIGURE 3

4. To couch with pearls, use regular sewing thread double threaded on a needle. Thread a strand of three pearls on each stitch (**fig. 4**). After each stitch, with a pointed object like the blunt end of a needle, pull up the flat ribbon to puff it. ▨

FIGURE 4

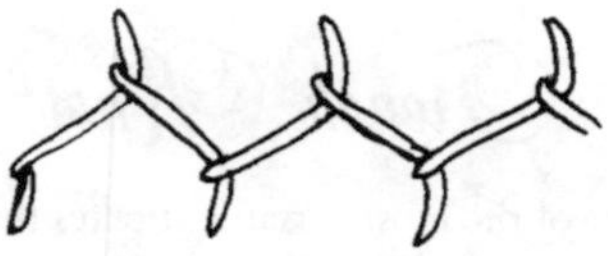

Cretan Stitch

The Cretan Stitch is a beautiful embellishment. This stitch is in the same family as the feather stitch. It takes a little practice at first, but if you have mastered the feather stitch it will be no problem. For beginners, it helps to mark the points on your fabric to practice the stitch until you get the hang of it.

1. To begin this line of stitching, bring the needle up through the fabric at B. Insert the needle through A and back up through B again in one stitch. Wrap the floss or ribbon around behind the needle (**fig. 1**).

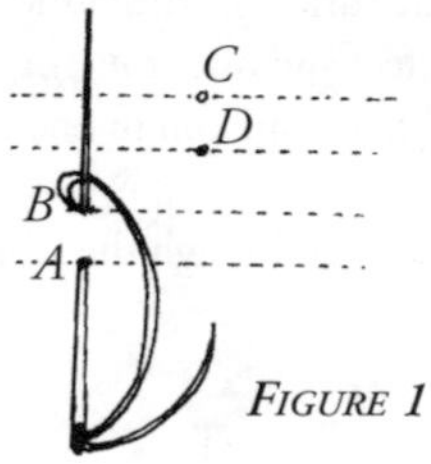

FIGURE 1

2. Pull the ribbon through and insert the needle through at C and D, keeping the needle over the floss or ribbon (**fig. 2**).

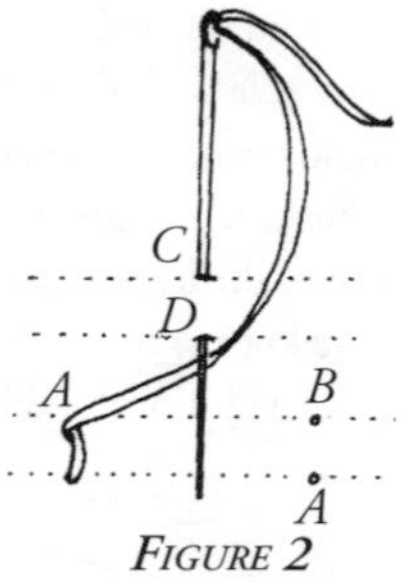

FIGURE 2

3. Repeat step 2 going in the opposite direction, inserting the needle in at A and up through B (**fig. 3**).

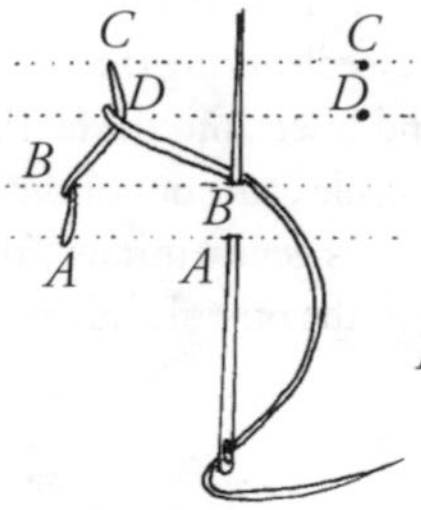

FIGURE 3

4. Continue repeating the A, B, C, D sequence and you will begin to see the pattern. ▩

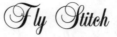

Fly Stitch

This stitch may be used for leaves at the base of flowers, it may be worked singly or in rows to give the appearance of ferns. This is an easy stitch to master and you will find many uses for it as fillers.

1. Come up at A . Insert the needle in the fabric at B, coming out of the fabric at C, making sure the loop of ribbon is below C (**fig. 1**). Keep the needle on top of the loop of ribbon.

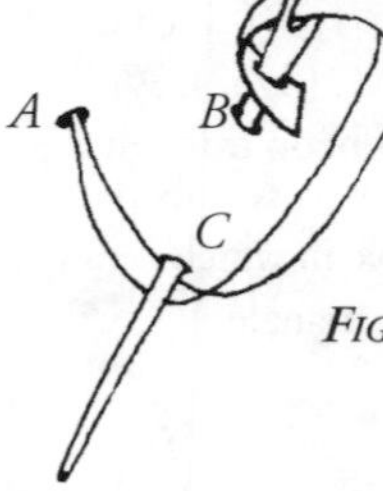

FIGURE 1

2. The length of the anchor stitch is determined by the length of the stitch taken between C and D. The floss or ribbon comes out of the fabric at C and the needle is inserted into the fabric at D. The longer the distance between C and D, the longer the anchor stitch. Gently pull the ribbon to the wrong side (**fig. 2 & 3**). ▩

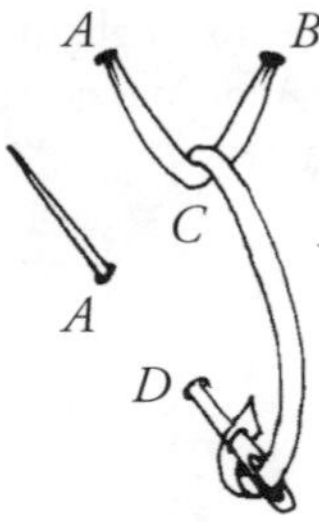

FIGURE 2

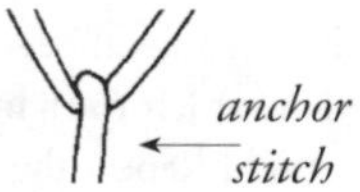

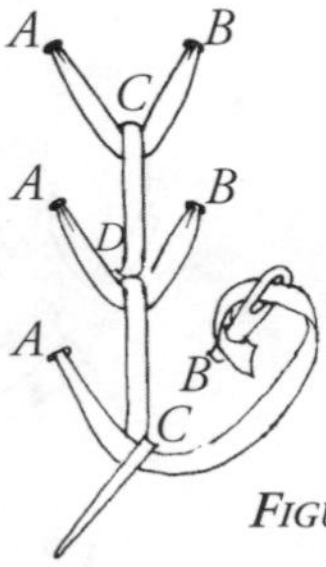

FIGURE 3

Elongated Fly Stitch

The elongated fly stitch is the basic fly stitch worked with a longer anchor stitch. I like to use this stitch to form leaves at the base of buds and the elongated anchor stitch makes the stem for the flower. I can take care of two steps at one time by using this stitch.

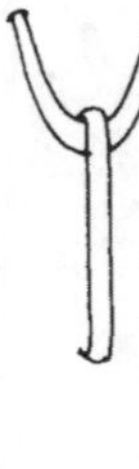

ELONGATED FLY STITCH

Feather Stitch

This is a great embellishing stitch that is frequently used for stems and vines. You may add beads at the ends of the Y in the feather stitch for another variation.

1. Bring the needle up through the fabric at A. (**fig. 1**). Insert the needle down about $^1/_4$ to $^3/_8$ inch across from A and into the fabric at B. In the same stitch bring the needle out of the fabric $^1/_4$ to $^3/_8$ inch down and slightly to the right of center at C (**fig. 2**). With the ribbon behind the needle, pull the ribbon through (**fig. 3**). This stitch is much like the lazy daisy only the needle does not insert into the same hole in which it came up. Notice that the stitch is simply a triangle.

FIGURE 1   FIGURE 2   FIGURE 3

2. Now you will begin working your triangle from right to left, or left to right. C will now become A for your next stitch. Repeat the stitch as in step 1 (**fig. 4**).

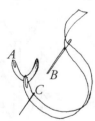

FIGURE 4

3. This time repeat the stitch on the other side (**fig. 5**). The trick is that A and B will always be straight across from each other and that A, B, and C will line up vertically (**fig. 6**). ▨

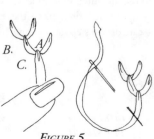

FIGURE 5

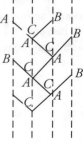

FIGURE 6

French Knot

This is one of the most versatile stitches that you will ever learn. The French knot is an easy stitch to use but it is one of the most intimidating stitches for embroiderers. The most asked question about French knots is "How many wraps?". The number of wraps will depend on the size of the knot desired, the type of thread or floss being used, and your personal preference. Generally, I recommend one strand of floss or 2mm silk ribbon with one to two wraps per knot. If a larger knot is needed, use more strands of floss or larger silk ribbon. Oftentimes, French knots will not lay flat on the fabric. To eliminate this problem, once the needle has been reinserted in the fabric (**fig. 3**), slip the wrapped floss or ribbon gently down the needle until it rests against the fabric. Hold the wraps against the fabric and slowly pull the floss or ribbon through the wraps to the wrong side. This will cause the knot to be formed on the surface of the fabric and not float above it. Practice makes perfect and once this gorgeous stitch is mastered, you will find a million in one uses for it.

1. Bring the needle up through the fabric (**fig. 1**).

FIGURE 1

2. Hold the needle horizontally with one hand and wrap the ribbon around the needle with the other hand (**fig. 2**). If you are using a single strand of floss, one or two wraps will create a small knot. If you are making French knots with 2mm silk ribbon, the knot will be larger. As stated above, the size of the knot varies with the number of strands of floss or the width of the silk ribbon being used.

FIGURE 2

3. While holding the tail of the ribbon to prevent it from unwinding off the needle, bring the needle up into a vertical position and insert into the fabric just slightly beside where the needle came out of the fabric (**fig. 3**). Pull the ribbon or floss gently through the fabric while holding the tail with the other hand. ▨

FIGURE 3

Hand Stitched Leaves

This leaf is perfect for large flowers where a lazy daisy, Japanese, or straight stitch is inadequate. For best results, use a 7mm or wider ribbon.

1. Beginning with a flat ribbon about 6 inches long, fold down one side at a right angle and leave about a 3 inch tail (**fig.** 1). Fold the other side the same so that the two sides meet edge to edge (**fig.** 2).

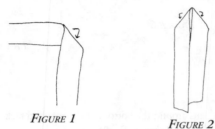

FIGURE 1   FIGURE 2

2. With a needle and thread, stitch across the flat edge of the ribbon. (**fig.** 3a) For a slightly different look using the same technique, simply wrap the ribbon across itself instead of meeting edge to edge and stitch across (**fig.** 3b).

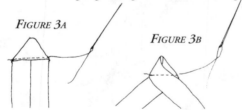

FIGURE 3A   FIGURE 3B

3. Pull the thread to gather the leaf. Wrap the thread around the stitching a couple of times to secure the gathers then insert the needle through the ribbon and tie a knot (**fig.** 4).

FIGURE 4

4. To apply the leaf to fabric, thread one of the dangling tails into a needle and insert into the fabric, pulling the ribbon to the back side. Repeat for the other tail and tie the tails together underneath. (**fig.** 5). You may apply these before or after making a flower. ▨

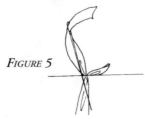

FIGURE 5

Herringbone Stitch

This beautiful line of stitching is a great decorative stitch. When doubled, this stitch becomes what Esther Randall calls a "Victorian stacking stitch". Use a 2mm ribbon for best results.

1. Bring the needle up at A. With the floss or ribbon on the right side of the fabric, make a long straight stitch from A to B (**fig.** 1). To practice, you may want to mark dots on your fabric and label each point until you get the hang of it.

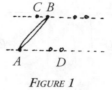

C B

A   D

FIGURE 1

2. Bring the needle up through the fabric at C and make another long straight stitch to D (**fig.** 2).

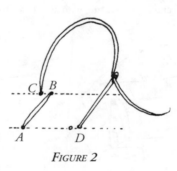

C B

A   D

FIGURE 2

3. Repeat steps 1 and 2 and continue the A, B, C, D pattern (**fig.** 3). Notice the sequence of overlaps; the current straight stitch overlaps the previous stitch. Also, notice that the crosses are high and low, not in the center. This is controlled by the distance set between points C and B and point A and D when bringing your needle up through the fabric for the next stitch. ▨

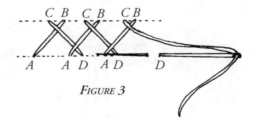

C B   C B   C B

A   A D A D   D

FIGURE 3

Hand Twisted Rose

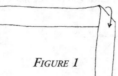

This rose adds a wonderful dimensional appearance to any floral design and can be made in a variety of sizes.

Use a 7mm or wider ribbon to make this rose.

1. Beginning with a flat piece of ribbon about 15 inches long, fold down about three inches at a right angle (**fig. 1**). Fold again, this time folding the ribbon back on itself. This will create a triangle in the corner (**fig. 2**)

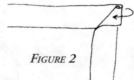

FIGURE 1   FIGURE 2

2. Place a pointed object such as the sharp tip of a chalk pencil or light colored pencil up through the "triangle" (**fig. 3**) and begin twisting with about two twists (**fig. 4**).

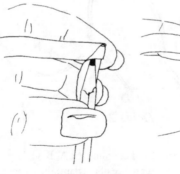

FIGURE 3   FIGURE 4

3. Begin folding the ribbon back while twisting the pencil (**fig. 5**). Continue folding and twisting until you have about 5 to 7 full twists for a full rose and about 4 twists for a small rosette.

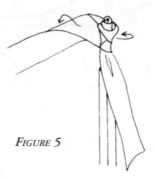

FIGURE 5

4. Remove the rose from the pencil and hold between your thumb and finger. Tack the bottom securely with a needle and thread, leaving the tails dangling (**fig. 6**). At this point you may apply the rose to your project or you may make a fuller rose by gathering about 1½ inch of the tail with a needle and thread (**fig. 7**).

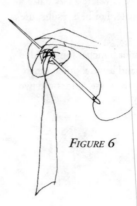

FIGURE 6

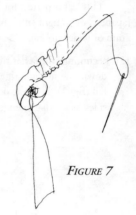

FIGURE 7

5. Wind this around the bottom of the rose and tack with the needle and thread (**fig. 8**).

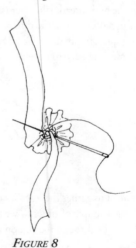

FIGURE 8

6. To apply the rose to fabric, thread one of the dangling tails into a needle and insert into the fabric, pulling the ribbon to the back side. Thread the other tail and insert underneath the rose into the fabric to the back side and tie the tails together (**fig. 9**). ▓

FIGURE 9

Japanese Ribbon Stitch

This stitch is simply a glorified straight stitch and may be used in as many variations. A rosebud is simply a Japanese ribbon stitch with straight stitches on both sides.

Use any size ribbon. Bring the needle up from under the fabric, loop it around and insert the needle down into the center of the ribbon a short distance in front of where the needle came up. Pull the ribbon so that the end curls in on itself loosely so that it does not disappear. ▓

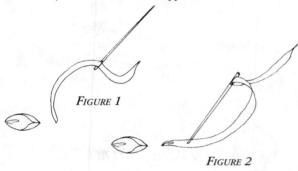

FIGURE 1

FIGURE 2

Leaf Ribbon Stitch

This versatile stitch is used for leaves and fern fronds. It also works well as leaves around small flowers or rosebuds.

1. Decide the length of the leaf or fern frond that you need and mark with a pencil or washout marker. As you begin to stitch, picture a leaf in your mind. It is narrow at the tip and becomes wider at the base. In order for the stitches to look like leaves or fern fronds, it will be necessary to gradually increase the width of the stitch.

2. Beginning at the top of the leaf, come up at A and go down at B. This will form a small straight stitch.

3. Come up at C and go down at D, bringing the needle out of the fabric at E and keeping D level with C.

4. Allow the needle to fall over the top of the ribbon loop.

5. Go down at F with a small straight stitch. This will anchor the stitch to the fabric.

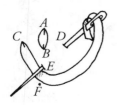

Lazy Daisy Stitch

This stitch is used in a variety of silk ribbon flowers and leaves. It is one of the most popular basic stitches.

1. Bring your needle up through the center point if you are stitching a flower, and up just next to a vine or flower for leaves. (fig. 1).

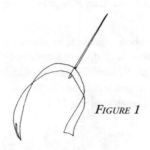

FIGURE 1

2. Insert the needle down into the same hole in which you came up. In the same stitch come through about $1/8$" to $3/8$" above that point (**fig. 2**). Wrap the ribbon behind the needle and pull the ribbon through, keeping the ribbon from twisting (**fig. 3**).

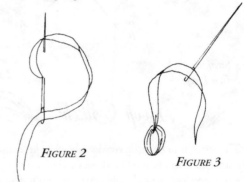

FIGURE 2

FIGURE 3

3. Insert the needle straight down into the same hole or very close to the same hole at the top of the loop (**fig. 4**). Notice in the side view of figure 4 that the needle goes down underneath the ribbon loop. The top view of figure 4 shows that the stitch is straight and will anchor the ribbon loop in place. ▓

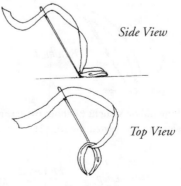

Side View

Top View

FIGURE 4

Loop Stitch French Knot

This is an unusual stitch that can be used as single flowers, grouped together, or as a filler.

1. Come up at A and make a loop. Hold the loop in place with a pin.

2. Wrap the ribbon around the needle two times. Insert the needle at B, close to the pin. Gently pull the two wraps down the needle until they rest on the fabric. Holding the ribbon tight, gently pull the needle through the fabric forming a French knot (**fig 1**). ▨

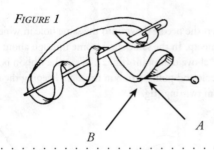

FIGURE 1

B   A

Straight Stitch Loop   *Japanese Loop*

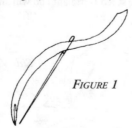

Loop Stitch

This stitch is to be made very loosely while keeping the ribbon straight. It can be used for daisies and bows or anywhere a loop look is needed. Experiment with different ribbon widths to achieve a variety of styles and uses.

Straight Stitch Method - Insert the needle up through the fabric and loop around away from you, inserting the needle just slightly beside where you came up (**fig. 1**).

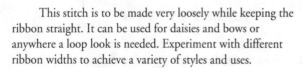

FIGURE 1

1. Pull the ribbon straight (without twists) and loosely adjust the loop to the desired size (**fig. 2**).

Straight Stitch Loop   FIGURE 2

Japanese Stitch Method - Insert the needle up through the fabric and this time loop it towards you, inserting the needle through the center of the ribbon just beside where the needle came up (**fig. 3**). Again, pull loosely while keeping the ribbon straight. ▨

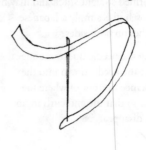

Japanese Loop

FIGURE 3

Loop Flower With French Knot

Pullen Knot

This stitch is a "mistake proof" stitch because it was created from an incorrectly formed French knot. It has proven to be a very versatile stitch that works great for floral clusters or simply as filler stitches. It adds so much depth and dimension to silk ribbon embroidery that you will find yourself using this stitch over and over again.

1. Bring the ribbon through the fabric at A and wrap the ribbon around the needle. The number of wraps depends on the size knot desired. Usually, from one to seven wraps is all that is needed. If you want a larger knot, simply use a larger ribbon. If you are doing a large number of wraps on the needle, it may be necessary to anchor the knot in place with monafilament thread after it is formed. The most important thing to remember about this knot is that all wraps must be kept loose on the needle.

2. Insert the needle into the fabric at B. When inserting the needle into the fabric, bring the needle as close to A as possible, but do not pierce the ribbon coming out at A. Pull the ribbon through the fabric but avoid pulling the stitch tight. The ribbon should be loose so that the knot appears to float on the fabric. ▨

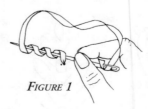

FIGURE 1   FIGURE 2

Pistil Stitch

This stitch may be used to form groups of flowers, flower centers, or grass.

1. Come up at A. Allow a short length of the ribbon to extend above A. Keep the ribbon flat and taut (**fig. 1**).

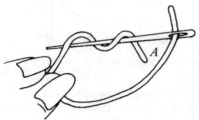

FIGURE 1

2. Wrap the ribbon around the needle two times. Insert the needle at B, gently pull the wrapped ribbon down the needle until it rests against the fabric. Hold the ribbon taut as you pull the needle through the fabric forming a two wrap French knot (**fig. 2**).

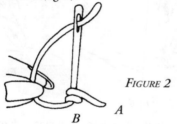

FIGURE 2

FINISHED STITCH

Pansy

A few pearls or a French knot in the center this flower will provide color, coverage and dimension. It is made by hand first and then tacked onto the fabric with a needle and thread. Four mm or wider ribbon works best.

1. Begin with a flat piece of ribbon 2$^1/_2$ inches long. Fold one end at a right angle and stitch across the edge with a needle and thread. Fold the end. (**fig. 1**).

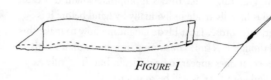

FIGURE 1

2. Pull the thread tightly to gather the ribbon (**fig. 2**)

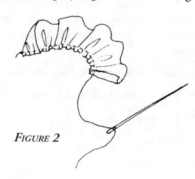

FIGURE 2

3. Curl the ribbon around so that the ends overlap. Tack the center with a couple of stitches to secure it and tie a knot (**fig. 3**). Tack to the fabric with thread and cover the center with pearls or a French knot. ❖

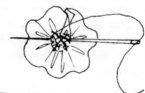

FIGURE 3

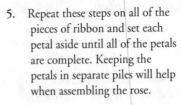

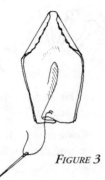

4. Make a tuck in the bottom at the raw edges of the ribbon and tack to secure (**fig. 3**).

5. Repeat these steps on all of the pieces of ribbon and set each petal aside until all of the petals are complete. Keeping the petals in separate piles will help when assembling the rose.

FIGURE 3

Petal by Petal Rose

This graceful, lifelike rose is appropriately named because each petal is literally made individually by hand before it is assembled into a rose. Janet Hyde taught me how to make this rose and though it is time consuming, it is more than worth the patience. It does appear to be difficult, but, it is truly easy to make and your friends will be so impressed.

This requires a 32mm ribbon. The petals vary in length and are prepared individually and then assembled from the smallest petals to the largest petals. A green wire edged ribbon bow is stitched to the bottom. Green silk leaves may be used instead of a bow.

Cut pieces of ribbon according to the following measurements.

3 - 3" pieces (these will be the center)

5 - 3$\frac{1}{2}$" pieces

5 - 4" pieces

5 - 4$\frac{1}{2}$" pieces

5 - 5" pieces

5 - 5$\frac{1}{2}$" pieces

Petal Directions

1. Fold the cut piece of ribbon in half and secure with a pin.

2. Fold in the corner of the folded end at an angle and roll toward the center of the ribbon (**fig. 1**). Whipstitch the roll in place, being careful to pick up only a thread or two so that the stitching does not show through to the other side of the petal (**fig. 2**).

3. Repeat this for the other corner so that the top of the petal is pointed (**fig. 3**).

Assembling the Petals

1. Start with the smallest petal (this will be a 3" one) and curl it inward with the stitching to the inside. With a needle and thread, take a couple of tacking stitches and wrap the thread around the bottom to secure the curl (**fig. 4**).

2. Wrap another 3" piece around the curled petal and tack at the bottom (**fig. 5**). Complete the center by wrapping and tacking the last 3" piece.

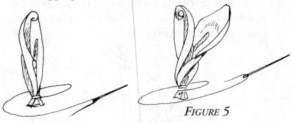

FIGURE 4   FIGURE 5

3. Continue layering and wrapping each of the 3$\frac{1}{2}$" petals (**fig. 6**). When the last 3$\frac{1}{2}$" petal is used, begin wrapping the 4" petals, then the 4$\frac{1}{2}$" petals, then the 5" petals, finishing with the 5$\frac{1}{2}$" petals and tacking as you go until they are all stitched together. When all the petals are stitched, take several stitches through all of the layers and then wind the thread around the bottom to secure.

4. At this point green silk leaves can be stitched to the bottom or a green wire ribbon bow can be tacked to the bottom as we have done on the sample (**fig. 7**). ▨

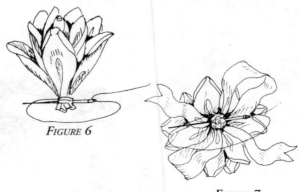

FIGURE 6   FIGURE 7

Fold

Wrong Side

FIGURE 1

FIGURE 2

Ruching

Ruching is an age old technique seen on many antique garments. Most often strips of fabric were pleated, fluted, or gathered to embellish women's and children's clothing. What we know as "puffing" was actually called ruching in the old days. In France, as ribbon became popular, it was used to adorn clothing as well. The ribbon was gathered or pleated and stitched directly on top of the garments since the edges were finished and raveling was not a concern. This particular "applied" type of ruching is the technique we use with silk ribbon.

1. On a flat strip of 7mm or wider silk ribbon, run straight stitching, by hand or by machine, down the length of the ribbon to be gathered in a back and forth, zigzag direction (**fig. 1**). If hand stitching, it helps if you have a long beading needle, because you can get more tiny stitches on the needle before you have to pull the thread through.

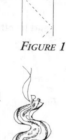

FIGURE 1

2. Once stitching is complete, pull the thread to gather the silk ribbon (**fig. 2**). Gather as loosely or tightly as desired and tack with needle and thread or glue to project.

FIGURE 2

3. For a ruched carnation, simply coil the ruching. Gather the center tighter and loosen the gathering as you complete the outer petals (**fig. 3**), tacking with needle and thread as you coil.

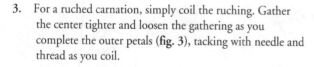

FIGURE 3

4. For a ruched iris, roll the ruching up until you have rolled about five scallops. Pull two scallops up and three scallops down and wrap with thread. Tack to project and flare the petals (**fig 4**). ▨

FIGURE 4

Satin Stitch

The satin stitch is used to fill in an area with color by using heavy ribbon coverage. All of the stitches line up in the same direction creating a smooth, sometimes shiny appeal when it catches the light, looking like satin. To fill a given area takes patience because it is a slow moving stitch; the end result, however, is very pleasing.

1. It generally helps if you have the area to be filled traced on the project so that you have two definite lines to guide and maintain the varying width of the stitch as it fills different shapes. Secure in an embroidery hoop.

2. Begin at one end and work the needle from one side to the other, stacking the thread up just below and next to the previous stitch (**fig 1**). Continue this wrapping process, keeping the fabric secured and taut while the stitches are pulled with light tension so that the fabric will not tunnel. ▨

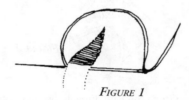

FIGURE 1

Running Stitch

1. Working from right to left, come up at A and go down at B.

2. Come up again at C making small, even stitches while working the needle into and out of the fabric. It is important that the stitches be kept the same length and that the distance between each space be consistent. ▨

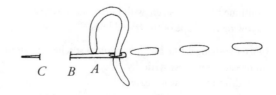

FIGURE 1

Silk Ribbon Weaving

Nothing is more elegant than a ribbon weave. Weaving ribbon adds surface interest to floral wreaths, and it's the perfect stitch to make baskets for silk arrangements. This technique is very easy and can be stitched in any shape. It is always done first, before the flowers are stitched.

Any size ribbon will make a weave, of course, it all depends on the size of your weaving shape. Once you get the hang of it, try different colors and different sizes together.

1. Trace the shape of the weave on the fabric. Begin at the top or the bottom of the shape and work to the other end. Bring the needle up through the fabric on one side of the traced line and insert it down through the fabric on the other side into the traced line (**fig 1**). Keep the ribbon completely flat and smooth. If fraying occurs switch to a bigger needle.

Front of weave

FIGURE 1

2. Make the next stitch come up through the fabric next to the last inserted stitch (**fig. 2**) so that the back side becomes simply an outline of the shape and not covered with ribbon (**fig. 3**). In other words you will not carry the ribbon across the back side of the fabric. When bringing the needle up for another stitch allow room for the ribbon width. You want the ribbon edges to touch but not to overlap.

Leave space between stitches

FIGURE 2

Back of weave

FIGURE 3

3. Continue filling the shape with horizontal stitches following the shape of the traced lines.

4. Once the shape is filled with horizontal stitches, it is time to repeat the process vertically, only this time you will weave the ribbon through the horizontal ribbons before you insert the needle on the other side (**fig. 4**).

FIGURE 4

5. Tie off when complete and embellish the edges with flowers and leaves. ▩

 ## Spider Web Rose

This rose is one of the prettiest and easiest of all the silk ribbon stitched roses. Use 13mm for large puffy roses, 7mm for medium roses, and 4mm for small roses. The spokes or "legs" on the spider will be shorter for 4mm ribbon than for 7mm ribbon. You will gain a good judgement for this after you have stitched a few roses and played with the different sizes.

Begin with a five legged "spider," or five spokes, stitched with either a single strand or a double strand of embroidery floss. For larger roses use a double strand. It may be helpful to mark a center with five evenly spaced dots around it using a washout pen or pencil as you are learning to make this rose.

1. To stitch the spider, come up from the bottom of the fabric with your needle through dot "a" then down in the center dot "b" (**fig. 1**). Come up through "c" then down in "b" (**fig. 2**). Continue around; up in "d" down in "b", up in "e" down in "b" etc… until the spider is complete and tie off underneath (**fig. 3**).

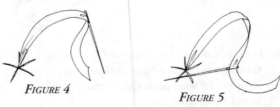

FIGURE 1   FIGURE 2   FIGURE 3

2. Now, with your silk ribbon, insert the needle up through the center "b" (**fig. 4**). Slide the needle under a spoke or "spider leg" and pull ribbon through loosely (**fig. 5**).

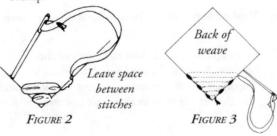

FIGURE 4   FIGURE 5

3. Skipping **over** the next spoke go **under** the third spoke (**fig. 6**) and begin weaving in a circle over and under every other spoke (**fig. 7**).

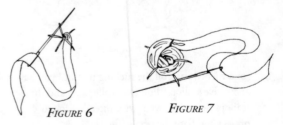

FIGURE 6   FIGURE 7

4. Continue weaving until the spokes are covered. Insert the needle underneath the last "petal" and pull through to the back.

You may stitch leaves first and then stitch the rose on top, or you may bring your needle up from underneath a "petal" and stitch leaves under the rose. ▩

Split Stitch

This stitch is a very old embroidery stitch. It is customarily made using floss or a slightly heavier thread. It works well with silk ribbon.

1. Come up at A and go down at B, making a small backward stitch (**fig.1**).

2. Come up at C piercing the ribbon in the center (**fig. 1**). ▓

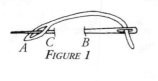

FIGURE 1   FIGURE 2

Stem/Outline Stitch

Worked from left to right, this stitch makes a line of slanting stitches. The thread is kept to the left and below the needle. Make small, even stitches. The needle is inserted just below the line to be followed, comes out to the left of the insertion point, and above the line, slightly.

1. Come up from behind at A and go down into the fabric again at B (**fig. 1**). This is a little below the line. Come back up a C (**fig. 1**). This is a little above the line. Keep the thread below the needle.

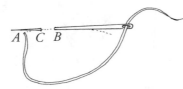

FIGURE 1

2. Go back down into the fabric at D and come up a little above the line at B (**fig. 2**).

FIGURE 2

3. Continue working, always keeping the thread below the needle (**fig. 3**). ▓

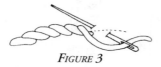

FIGURE 3

Straight Stitch

This stitch is used for almost everything. By itself or in combination with other stitches it becomes leaves, flowers, stems, vines, rose buds, and more. Use any size ribbon. Narrow ribbons are good for vines, stems and tiny leaves, while wide ribbons are great for flower petals and big leaves.

Simply bring the needle up from under the fabric and insert it down into the fabric a short distance in front of where the needle came up. It is an in–and–out stitch. Remember to pull the ribbon loosely for nice full stitches. ▓

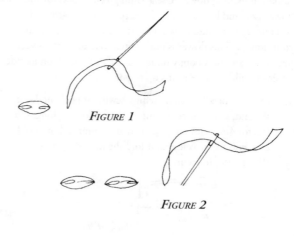

FIGURE 1

FIGURE 2

Twisted Loop

This stitch can be used to form loop flowers or as a filler. It will add dimension to any design you choose to use it on.

1. Come up at A and twist the ribbon (**fig. 1**).

2. Insert the needle at B and pull through the fabric, holding the loop in place with your thumb (**fig. 1**).

3. Insert the needle from the back at C, piercing the ribbon slightly above B (**fig. 2**).

4. Holding the loop in place with your thumb or a laying tool, make the next loop, being careful not to pull the previous loops out of shape (**fig. 3**). ▓

FIGURE 1   FIGURE 2   FIGURE 3

Sweet Pea

Here is dainty little flower to add to your floral bouquet. This one is so fun to make and can be made with several sizes of ribbon. Again, it is an individually hand–made flower that is later stitched to the project. The stitching on this flower is covered by the stem.

Sizes 7mm and 13mm ribbon are easiest to handle; however, for tiny projects a 4mm works well and looks like a blossom. For very large projects, a 32mm will create a huge carnation looking flower. Use a 7mm green ribbon for the flower base and leaves. Since sweet peas actually grow on vines you may want to stitch a wrapped stitch vine before adding your flowers. This flower is not limited to being just a sweet pea, it can also be a poppy on its side or a carnation on its side by simply adding a stem. It's up to you.

1. Thread a needle with matching sewing thread and knot the end. Cut a piece of 7mm ribbon about 7" long. Use less for 4mm ribbon and more for 13mm ribbon. Fold each end to the center and fold the raw edges down (**fig. 1**). Pin to secure.

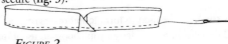

FIGURE 1   Back of flower

2. With tiny stitches, run a gathering stitch across the bottom through both layers (**fig. 2**). Pull the thread to gather the ribbon and take a couple of tack stitches to secure (**fig. 3**).

FIGURE 2

FIGURE 3

3. Place on the fabric with the folded edges to the back and tack stitch to secure (**fig. 4**).

FIGURE 4

4. Thread a 7mm green ribbon and make a straight stitch wrapping over the bottom of the flower to cover the tack stitches (**fig. 5**). This will also hold the sides of the flower up. Add leaves to complete. ▩

FIGURE 5

174

Tulip

With the appearance of tulips in the spring, everyone realizes that winter is almost over and the renewal of life is about to begin. Tulips are easy to make with silk ribbon. They are made using straight stitches and Japanese ribbon stitches. You may want to review these two stitches before beginning your tulips.

1. With a 4mm or 7 mm ribbon, start by taking two small horizontal straight stitches (**fig. 1**).

FIGURE 1

2. Bring the needle up below and to the center of the previous stitches and make a vertical Japanese ribbon stitch to the left (**fig. 2**). Come up in the same center point and make another vertical Japanese ribbon stitch to the right (**fig. 3**).

FIGURE 2   FIGURE 3

3. Bring the needle up, once again, through the same center point and make a Japanese ribbon stitch between and on top of the two previous stitches (**fig. 4**).

FIGURE 4

4. Add a stalk and long straight stitch leaves to complete this beautiful spring flower ee finished drawing at top of page). ▩

Wrapped Stitch or Whipped Straight Stitch

This is a very effective stitch to use as a filler or to form stems for vines and flowers, seeds, small buds, or roses. It is a simple stitch but will add so much to the overall look of the design.

Single

1. Keep the ribbon flat.

2. Come up at A, go down at B, making a straight stitch the length needed.

3. Bring the needle up again at A. The straight stitch just made should be flat on the fabric but not tight (**fig.** 1).

FIGURE 1

4. Slip the needle underneath the ribbon (**fig.** 1), making sure that you do not catch the fabric with the needle, gently pulling the ribbon around the straight stitch previously made. Do not allow the ribbon to twist (**fig.** 2).

FIGURE 2

5. The number of wraps will depend on the desired effect you want your design to have and the length of your straight stitch. Most of the stitches are wrapped 2 or 3 times. If you want a thicker wrapped stitch, simply wrap more times (**fig.** 3).

FIGURE 3

6. To tie off the stitch, slip the needle through the fabric to the wrong side and tie off.

Curved Whip Stitch

This simple stitch works wonders when used in a silk ribbon project.

1. Keep the ribbon flat. Come up at A, go down at B, making a straight stitch the length needed.

2. Bring the needle up again at A. The straight stitch just made should be flat on the fabric but not tight (**fig.** l).

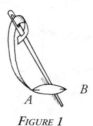

FIGURE 1

3. Slip the needle underneath the ribbon at b, making sure that you do not catch the fabric with the needle. Gently pull the ribbon around the straight stitch just made, pulling in the direction of a. Wrap the stitch two or three times inserting the needle under b and coming out at a. Make sure that you "squeeze" the stitch to make it curve (**fig.** 2).

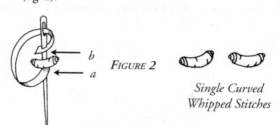

FIGURE 2

Single Curved Whipped Stitches

Interlocking Curved Whipped Stitch

The interlocking curved whipped stitch is referred to in several of the designs in this book. As you see, this simply means that the stitches will face each other like puzzle pieces that are being fitted together.

Interlocking Curved Whipped Stitches

Whipped Running Stitch

This stitch is used for vines, stems and stalks.

Use a 2mm or 4mm ribbon. You may also use embroidery floss.

1. Stitch a line of straight stitches along the design line (**fig. 1**). Refer to straight stitch instructions.

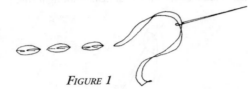

FIGURE 1

2. Bring the needle up at the end of the line of straight stitching (**fig. 2**).

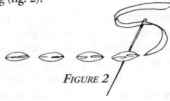

FIGURE 2

3. Begin wrapping the ribbon under and around the straight stitches (**fig. 3**). ▓

FIGURE 3

Wisteria

This blossom is simply a cluster of colonial or French knots arranged in a loose triangular shape. Keep in mind that wisteria grows on a vine. So, stitch the vine first and add the blossoms and leaves later.

1. It is a good idea to mark dots on your fabric to create the shape of the cluster when you are learning to make this blossom (**fig. 1**). Once comfortable with the concept, dots are no longer needed as a guide.

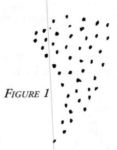

FIGURE 1

2. Refer to the French knot or colonial knot instructions if necessary. Starting at the top of the blossom (this is the thickest part of the cluster), stitch plump knots by wrapping the needle two or three times with a colonial knot and four or five times with a French knot. As you work down the cluster, reduce the number of wraps to two and three. As you reach the bottom, the last three or four knots should be wrapped once or twice (**fig. 2**).

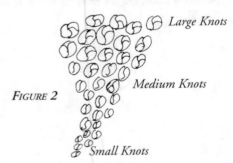

Large Knots

Medium Knots

FIGURE 2

Small Knots

This blossom can also be made entirely out of the same size knot. Try both ways and choose your favorite method.

3. To complete the blossom, add a small twisted straight stitch stem and a couple of Japanese ribbon stitch leaves. ▓

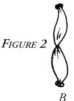

Twisted Chain

To create a truly luscious rosebud, use 7mm ribbon and this stitch. The wrapped effect it gives makes the rosebud more realistic. When making large roses, this stitch and 7mm ribbon used to form leaves will prevent the leaves from becoming lost in the design. It truly is a versatile stitch that you will find hundreds of uses for.

1. Bring the ribbon or floss up at A and form a loop (**fig. 1**).

FIGURE 1

2. Hold the loop in place and insert the needle through the fabric at B, slightly to the left of A and out at C (**fig. 2**). Make sure that the ribbon or floss is underneath the needle at C. ▩

FIGURE 2

Straight Stitch Rose

A straight stitch rose is simple and easy to make. Refer to the instructions given for a straight stitch in this section.

1. Work 3 French knots or Colonial knots in the center (**fig. 1**).

2. Work a 3 straight stitches in a triangle around the center French knots. The straight stitches need to partially cover the stitch before (**fig. 2**).

3. Continue making rows of straight stitches being careful to overlap the stitches slightly as you work around the rose. The size of the rose is determined by the number of rows worked (**fig. 3**). ▩

FIGURE 1   *FIGURE 2*

FIGURE 3

Stem Stitch Rose

A stem stitch rose is a quick and easy flower to make. The rose begins with French knots in the center. The rows of stitches that follow are simple stem stitches worked in a circle. The more rows of stem stitches worked, of course, the larger the rose will be. You may shade this rose by making each row of stitches a lighter color. It will give the flower a more realistic look. As you stitch, you will notice the stitches are overlapping each other filling in all areas.

1. Work a small cluster of French knots for the center of the rose. You may want to review the French knot instructions given in this section (**fig. 1**).

2. Begin the first row of the rose by working loose stem stitches counter clockwise around the knot. Bring the ribbon up at A, insert the needle in at B and out again at C, making sure that the ribbon or floss is underneath the needle (**fig. 2**).

3. The stem stitches will need to be made longer with each round of stitches that you make. ▩

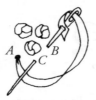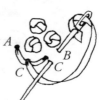

FIGURE 1   *FIGURE 2*

Twisted Straight Stitch

This stitch makes a lovely addition to the normal straight stitch and the only difference is a deliberate twist in the ribbon. Let your imagination dictate where to put this stitch.

1. Following the instructions given for the straight stitch, bring the ribbon up at A and twist it one time, going back into the fabric at b (**fig. 1**).

2. Allow the twisted straight stitch to sit on top of the fabric. If pulled tightly against the fabric, you will loose the curl of the ribbon (**fig. 2**).

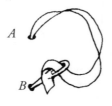

FIGURE 1   *FIGURE 2*

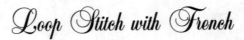

Loop Stitch with French Knot Anchor

This stitch is one of the more versatile stitches in silk ribbon embroidery because of its many uses. If using larger ribbon, the ribbon takes on the look of a bow. If you want to make a stem of flowers, it will work for the flowers on either side of the stem. It is also great used simply as a filler.

1. Following the instructions for the loop stitch, complete the loop of ribbon (**fig. 1**). Make sure that you keep the loop larger than normal.

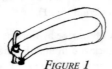

FIGURE 1

2. Flatten the loop until it is centered between A and B. Bring the needle up between A and B, piercing the flat ribbon (**fig. 2**).

FIGURE 2

3. Using the instructions for a French knot, work a single wrap French knot in the center of the ribbon (**fig. 3**).

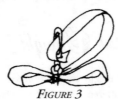

FIGURE 3

4. Pull the French knot until it rests tightly against the ribbon. The French knot serves as an anchor for the ribbon loop (**fig. 4**). ▨

FIGURE 4

Twisted Chain Stitch Rose

This stitch makes a beautiful rose that makes one feel they are looking down on the rose. If you need a quick and easy rose for a project, this would be the stitch to use. Keep in mind that when a rose opens, the center is always tighter than the last row of petals. As you finish the center stitches of the rose, the stitches should gradually become looser as you progress to the outer row of petals. The size of the rose is determined by the number of rows worked.

1. Work a French knot or colonial knot in the center.

2. Come up at A beside the knot and wrap the ribbon around the know counterclockwise (**fig. l**). Remember, when beginning a stitch, stay as close to the previous petal as you can to avoid holes in the flower. Insert the needle at B, close to the knot and take a small stitch coming up at C, next to the knot (**fig. l**).

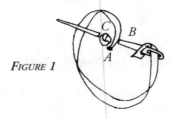

FIGURE 1

3. Pull your ribbon toward yourself until taut. Wrap the ribbon around the knot counterclockwise. Repeat the instructions given in step 2 for stitches 2 and 3 (**fig. 2**).

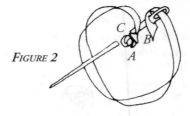

FIGURE 2

4. Continue working the stitches in a circle until you have the size rose desired (**fig. 3**).

5. To complete the last stitch, pierce the fabric angling the needle toward the rose. ▨

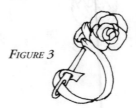

FIGURE 3

Preparing To Smock

Needles

Generally, a #8 crewel embroidery needle is used in smocking. If you are using silk ribbon, please refer to "Tips for Smocking with Silk Ribbon."

For smockers with bad vision, it may not be comfortable to thread a #8 crewel needle with three or four strands of embroidery floss. If this is the case, use a #6 or #7 crewel needle.

 # 6 CREWEL

Some needles work better for certain fabrics. For example:

a. For fine batiste or batiste blends, use a #8 or #9 crewel needle. Use a smaller size when using fewer strands of floss.

b. For fine to medium fabrics, such as broadcloth or quilting fabric, use a #7 or #8 crewel needle.

 # 8 CREWEL

c. Personal preference for some smockers is to use a milliner's needles. These needles are long and have a straight needle eye opening. Other smockers prefer to use #7 darners or #7 long darners.

#7 DARNER

Needles also have a right and wrong side. Think about sewing machine needles that only go in one way. If you have difficulty threading a needle, flip it to the other side. One side will usually thread more easily than the other. ▨

Embroidery Floss

The general rule of thumb is to use three strands of embroidery floss when working with fine to medium fabrics.

THREE STRANDS OF FLOSS

However, there are exceptions:

a. For a different look with fine fabrics, try using two strands. It is pretty and delicate.

TWO STRANDS OF FLOSS

b. For picture smocking, most designers recommend four strands.

FOUR STRANDS OF FLOSS

c. For some heavier fabrics, such as corduroy and velveteen, use up to five or six strands. Experiment with heavier fabrics to find the right weight of floss for the desired look.

FIVE STRANDS OF FLOSS   *SIX STRANDS OF FLOSS*

d. It is perfectly acceptable to use #8 perle cotton for smocking.

e. In order to prepare your embroidery floss for smocking, you must first make sure that it is put on grain properly. All thread has a grain. With DMC floss, it is easy to make sure the floss is on grain properly. Look at the two paper wraps on the embroidery floss. One has the round DMC symbol. The other has the color number and a picture of two hands pulling the floss out of the package. Follow these directions. Place your left hand on the floss, and with your right hand, pull the floss out of the package. Always knot the end that you cut. If I am smocking, I separate all six strands, put back together the number of strands needed for my project and knot those ends. I put the other strands back together and mark the ends to be knoted. If I have the correct number of strands for another needle, I will knot them at this time. If I do not have enough strands for another needle, I mark the end to be knotted.

f.   If for some reason you forget which end you cut and therefore, which end to knot, here is a simple solution. One end of the floss "blooms" more than the other. The cut end of the floss does not fuzz out as much. The knot will go on the less fuzzy end. ✻

Fabric

Some favorite fabrics to smock are the blends of 65 percent polyester and 35 percent cotton. Sometimes, a higher polyester count does not pleat well. However, using all of the half spaces of the pleater, we have pleated lingerie - 100 percent nylon - without a pucker. Ginghams, Pima cottons, 100 percent cottons for quilting, challis, Swiss batiste, velveteen, soft corduroy, and silks are also good for smocking. Fabrics, such as calico prints, which are 100 percent cotton, should be washed and dried before pleating. Fabrics with a polyester content generally do not shrink, and thus do not need to be washed prior to pleating. It is not necessary to preshrink Imperial batiste, Imperial broadcloth, 100 percent cotton Swiss batiste, wool challis from Switzerland, and velveteen.

> **Note:** When a 45 inch piece of fabric is necessary for the front and back of a yoke dress, it is easier to tear these skirt lengths first and preshrink them separately. Then, preshrink the remaining fabric from which the bodice, sleeves, and collars will be cut. It is easier to preshrink and put fabric "on grain" in smaller pieces. ✻

Putting Fabric On Grain

Follow these directions for putting fabric on grain.

Tear both ends. Most fabric stores tear wovens (**fig. 1**).

Snip Fabric   FIGURE 1   *Tear*

Or, pull a thread and clip across from selvage to selvage. I always do this on Swiss batiste (**fig. 2**).

Pulling Thread and Cutting

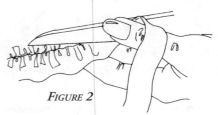

FIGURE 2

Fabric may be preshrunk after having "torn" or "pulled a thread" and cut the fabric. ✻

Tying Off Pleating Threads Before Smocking

Much of the fitting is done before any smocking is done. Measure the piece to which the smocking is to be attached. A good rule of thumb to follow is to fit the pleated piece to the yoke and then tie off the pleating threads. If you will get in the habit of blocking your pleated fabric before smocking, you will find that the piece will stay more true to size.

Figure 3 is an example to show that the whole skirt will be used in the smocked garment.

FIGURE 3

This is a "longish" yoke dress where the whole 45" gathered skirt will be used in the garment. Tie off the skirt gathering threads before smocking so that the top of the skirt matches the bottom of the yoke. In regular smocking, if you are a loose smocker, it is acceptable to tie off the skirt from 1" to $1^1/2$" smaller than the yoke to which it will be attached after the smocking is completed.

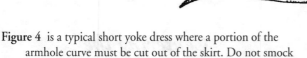

Figure 4 is a typical short yoke dress where a portion of the armhole curve must be cut out of the skirt. Do not smock that portion.

Draw the armholes and remove the pleating threads from the area that will be cut away. Tie off so that the area between the armholes will fit the bottom of the yoke. Smock before cutting out the armholes.

FIGURE 4

This rule is sometimes called "smocking to size." It is a must to size the pleating before beginning to smock. If this rule is not followed, the smocking will have to be stretched too much to fit the dress. This excess stretching will cause ripples and waves at the yoke after the dress is constructed. I suppose that the opposite could be true (smocking too loosely); however, I have never found beginning smockers to smock too loosely.

The width of fabric, before being pleated, should be three times as wide as the finished smocked piece will be. A little more or a little less fullness is acceptable. ▩

Right and Wrong Side of Pleated Fabric

Pleated fabric has a right and wrong side. The secret to figuring out which side of the fabric to smock, assuming that the fabric does not already have a designated right or wrong side, is easy to remember - **Long is Wrong.**

Stretch out the pleated fabric (**fig. 5**). Look at the length of stitches on both sides. The flat stitches are longer on one side than they are on the other . This is the wrong side. The right side of the fabric, the side to be smocked, has the shorter stitches (**fig. 6**). Hence, the rule - **Long is Wrong.**

"Long Is Wrong"

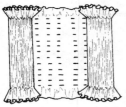

FIGURE 5

Roll the fabric down to see which side has the long sitches

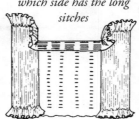

FIGURE 6

Another way to determine the right and wrong side of the pleated fabric is by the height of the pleats. Flip the pleated fabric back and forth to see which side has the tallest pleats from the gathering row up to the top of the pleat. The right side of the pleated fabric has the tallest pleats.

When running fabric through the pleater, the right side of the fabric should face the floor or the bottom of the pleater. If you are using a fabric with a designated right or wrong side (corduroy or printed fabric), run it through the pleater with the right side facing down to the floor. ▩

Tying Off Gathering Threads Before Smocking

After opening the pleated fabric to the desired width, it is time to tie off the excess gathering threads (**fig. 7**).

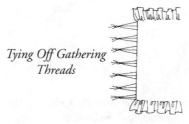

How do you tie off?

FIGURE 7

Tie off as many threads as is comfortable. I usually work with three threads (**fig. 8**).

Tying Off Gathering Threads

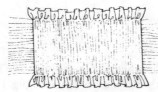

FIGURE 8

It is not necessary to tie off gathering threads at all. Many smockers will work with them hanging long. As a beginner, you might find that the long hanging threads tangle. If so, tie them.

It is hard to keep the spongy quilting thread from coming untied. I find that a surgical knot does the trick. ▩

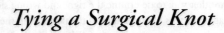

Tying a Surgical Knot

1. Tie one knot. Do not take this first knot down to the fabric, but leave it about one inch away from the fabric edge (**fig. 9**).

FIGURE 9

2. Hold the knot with your right hand. Wrap the left hand strings around the knot one more time (**figs. 10 and 11**). Reverse if you are left handed.

| FIGURE 10 | FIGURE 11 |

3. Tie one more knot, just like the first one (**fig. 12**). This last knot is pulled tightly for a very tight knot (**fig. 13**).

| FIGURE 12 | FIGURE 13 |

4. Clip off the excess threads after tying the knot. Clip the threads to within two inches of the knot. ▧

Centering the Smocking Design

The easiest way to mark the center of the fabric is to fold it in half and mark before pleating. Counting the pleats to determine the center will also work. There are two methods of centering the smocking.

• *Method One*

1. Begin smocking in the exact center of the skirt or dress. Tie knots at this point, as if this were the left hand side of the smocking.

2. Knot the floss. Bring it in on the left hand side of the middle pleat of the skirt. Smock half the skirt to the right side.

3. Turn the work upside down. Smock the other side, working from the middle to the other side.

• *Method Two*

This method avoids the two knots on the center pleats (**fig. 14**).

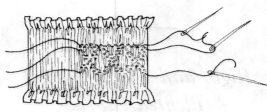

FIGURE 14

1. Leave a long thread with the first stitch.

2. Take this first stitch from the front of the smocking. Do not bring the thread from the back. Leave your long, unknotted thread hanging on the front.

3. Smock all the way over to the right and tie off.

4. Turn the work upside down. Re-thread the long thread. Finish the first stitch you started. Smock the rest of the work to the other side. ▧

Crazy Cat and the Courthouse Story

Many beginner smockers get frustrated with the rule: When you move up, the thread is down, when you move down, the thread is up. For a beginner, this is the most difficult concept to learn. I made up a simple, and very silly, story to help beginners remember this principle. I was a little embarrassed the first time I told the story, but several years and smockers later, I can honestly say the story works.

> **Setting** - a courthouse with lots of tall steps leading to the door

> **Characters** - A Tabby cat with a very long tail, and Martha Pullen

> **Time** - During business hours

Tabby Cat wants to drive a car and knows she must first have a driver's license. Martha Pullen drives Tabby Cat to the courthouse and parks at the side of the building to let Tabby Cat out. Tabby Cat climbs the long steps until she gets almost to the top. There, she remembers that you have to have money to pay for a license. Tabby Cat turns around, climbs down the long flight of steps and goes back to the car to get some money from her purse.

• *Important Points To This Story:*

Point A. Tabby Cat's tail is the thread.

Point B. When Tabby Cat climbs the stairs, her tail points downward (**fig. 15**).

In smocking, when the needle is moving up, the tail of the thread is down.

Point C. When Tabby Cat climbs down the steep stairs, her tail points upward (**fig. 16**).

In smocking, when you are moving to take a stitch downward, the tail of the thread is up.

Point D. When Tabby Cat turns around at the top of stairs, at the landing, her tail swings around before she can begin to climb back down the stairs. This symbolizes a top cable before the wave or trellis moves downward. When Tabby Cat turns around at the bottom of the stairs to begin upward, this symbolizes a bottom cable before the climb back up. ▨

FIGURE 15

FIGURE 16

Bringing in the Needle to Begin Smocking

There are two schools of thought on where to make the first stitch.

Method One

1. Bring in the needle on the left hand side of the first pleat that begins your smocking (**fig. 17**).

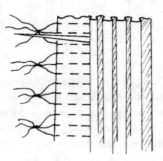

FIGURE 17

2. Bring in the needle just above the gathering thread (**fig. 18**).

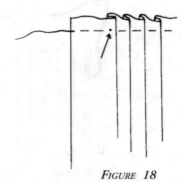

FIGURE 18

3. It is acceptable to bring in the needle in the same hole as the gathering thread, on this left side of the pleat.

4. This method leaves the knot of the floss hidden within the first pleat on the back of the smocking.

183

Method Two

1. Bring in the needle on the left hand side of the second pleat, rather than on the left hand side of the first pleat (**fig. 19**). Pull the thread through (**fig. 20a**).

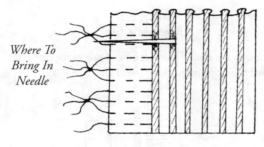

Where To Bring In Needle

FIGURE 19

2. Go through the gathering holes of the first pleat to bring the needle out of the left hand side of the first pleat where smocking begins. This hides the knot in the second pleat and is stronger and more secure. The knot will less likely pull out with wear and washing since it is one pleat over from the edge of the smocking (**fig. 20b**). ▓

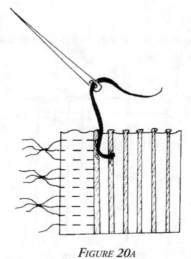

FIGURE 20A

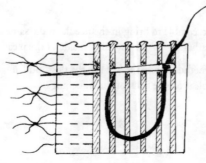

FIGURE 20B

Stitch Bite

Nearly all smocking books advise picking up from $^1/_3$ to $^1/_2$ of the pleat above the pleating threads (**fig. 21**).

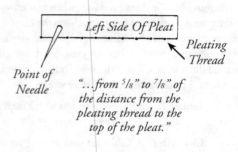

Left Side Of Pleat

Pleating Thread

Point of Needle

"…from $^5/_8$" to $^7/_8$" of the distance from the pleating thread to the top of the pleat."

FIGURE 21

I have tried my best to figure out how there is enough space using a #8 crewel embroidery needle to pick up $^1/_3$ of the space above the gathering threads, when there is only about $^1/_{16}$ of an inch in that distance. A #8 crewel needle is almost that wide.

I suggest picking up $^5/_8$ to $^7/_8$ of the distance from the gathering thread to the top of the pleat. Some people may pick up as little as $^1/_2$ of the pleat above the gathering row. ▓

Tangled Thread

Your thread may become tangled after making some stitches. There are several ways to fix this. Hold the smocking over, so that the threaded needle can hang loose. Let the thread untangle by twirling around until it stops (**fig. 22**).

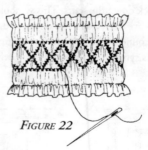

FIGURE 22

With the needle still threaded, push the needle all the way down to the fabric. Separate the strands of floss, untangling them all the way down to the needle. After separating

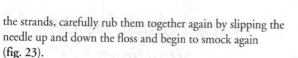

the strands, carefully rub them together again by slipping the needle up and down the floss and begin to smock again (**fig. 23**).

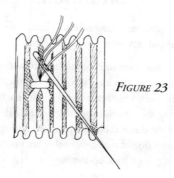

FIGURE 23

Some people use beeswax for smocking. It does help to keep threads from tangling, somewhat. Be aware that beeswax may compress the threads more than you like (**fig. 24**).

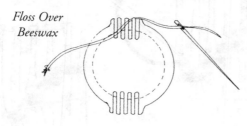

Floss Over Beeswax

FIGURE 24

I think a better substitute for beeswax is to run the threads (already threaded and knotted) over a dry bar of Ivory Soap. This gives a little lubrication (**fig. 25**).

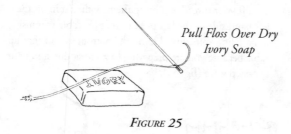

Pull Floss Over Dry Ivory Soap

FIGURE 25

Always remember to have floss running with the grain with the cut end knotted (**fig. 26**). Always remember to separate the floss, strand by strand, before knotting. ▨

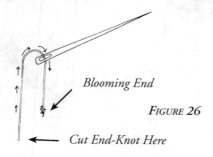

Blooming End

FIGURE 26

⟵ *Cut End-Knot Here*

Slip-Snail Knot

Tying Off Your Floss

When you run out of floss in the middle of a row, when you change colors, or when you end a row of smocking, you must properly tie off your floss. I like to use a slip snail knot.

1. Take the floss to the back of the smocking.

2. Turn the work to the back and notice that the needle is in one pleat. This is the pleat on which you will want to put the knot.

3. Make a small stitch in that one pleat (**fig. 27**).

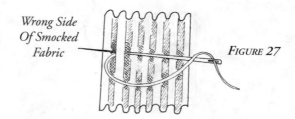

Wrong Side Of Smocked Fabric

FIGURE 27

4. Tighten that stitch but leave a little loop (**fig. 28**).

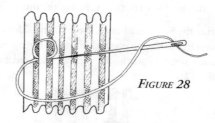

FIGURE 28

5. Take the needle around and slip it through the loop (**fig. 29**).

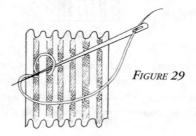

FIGURE 29

6. Pull the thread to form a little knot (**fig. 30**). This is where the slip snail knot comes in. Slip the needle through the loop and slip a little knot in the thread. This knot should look like a snail. If you want to tie the second knot, follow the same instructions in the same pleat. ▨

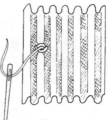

FIGURE 30

185

Tie Off, Re-thread, and Begin Again In Middle

Since smocking is best worked with 15 to 20 inch lengths of thread, tie off and begin again in the middle of the row. It is easiest to tie off on a level cable stitch, using the following technique.

1. Take the smocking stitch, whatever that stitch may be.

2. Take the needle to the back by going between the last two pleats involved in that last stitch. Slip the needle down very close to the stitch before taking the thread straight back to the back (**fig. 31**).

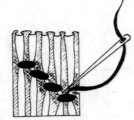

FIGURE 31

3. Tie a slip snail knot. You may want to tie two.

4. Re-thread. Tie a knot in the end of the thread.

5. Bring the new thread in on the left hand side of the last pleat that already has smocking on it. It may be difficult to do, since the stitch will already be secured and tied off (**fig. 32**).

FIGURE 32

6. Try to bring the needle in at exactly the same place where the smocking thread has travelled in the left hand side of that last pleat. The thread will appear as if it were not tied off at all, coming through the same hole as described. ▩

Specific Stitch Tie Off Situations

Thread placement depends on whether the next stitch moves upward or downward.

• **Example A.** You have just completed a two-step wave, coming down. You have made the down cable, at the bottom. This is the turnaround stitch. Tie off the floss, and bring the new floss in the left hand side of the last pleat of the down cable you just took. Bring the thread in on the top side of that down cable because you are preparing to go back up in your two-step wave (**fig. 33**).

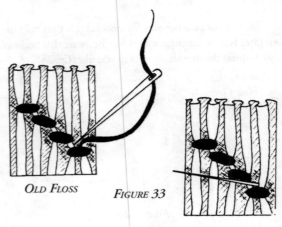

OLD FLOSS   FIGURE 33

NEW FLOSS

• **Example B.** You have just completed a two-step wave, going up. You have made the up-cable at the top of the wave. Tie off your thread and bring the new thread in on the left hand side of the last pleat of that up-cable you just took. Bring your thread in on the bottom side of that up-cable because you are preparing to go back down in your two-step wave (**fig. 34**). ▩

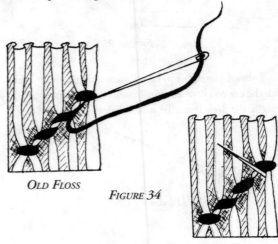

OLD FLOSS   FIGURE 34

NEW FLOSS

Blocking

1. Always block your smocking before constructing the garment. After smocking is completed, carefully remove all pleating row threads except the top thread.

2. Set your steam iron on the lowest setting you can get and still have steam.

3. Pin the smocked piece to the board at the top, middle, and sides (**fig. 35**). Gently stretch it out to the exact measurement of the yoke to which it will be attached. I pin the smocking right side up to be sure the smocking design is straight.

Front View: How To Pin

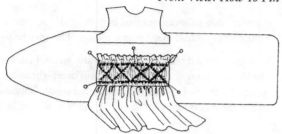

FIGURE 35

4. Hold the steam iron at least one or two inches above the smocking. Do not touch the smocking with the iron. Steam the piece (**fig. 36**). Allow it to dry thoroughly before unpinning the piece from board. ▨

Side View:
How To
Steam

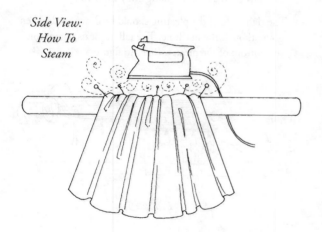

FIGURE 36

The Pleater

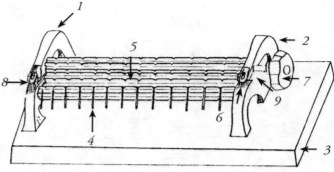

PLEATER

Important Parts

1. Left hand end plate

2. Right hand end plate

3. Base of the machine

4. Needles inserted into the grooves

5. Drop-in roller

6. Keeper and keeper screw

7. Knob

8. Left hand slot underneath keeper screw that allows the fabric to pass through the pleater and off the needles

9. Right hand slot underneath keeper screw that allows the fabric to pass through the pleater and off the needles

Pleater Needles

1. Loosen the keeper screw. Complete removal of the keeper and the screw is not necessary; just slide the keeper forward on the loosened screw (**fig. 1**).

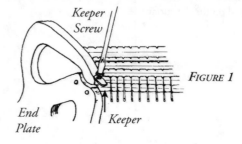

Keeper
Screw

FIGURE 1

End
Plate   *Keeper*

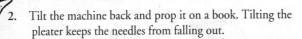

2. Tilt the machine back and prop it on a book. Tilting the pleater keeps the needles from falling out.

3. With the thumb, gently roll the small, drop-in roller up and off of the machine (**fig. 2**).

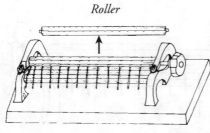

Roller

FIGURE 2

4. Reposition the needles according to the specific pleating needs (**fig. 3**). Slide the elbow (crook) of the needle in first, do not jab the point in.

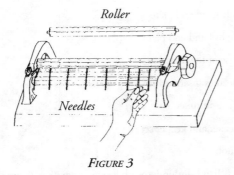

Roller

Needles

FIGURE 3

5. Gently roll the drop-in roller back into place. Be sure to align the half spaces of the drop-in roller with the half space grooves on the pleater.

6. Tighten the screw just until resistance is felt, then turn just a tiny bit more. Do not overtighten. Loosen the screws when pleating heavier fabrics; tighten them for sheer fabrics.

7. To hold your pleater in place during pleating, tape it in place using two inch duct tape.Cut enough of this tape to put across the back of the pleater. Put the pleater on a flat surface with the duct tape across the back of the pleater and on the flat surface. ▓

Preparing To Pleat

1. Thread the required number of needles using a 36 inch long piece of quilting thread for each needle. Thread from the top. Pull 6 inches through. Let the long end hang (**fig. 4**).

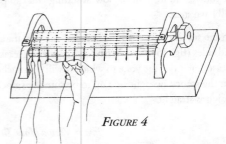

FIGURE 4

2. If you are usig a continuous feed bobbin holder or system, your quilting thread may become spongy. This may help.

3. Soak your spool if quilting thread in warm water. Pleace the spool in front of the refrigerator vent overnight to gently dry the thread. You may then wind it onto bobbins or put the spools into your smocking machine holder. ▓

Pleating a Skirt Piece

1. Do not cut off the armholes of the dress until after the fabric has been pleated.

2. Place the skirt piece wrong side up, with the top edge to your left. Beginning at the side edge nearest to you, roll the skirt onto a dowel, rolling away from you.

3. The right side of the pleating should be downwards when going though the machine. The tallest pleats come from the bottom of the pleater. Refer to figure 5. ▓

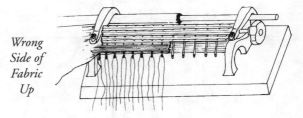

Wrong Side of Fabric Up

FIGURE 5

Pleating a Bishop

1. Lay the fabric flat with right sides down, and roll onto a dowel stick in the direction shown. Run the fabric through the pleater, right side down (**fig. 6**).▨

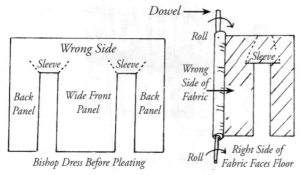

Bishop Dress Before Pleating

FIGURE 6

Pleating With A Dowel Stick

Usually I use a ¼ inch, wooden, craft-type dowel stick, about 36 inches long. However, some people like small, thin, steel rods which give some weight for holding the fabric and dowel in place while pleating. Others like a cafe curtain rod which opens or closes as much as needed for garments. The size of the dowel should be compatible with the type fabric used, no larger than 1 inch (**fig. 7**).

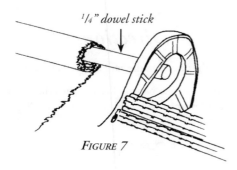

FIGURE 7

1. Put the dowel stick, covered with the rolled fabric, through the left hand side of the pleater.

2. Line up the exact rows to pleat. Eyeball the groove that you must use as a guideline in order to run the pleating through evenly, leaving one whole pleater space for the guideline. (**fig. 8**).

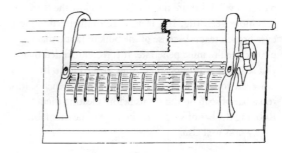

FIGURE 8

4. Hold the fabric and begin to guide it through.

5. As your fabric goes through the pleater it is important to gently pull the fabric edge hanging out the left side. Gently pull parallel with the rollers. This will keep bumps from forming in the pleats. Let the rollers and the handle pull the fabric through (**fig. 9**). As the fabric comes onto the needles, stop and gently guide the fabric off of the needles. Do not force or jerk, since this could bend the needles. ▨

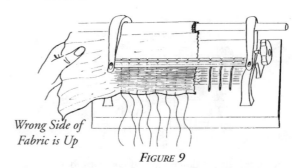

Wrong Side of Fabric is Up

FIGURE 9

With your left hand gently pull the fabric which hangs out the left side. Pull parallel with the rollers.

Pleater Tips

1. The fabric edge to be fed into the machine should be cut straight and started evenly to avoid a crooked pleat and for pleating with ease. Gently "rocking" the fabric into the pleater may get it going.

2. Do not force or pull the fabric into the roller gears to get it started. Align the fabric straight into the gears and let the gears grab the fabric as you start turning. Although unlikely, if the fabric should jam and some of the needle start moving wildly, the pleater may become very difficult to turn. Remove the drop-in roller gear and remove the needles and fabric. "Cutting out the pleating" will be avoided this way.

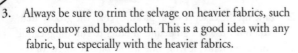

3. Always be sure to trim the selvage on heavier fabrics, such as corduroy and broadcloth. This is a good idea with any fabric, but especially with the heavier fabrics.

4. A strip of wax paper run through the pleater prior to pleating, will lubricate the needles and allow the fabric to pass more freely (**fig. 10**). It is not recommended to pleat over French seams because of the bulk of fabric that the pleater needles must penetrate. It is recommended that you serge the seams together using a rolled hem. If, however, you find it necessary to pleat over French seams, rub a bar of soap on the seams before pleating them. Rubbing the bar of soap over the edge of heavier fabric edge works well also.

Rub a bar of Ivory soap over French seams before pleating them.

A strip of wax paper, run through the pleater prior to pleating, will lubricate the needles and allow the fabric to pass more freely.

FIGURE 10

5. Fabric may tend to pile up on the needles as it comes out of the pleater and make it hard to turn. If this occurs, gently slide the fabric along the needles onto the thread as it accumulates on the needles (**fig. 11**).

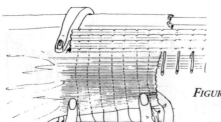

FIGURE 11

6. Replace bent and dull needles. If not replaced, they can jam the cloth and break in the machine. A bent needle is easy to identify: it moves excessively while the pleater is turning, it has an unusual angle compared with the other needles, and it makes pleating more difficult.

7. Needles do need to be changed after excess usage because they will dull.

8. If the machine becomes stiff to operate, chances are that you have wound some threads into the machine or around the shaft of the roller. Pick these out carefully with a small needle and cut them.

9. Because the pleater's needles will rust when exposed to moisture, keep the pleater in a dry place. ✄

Smocking Stitches

Cable Stitch

General Instructions

- This stitch is worked from left to right. It consists of alternating up and down cables. Start the thread on the left hand side of the pleat to smock.

- Take every stitch with the needle running parallel to the gathering line, taking care to keep the needle parallel as you take the stitches.

- The needles always "bite the fabric" exactly on top of the gathering row. It may appear that one stitch goes a tiny bit above the gathering thread and one stitch goes a tiny bit below. The up cable (top cable) and down cable (bottom cable) portions of the stitch give this appearance. Be sure you keep each stitch exactly on top of the gathering thread.

- A down cable is made by stitching into the pleat with the thread below the needle. An up cable is made by stitching into the pleat with the thread above the needle.

- Take one cable stitch in every pleat. Throw the thread to the bottom in one stitch, to the top in the next.

Directions

1. Bring in the thread on the left hand side of the first pleat.

2. Move to the second pleat and take a stitch there with the thread below the needle. This is a down cable (**fig. 1**).

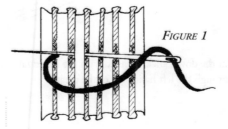

FIGURE 1

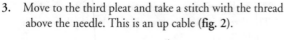

3. Move to the third pleat and take a stitch with the thread above the needle. This is an up cable (**fig. 2**).

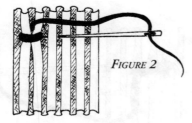

FIGURE 2

4. Move to the fourth pleat and take a stitch with the thread below the needle. This is another down cable.

5. Move to the fifth pleat and take another stitch with the thread above the needle. This is another up cable.

6. Every two to four stitches, with the needle or a fingernail, push the cable stitches together to be sure the fabric does not show through.

7. To make beautiful cable stitches, try this. After taking the stitch, begin to tighten by pulling upward on a down-cable and downward on an up-cable.

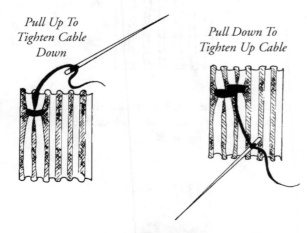

Pull Up To Tighten Cable Down

Pull Down To Tighten Up Cable

8. Before actually pulling the final stitch to the fabric, place your thumbnail next to the stitch and guide the stitch into its exact position. ▨

Push Up Cable Down To Level It

Push Down Cable Up To Level It

Outline Stitch

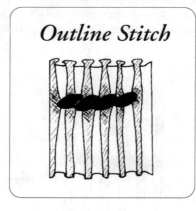

Directions

This stitch is worked from left to right.

1. Bring the thread in on the left hand side of the first pleat (**fig. 1**).

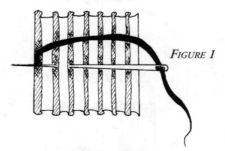

FIGURE 1

2. The outline stitch is a continuous row of up cables. The thread is thrown above the needle for every stitch (**fig. 2**).

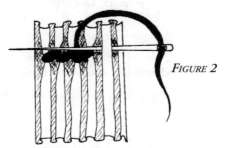

FIGURE 2

3. Run the needle in parallel to the gathering row, on exactly the top of the gathering row. Tighten each up-cable by pulling down. Always tighten up cables in this manner (**fig. 3**).

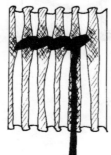

FIGURE 3

4. After tightening each stitch, gently pull upward to align the whole row with the gathering row (**fig. 4**). ▨

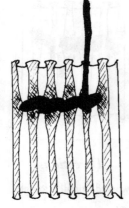

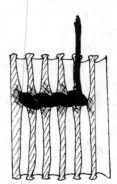

FIGURE 4

Stem Stitch

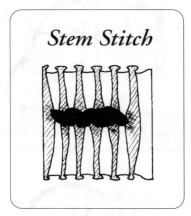

This stitch is worked from left to right.

1. Bring the thread in on the left hand side of the first pleat (**fig. 1**).

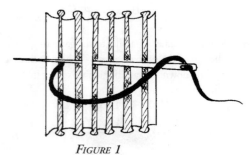

FIGURE 1

2. The outline stitch is a continuous row of down cables. The thread is thrown down below the needle for each stitch (**fig.2**).

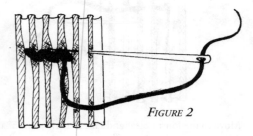

FIGURE 2

3. Take each stitch by running the needle in parallel to the gathering row on exactly the top of the gathering thread. Next, tighten each down cable by pulling up (**fig. 3**).

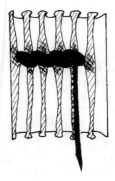

FIGURE 3

4. After you do the up tighten on each stitch, gently pull downward to pull the whole row back in line with the gathering row (**fig. 4**). ▨

FIGURE 4

Wave/Chevron Stitch or Baby Wave

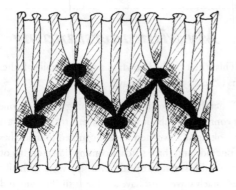

Directions

1. Bring the thread in on the left hand side of the first pleat.

2. Move to the second pleat and make a down cable (**fig. l**).

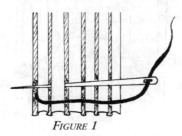

FIGURE 1

3. Make another down cable at the half-space line (marked with a gathering thread on the pleat). Remember the Cat and the Courthouse story. When the cat goes up the courthouse steps, the tail drops down (**fig. 2**).

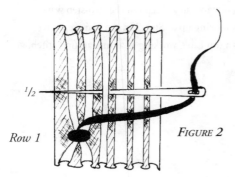

FIGURE 2

Row 1

4. Make an up cable on the half-space line also (**fig. 3**). It may look as if the second stitch went in between the bottom row and the half-space row. Looks are deceiving.

The second down cable and the up cable (the turnaround stitch) are placed on exactly the same line - the half-space line.

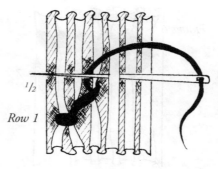

Row 1

FIGURE 3

5. Now move back down to the whole line. Make an up cable at the starting line (**fig. 4**). Remember the Cat and the Courthouse tale.

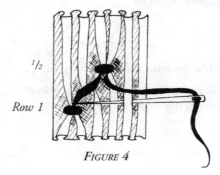

Row 1

FIGURE 4

6. At the same bottom row, make another down cable. This is the turnaround stitch (**fig. 5**).

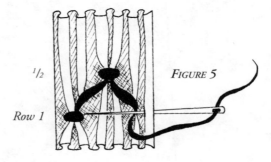

FIGURE 5

Row 1

7. Half-space chevrons end at the half space on the smocking rows. Whole-space chevrons are taller and go all the way to another row.

8. Half-space chevrons are easy if you own a pleater because you are able to pleat half spaces in addition to the whole spaces. Half-space refers to the stitch going from the row you are smocking on to the halfway point of the next row, and back again to the row you began smocking on.

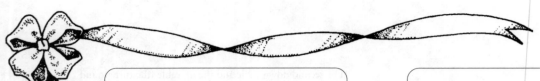

Wheat Stitch

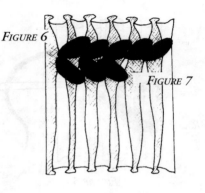

FIGURE 6

FIGURE 7

A wheat stitch derives its name from its similarity to wheat. The wheat stitch is really two rows of stitching that gives the appearance of one.

Directions

1. The first row is the outline stitch (**fig. 6**).

2. Work a row of stem stitches directly under the outline stitch row (**fig. 7**). ▨

Two, Three or Four-Step Wave (Trellis)

My Misunderstanding

This stitch can be known as a wave or trellis. Either is correct. I choose to call it a wave.

When I was a beginner, just learning to smock, one thing always confused me about waves. So, let's try to clear it up. When looking at a two-step wave, I counted four stitches going up on one side and three stitches coming down on the other. How could this stitch be called a two-step wave with all these stitches? Each wave must have a cable at the bottom and a cable at the top. These are "level" or "turn-around" stitches. Counting these as steps to the two-step wave is where I got confused.

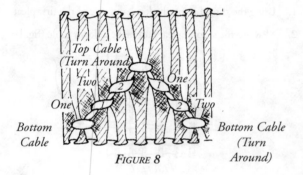

FIGURE 8

Correct Way To Count A Two-Step Wave (Figure 8)

Stitch 1 is a bottom-cable working as a turn-around stitch.
Stitch 2 is moving up as Step l in the two-step wave.
Stitch 3 Is moving up as Step 2 in the two-step wave.
Stitch 4 is a top-cable working as a turn-around stitch. ▨

Two-Step Wave (Trellis)

Directions

This is worked from left to right. Move over one pleat at a time as you move up and down between the rows.

A two-step wave can have various heights, depending on your design. **Example:** A two-step wave which goes from row 1 to row $^1/_2$ above it (technically called a half-space, two-step wave) is done like this:

1. Bring the needle in on the left side of the first pleat. Begin with a down-cable on Row 1 (**fig. 1**).

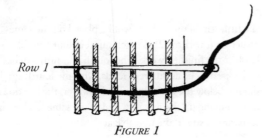

FIGURE 1

2. Move up halfway between row 1 and row $^1/_2$ (a $^1/_4$ space) for the next stitch, a down cable (**fig. 2**).

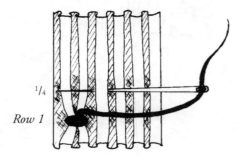

FIGURE 2

3. Move up to the half-space for the next stitch, another down cable (**fig. 3**).

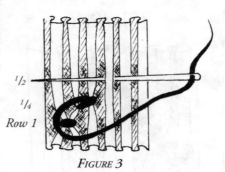

FIGURE 3

4. At this same half-space point, move over one pleat and do a top cable (turn-around stitch) (**fig. 4**).

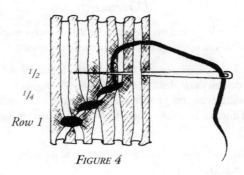

FIGURE 4

5. Move down $^1/_4$ space, do a top cable.

6. Move down to row 1 and do another top cable.

7. Complete the stitch sequence with another turn-around stitch (a bottom cable - refer to finished drawing).

"Now, there is a common misunderstanding concerning two-step waves. I will try to clear this up. Look at the illustration showing a completed two-step wave. It appears that the two middle steps are stitched on the $^1/_3$ and $^2/_3$ points between the bottom cable and the top cable. That is only its appearance! In reality the two stitches are taken at the $^1/_4$ point and at the $^1/_2$ space itself."

Three-Step Wave (Trellis)

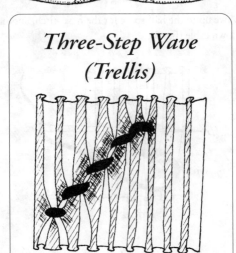

Directions

This is worked from left to right. Move over, one pleat at a time, as you move up and down between the rows.

A three-step wave can have various heights, depending on your design. **Example:** A three-step wave, which goes from one major gathering row to the next, for a distance of $3/8$ inch (the usual distance between gathering rows on a pleater) is done like this:

1. Row 1 begins with a down-cable on the gathering row (**fig. 1**).

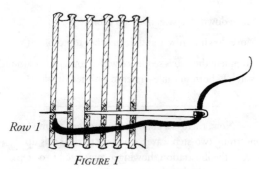

FIGURE 1

2. The second stitch, a down cable, will be placed $1/3$ of the way up (**fig.2**).

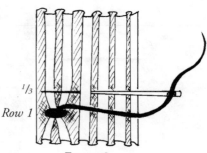

FIGURE 2

3. The third stitch, a down cable, will be placed $2/3$ of the way up (**fig. 3**).

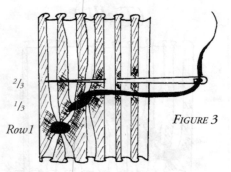

FIGURE 3

4. Row 2 is the fourth stitch, a down cable, placed on the next gathering row line (**fig. 4**).

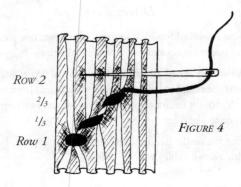

FIGURE 4

5. The fifth stitch, up cable. It will be placed on the same gathering row (Row 2) as stitch number four (**fig. 5**). Look at the finished work. The fourth and fifth stitches will appear to be at different levels, with the fourth stitch slightly below the gathering row. However, the last down cable moving up the row is placed at the same level as the turnaround stitch, the up-cable at the top.

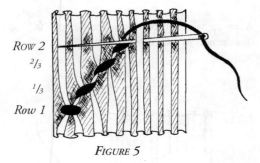

FIGURE 5

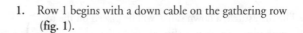

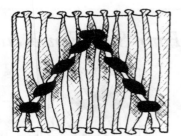

COMPLETED THREE-STEP WAVE

Sitting In Martha's Smocking Class

"An easy way to count three step waves when going across a row is to say, 'bottom cable, 1, 2, 3, top cable, 1, 2, 3, bottom cable,1, 2, 3, top cable, 1, 2, 3.' Some people like to say, 'turn around, 1, 2, 3, turn around, 1, 2, 3, turn around 1, 2, 3.' There will always be three steps in the middle with a cable at the top and a cable at the bottom." ▨

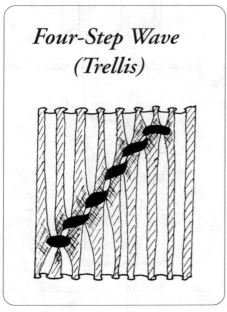

Four-Step Wave (Trellis)

Directions

This is worked from left to right. Move over, one pleat at a time, as you move up and down between the rows.

A four-step wave can have various heights, depending on your design. It goes from one major gathering row (Row 1) to the next gathering row (Row 2) in this example.

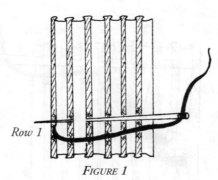

1. Row 1 begins with a down cable on the gathering row (**fig. 1**).

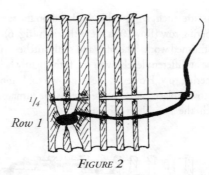

FIGURE 1

2. The second stitch, a down cable, will be placed $^1/_4$ of the way up (**fig. 2**).

FIGURE 2

3. The third stitch, a down cable, will be placed on the half-space (**fig. 3**).

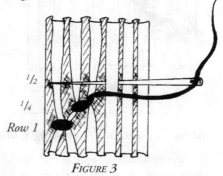

FIGURE 3

4. The fourth stitch, a down cable, will be placed on the $^3/_4$ space (**fig. 4**).

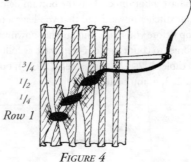

FIGURE 4

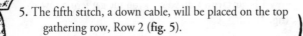

5. The fifth stitch, a down cable, will be placed on the top gathering row, Row 2 (**fig. 5**).

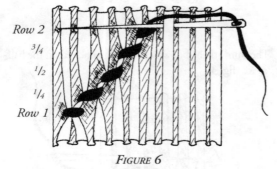

Row 2
³/4
¹/2
¹/4
Row 1

FIGURE 5

6. The sixth stitch, an up cable, is placed on the same gathering row (Row 2) as the fifth stitch (**fig. 6**). Look at the finished work. The fifth and sixth stitches will appear to be at different levels, with the fifth slightly below the gathering row. However, the last down cable moving up the row is placed at the same level as the turnaround stitch, the up cable at the top. ▨

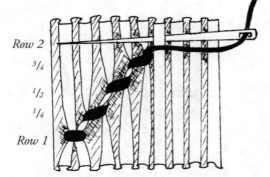

Row 2
³/4
¹/2
¹/4
Row 1

FIGURE 6

Sitting In Martha's Smocking Class

"Just because we have stopped our instructions with a four-step wave doesn't mean that you can't make a five-step wave or a six-step wave or even more. Always remember that when you call a stitch a four-step wave, that you have a bottom cable at the bottom before you make four stitches upward and that you have a top cable at the top before you make four stitches downward. Don't forget to count the four-step wave as follows. Bottom cable, 1, 2, 3, 4, top cable, 1, 2, 3, 4, bottom cable, 1, 2, 3, 4, top cable." ▨

Four-Step Flowerette

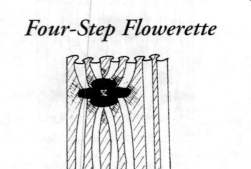

Directions

This stitch is worked from left to right. Begin the stitch by bringing the needle in on the left side of the first pleat (**fig. 1**).

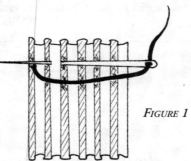

FIGURE 1

1. Move over to the second pleat and make a down cable (**fig. 2**).

FIGURE 2

2. Move over to the third pleat, and make an up cable (**fig. 3**).

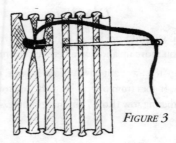

FIGURE 3

3. Move to the fourth pleat and make another up cable (**fig. 4**).

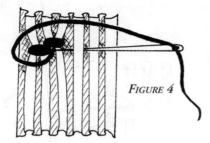

FIGURE 4

4. Look at the finished work. There are four pleats involved at this time with the flowerette stitching (**fig. 5**).

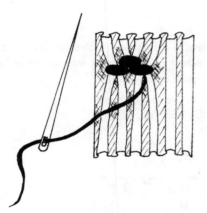

FIGURE 5

5. Take the needle to the back of the garment, going between the first and second pleats. This will complete the flowerette stitching sequence (**fig. 6**).

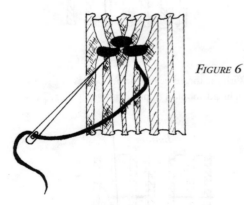

FIGURE 6

6. Tie off each flowerette on the back of the garment by using the slip-snail knot instructions given earlier. ▨

Double Wave or Diamond Stitch

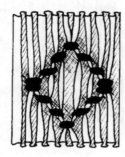

Directions

A double wave means the second wave is worked in the opposite directions of the first, making a diamond shape.

1. The top portion of the diamond wave (one-, two-, three-, four-wave) begins with a down-cable, and moves upward.

2. The bottom portion of the diamond wave begins with a top cable and moves downward.

3. Stack the cables the to meet in the middle. A trick to matching the cables perfectly is to slip your needle between the pleats and slide it up. This will enable you to stitch very close to the first pleat. ▨

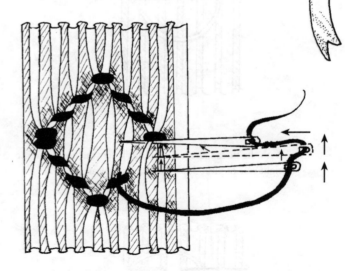

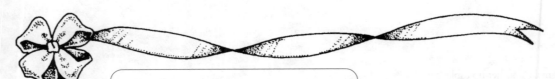

Six-Step Flowerette

Directions

Work from left to right.

1. Bring the needle up on the left side of pleat 1 or the left side of the first pleat to be involved in the flowerette.

2. With the thread below the needle, insert the needle on the right side of pleat 2 , picking up only pleat 2 (**fig. 1**).

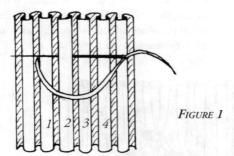

FIGURE 1

3. With the thread above the needle, insert the needle on the right side of pleat 3, picking up only pleat 3 (**fig. 2**).

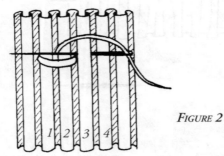

FIGURE 2

4. With the thread below the needle, insert the needle on the right side of pleat 4, picking up only peat 4 (**fig. 3**).

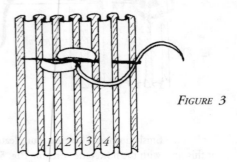

FIGURE 3

5. Carry the thread to the back of the fabric between the last two pleats (pleats 3 and 4). Turn the work, as well as the illustration, upside down.

6. Bring the needle out on the left side of pleat 4, below the last down cable made (**fig. 4**).

Bottom

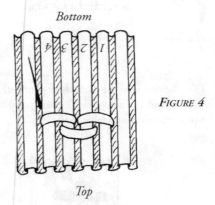

FIGURE 4

Top

7. With the thread below the needle, insert the needle on the right side of pleat 3, picking up only pleat 3 (**fig. 5**).

Bottom

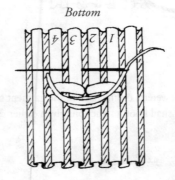

FIGURE 5

Top

8. With the thread above the needle, insert the needle on the right side of pleat 2, picking up only pleat 2 (**fig. 6**).

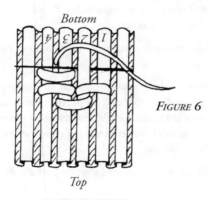

Bottom

Top

FIGURE 6

9. With the tread below the needle, insert the needle on the right side of pleat 1, picking up only pleat 1 (**fig. 7**).

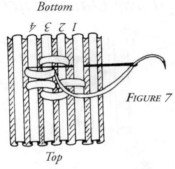

Bottom

Top

FIGURE 7

10. Carry the thread to the wrong side of the fabric by inserting in between the last two pleats used, (pleats 1 and 2), and tie off. ▓

Bullion Rose

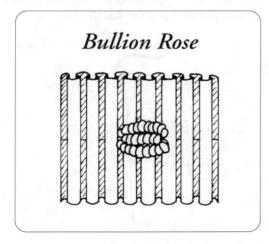

Directions

This stitch is the one stitch that frightens smockers the most; when, in fact, it is one of the easiest. It is frequently used to make flowers and for surface embellishments. The key to a

good bullion is using a long needle that is slightly tapered such as an 8 crewel. The wraps forming the bullion rose are made on the pointed end of the needle. The needle is then pulled through the wraps forming the bullion. If the needle tapers too much, it is extremely difficult to pull the needle through the wraps and oftentimes distorts the stitch. Another needle you can use is a 7 long darner.

The number of threads used in making a bullion rose is determined by the type of thread used. For a thick bullion rose use two to three strands of embroidery floss. If you are using pearle cotton, use only one strand.

1. Bring the needle up in the **center** or top of pleat 1 (**fig. 1**).

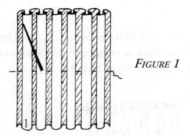

FIGURE 1

2. With the thread below the needle, insert the needle into the center or top of pleat 4.

3. Insert the needle through pleats 3 and 2, making sure that you come up on the center of pleat 1 directly beside the previous stitch (**fig. 2**).

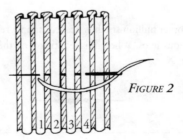

FIGURE 2

4. Wrap the thread around the needle as many wraps as desired (**fig. 3**). Keep the wraps close together and hold them taut.

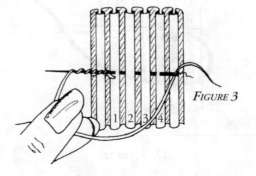

FIGURE 3

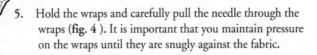

5. Hold the wraps and carefully pull the needle through the wraps (**fig. 4**). It is important that you maintain pressure on the wraps until they are snugly against the fabric.

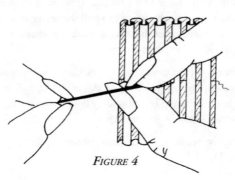

FIGURE 4

6. Once you have your bullion stitch in place and have no need to make changes, insert the needle again in pleat 4 and carry it through to the back (**fig. 5**).

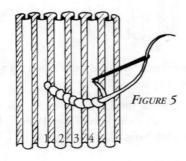

FIGURE 5

7. If another bullion stitch is needed, simply refer to the previous steps. When finished, tie off on the back with a knot. ❖

Satin Stitch Flowerette

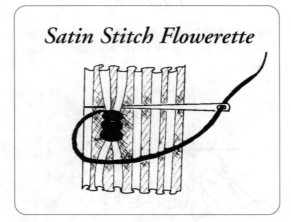

Directions

Satin-stitch flowerettes may be worked over two, three, or four pleats. I think two is usually prettiest.

1. Bring the thread in on the left side of the first pleat of the satin stitch flowerette.

2. Use the satin embroidery stitch. Stitch through the pleats as if making smocking stitches. Be sure the stitches lay close to each other.

3. Use the needle tip or your thumb to place the stitches just right.

4. After stitching across the desired number of pleats, take the needle to the back, on the right hand side of the smocked pleats. Continue at the point where another whole stitch would be taken if more bars were added to the flowerette.

5. Tie off with a slip-snail knot on the back. ❖

Lazy Daisy Stitch

Directions

This is actually an embroidery stitch used to represent flower leaves or an actual daisy-type flower. It is a smocking embellishment technique.

1. Knot the floss. Bring the threaded needle, from the back, up through the center of the pleat (**fig. 1**).

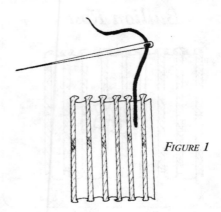

FIGURE 1

2. Insert the needle right above the hole you just came through, run it through two complete pleats, and up in the center of the third pleat (**fig. 2**). Make sure to use four pleats in this stitch. A review: Bring the needle up

through the fabric in the center of one pleat. Then, run the needle through that pleat and the next two pleats. And finally, bring the needle through the center of the fourth pleat for the other side of the stitch. The thread should lay to the bottom of the needle while running the needle form the first pleat to the fourth.

3. Before pulling the thread through, form a loop around and under the tip of the needle (**fig. 2**).

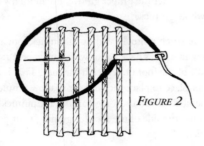

FIGURE 2

4. Pull the thread, holding the loop carefully to shape it and place it with your fingers.

5. Shape the loop as desired, and pull the thread through the smocking to tighten the loop.

6. Take the tip of the needle over the loop and through the same hole it came up out of in the fourth pleat (**fig. 3**). Do not pull too tightly.

FIGURE 3

7. Tie off on the back with a slip-snail knot after making all the lazy daisy stitches you want. When you move to another location for more lazy daisy stitches, knot a new thread and start all over again. ▦

Reflections From Martha On Smocking

The very thought of the word, smocking, brings joy to my heart. The first smocking I ever stitched was begun in 1968 when I bought a soft coral fabric and a McCall's pattern with iron on dots. This lovely little bishop dress was lovingly begun by me and then those dratted dots were ironed on. The commercial pattern instructed me to draw up each dot as I stitched a little wave design. My very nerves were shattered as I hunted among the stitches for the next dot to draw up. Actually, I gave up on completing the dress; however, I didn't throw it away. Years later, about 1978 to be exact, I found the little unfinished dress. Since I had begun my first smocking class at that time, I decided that it would be good to finish it for Joanna. The original plans for the dress were for a friend's little girl. Those plans fell through! I was so proud of my completing it, I even took Joanna for a picture in the dress which took 10 years to make!

I had a pleater ordered at that time and was very grateful for a teacher who would pleat for me until mine came. Back in the "olden days of smocking" (around 1978) you had to wait about a year for a smocking machine. Worse yet, the price was $165 for a small pleater. My pleater finally came and the rest is history, I suppose. Smocking has been one of the great joys of my life and smocking for grandchildren has brought the smocking bug back into my life in full swing. I'm even perfecting picture smocking.

I have a funny story to relate to you. About 1982, when I still had a smocking shop, the phone rang one day and a sweet sounding lady asked me to mail order her a smocking needle. Customarily, one orders several needles for the pleater, but I figured that she had broken only one pleater needle and that she only wanted to spend $1. I wrapped a pleater needle carefully and mailed it to her. A few weeks later she wrote me a letter thanking me for this wonderful needle. She related that it had taken hours off of her smocking to have that interesting little crooked needle! Mortified, I picked up the phone and reconfirmed my fear that she had used that pleater needle to smock a whole dress. I apologized profusely, telling her that I thought she had wanted a pleater needle. Since she had never heard of a pleater, I sold her a pleater over the phone and she promised that she would never again use her crooked needle for hand smocking. ▦

203

Corded Pintucks And Raised Pintucks

Cords make pintucks more prominent. Use Mettler gimp or #8 pearl cotton. Cording comes in handy when pintucks are being shaped. When pintucking across a bias with a double needle, you may get some distortion. The cord acts as a filler and will keep the fabric from distorting. Sometimes you might choose to use cording in order to add color to your pintucks. If you asked me, "Martha, do you usually cord pintucks? my answer would be no." However, just because I don't usually cord pintucks, doesn't mean that you won't prefer to cord them.

Some machines have a little device which sits in the base of the machine and sticks up just a little bit. That device tends to make the pintucks stand up a little more for a higher raised effect. Some people really like this feature.

1. If your machine has a hole in the throat plate, run the cord up through that hole and it will be properly placed without another thought (**fig. 1**).

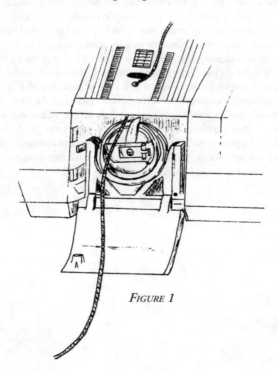

FIGURE 1

2. If your machine does not have a hole in the throat plate, put the gimp or pearl cotton underneath the fabric, lining it up with the pintuck groove. Once you get the cording lined up under the proper groove, it will follow along for the whole pintuck.

3. You can stitch pintucks without a pintuck foot at all. Some sewing machines have a foot with a little hole right in the middle of the foot underneath the foot. That is a perfectly proper place to place the cord for shadow pintucks. Remember, if you use a regular foot for pintucking, you must use the side of the foot for guiding your next pintuck. ▒

Index

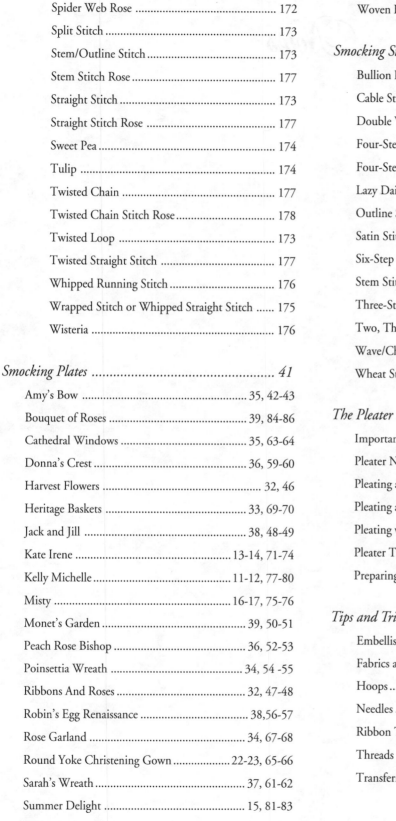

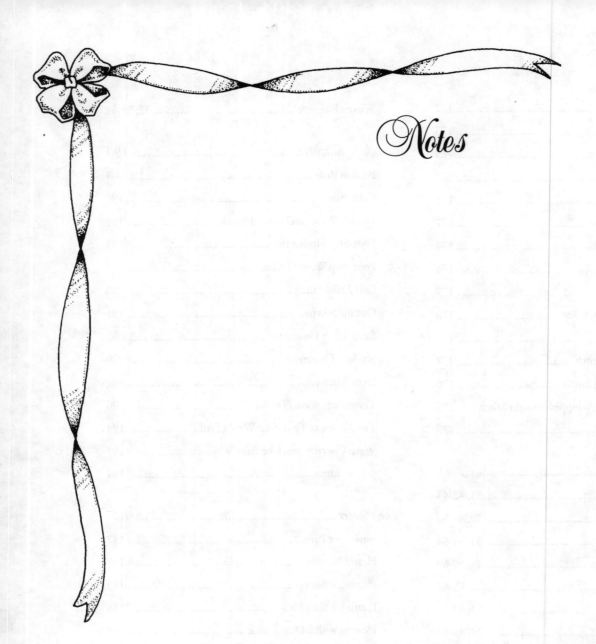

Notes